CITY-REGIONS IN PROSPECT?

MCGILL-QUEEN'S STUDIES
IN URBAN GOVERNANCE
Series editors: Kristin Good and Martin Horak

In recent years there has been an explosion of interest in local politics and
the governance of cities – both in Canada and around the world. Globally,
the city has become a consequential site where instances of social conflict
and of cooperation play out. Urban centres are increasingly understood as
vital engines of innovation and prosperity and a growing body of interdisciplinary research on urban issues suggests that high-performing cities
have become crucial to the success of nations, even in the global era. Yet at
the same time, local and regional governments continue to struggle for
political recognition and for the policy resources needed to manage cities,
to effectively govern, and to achieve sustainable growth.

The purpose of the McGill-Queen's Studies in Urban Governance series
is to highlight the growing importance of municipal issues, local governance, and the need for policy reform in urban spaces. The series aims
to answer the question "why do cities matter?" while exploring relationships between levels of government and examining the changing dynamics
of metropolitan and community development. By taking a four-pronged
approach to the study of urban governance, the series encourages debate
and discussion of: (1) actors, institutions, and how cities are governed;
(2) policy issues and policy reform; (3) the city as case study; and
(4) urban politics and policy through a comparative framework.

With a strong focus on governance, policy, and the role of the city,
this series welcomes manuscripts from a broad range of disciplines and
viewpoints.

City-Regions in Prospect?

Exploring Points between
Place and Practice

Edited by

KEVIN EDSON JONES, ALEX LORD,
AND ROB SHIELDS

McGill-Queen's University Press
Montreal & Kingston · London · Chicago

© McGill-Queen's University Press 2015

ISBN 978-0-7735-4603-5 (cloth)
ISBN 978-0-7735-4604-2 (paper)
ISBN 978-0-7735-9778-5 (ePDF)
ISBN 978-0-7735-9779-2 (ePUB)

Legal deposit third quarter 2015
Bibliothèque nationale du Québec

Printed in Canada on acid-free paper that is 100% ancient forest free
(100% post-consumer recycled), processed chlorine free

This book was published with the help of a grant from the Canadian
Federation for the Humanities and Social Sciences, through the Awards
to Scholarly Publications Program, using funds provided by the Social
Sciences and Humanities Research Council of Canada.

McGill-Queen's University Press acknowledges the support of the
Canada Council for the Arts for our publishing program. We also
acknowledge the financial support of the Government of Canada
through the Canada Book Fund for our publishing activities.

Library and Archives Canada Cataloguing in Publication

City-regions in prospect?: exploring points between place and practice/
edited by Kevin Edson Jones, Alex Lord, and Rob Shields.

(McGill-Queen's studies in urban governance; 2)
Includes bibliographical references and index.
Issued in print and electronic formats.
ISBN 978-0-7735-4603-5 (bound). – ISBN 978-0-7735-4604-2 (paperback). –
ISBN 978-0-7735-9778-5 (ePDF). – ISBN 978-0-7735-9779-2 (ePUB)

1. Cities and towns – Case studies. 2. Regionalism – Case studies.
3. Globalization – Case studies. 4. Urbanization – Case studies. 5. City
planning – Case studies. 6. Municipal government – Case studies. I. Jones,
Kevin Edson, 1973–, author, editor II. Lord, Alex, 1961–, author, editor
III. Shields, Rob, 1979–, author, editor IV. Series: McGill-Queen's studies
in urban governance; 2

HT151.C58 2015   307.76   C2015-903008-0
                                        C2015-903009-9

This book was typeset by Interscript in 10.5/13 Sabon.

Contents

Figures and Tables

CITY-REGIONS IN PROSPECT?

Introduction: City-Regions in Prospect?

KEVIN EDSON JONES, ALEX LORD,
AND ROB SHIELDS

The "city-region" has become a core concept in urban and regional planning scholarship, as well as an ever-present logic guiding urban planning approaches internationally. As an idea about the appropriate scale at which to consider and organize local governance, economies, and communities, the city-region has evolved to take on multiple meanings at multiple levels. Likewise, in practice, city-regionalism encapsulates a wide range of international experience and experimentation. The essays and case studies contained in this volume, and presented by an interdisciplinary and international collection of scholars, explore the "city-region" as both an evolving concept and a growing area of experiential knowledge. More specifically, the book explores the tensions and uncertainties existing between the conceptual aspirations of city-regions, and the contextual experiences of local communities and local governments. The instabilities and heterogeneities of the city-region are readily apparent. Our more substantial aim is to explore this congested topography by addressing how city-regions are being made, to shed light on how they are being contested, and to examine the prospect of city-regionalism to make sense of, and respond to, the challenges of an increasingly urban world.

The attempt to capture a spatial category which looks across traditional boundaries – for example, those between town and country; between multiple levels of national and local governments; or between individual metropolitan regions – has much history (see Harrison, this volume). There have been flirtations with re-territorialization, experiments in regional governance, and other attempts to redraw the spatial, economic, and cultural boundaries of the city.

Yet such ardour, as we have already noted above, provides neither a unified image of a re-territorialized world, nor a clear trajectory towards one. An impression is often left that talk about cities and regions, particularly as it relates to planning policy, is cyclical and recurrent. This may be because while the motivations for re-territorialization persist, or are even exacerbated over time, how we understand and shape our responses to these perceived factors is articulated in varying ways across time and place. In this sense, city-regionalism is less well articulated as either a captured concept (Harrison, this volume), or even a move towards a pre-determined endpoint. Rather, the city-region can embody many articulations, both in concept and practice, shifting across time and context. Such a revelation is important because it draws our attention to the contingency and fluidity of the concept, and in doing so, further highlights its locally contested and political construction.

Yet, despite the heterogeneity of the "city-region," its momentum has often carried with it a unified sense of purpose, and even a self-reinforcing logic (see Smart and Tanasescu, this volume). Not a clearly defined toolkit, its influence and appeal occur directly in relation to its conceptual and practical elasticity. In a contemporary context in which the importance of urban and metropolitan forms of life, economy, and governance are accelerating, the "city-region" has been an influential means of trying to understand, account for, and respond to this changing dynamic and the many uncertainties associated with it.

Foremost, current articulations of the "city-region" attempt to capture the growing relevance of cities in a rapidly urbanizing world. For the first time in human history, half of the Earth's population is now expected to be living in cities (Cohen 2003). Indeed, of the 2.2 billion members of the projected population increase between 2000 and 2030, 2.1 billion are expected to be city dwellers (UN Population Division 2002). Cities are growing, both in terms of population and geography. Such is the scale of growth that the boundaries of city-regions have extended beyond the traditional peri-urban neighbourhoods lying between town and country, to create large polycentric conurbations. In the early twentieth century, Patrick Geddes noted the prevalence of agglomeration in urban growth patterns, and in doing so, realized the necessity of adopting regional perspectives on the evolution of the city. The scale and pace of today's change have made Geddes' challenge seem even more pressing. In today's language we now not only speak of the mega-city, but of mega-regions,

interdependent urban clusters, and urban corridors. Cities are growing, but so too are the infrastructures, transportation roots, and social
and cultural networks that link them together.

Perhaps nowhere is urbanization more visible than in China,
in the scale and rapidity with which its cities are growing, often
being constructed from the greenfield up. The Pearl River Delta
(PRD), the name given to the area around Hong Kong, Shenzen, and
Guangzhou, is the most obvious example. The PRD has an estimated
population of 120 million. Though such claims have been refuted by
the Guangdong Provincial Authority, the prominence afforded the
PRD has been accentuated of late by suggestions that plans are afoot
to merge the nine mainland cities of the PRD to form a single urban
metropolis in excess of 240 million people and twenty-six times larger geographically than Greater London (Moore and Foster 2011).

This trend is repeated in many other places around the globe. The
Yangtze River Delta is a mega-region encompassing sixteen cities
(including Shanghai, Nanjing, and Hangzhou) covering an area of
110,115 square kilometres and with over 90 million inhabitants,
and the Bohai Economic Rim, the urban area centred on Beijing and
Tianjin, has a growing population of 60 million. In Japan, Tokyo–
Kobe–Osaka–Kyoto–Nagoya is predicted to reach a population of
60 million by 2015; this is double the size of the largest global city-
region identified by Scott (2001). A super-urban area for Central
Asia is said to be emerging in India along the 1,500-kilometre urban
corridor stretching from Jawaharlal Nehru Port in Navi Mumbai
to Dadri and Tughlakabad in Delhi – currently home to in excess of
40 million people. Finally, Rio de Janeiro–São Paulo is Brazil and
South America's super-urban area, based on the 430-kilometre urban
corridor between the two cities, which has a current population of
43 million.[1]

What is important is not simply that cities and regions are growing demographically and geographically. The transition to an urban
world carries consequences for how we understand our future and
the politics that guide this transition. The social, economic, and
environmental questions that arise from the emergence of the next
century's principal urban centres have fascinated researchers, from
the fundamentals of food security (Umali-Deininger and Deininger
2001) and waste management (Sudhir et al. 1997) to the provision
of infrastructure and an urban environment of sufficient scale to
match the demands of the "megalopolis" (Gottman 1961; Jenkins et
al. 2007; Yokohari et al. 2000).

A recent report from the UN Habitat (2013) program on the State of the World's Cities (from 2012 to 2013) identifies the city as the appropriate scale and context to meet the many uncertainties of our current world and communities. As the report defines it, the challenge is to foster cities that promote prosperity within a variety of contexts including, but not limited to, a traditional focus on infrastructure and economic growth. Interlinked policy approaches to equity, sustainability, liveability, health, and welfare alongside service provision and productivity are the business of what the UN identifies as the people-centred cities of the twenty-first century. Stated simply, urban cities (and city-regions) and future aspirations for human development are inextricably interlinked: "As the world moves into the urban age, the dynamism and intense vitality of cities become even more prominent. A fresh future is taking shape, with urban areas around the world becoming not just the dominant form of habitat for humankind, but also the engine-rooms of human development as a whole" (UN Habitat 2013, 5).

The city-region has taken centre stage as a means of capturing and responding to the compelling, if equally uncertain, logics of globalization (Sassen 2000; 2001; Scott 2001). It promises to bridge local geographies, economies, and communities with global networks of knowledge, capital, and culture. At its most abstract, the city-region can be understood as an ambition, although without a clear endpoint or agreed-upon path towards its achievement. It is a means of theorizing and acting out aspirations for growth, prosperity, and cultural development in an uncertain global world. The city-region is an articulation of attempts to overlay the functional geographies of urban spaces with the transformative and developmental ambitions being affixed to cities.

Finally, as an object of ambition, the city-region has motivated extensive experimentation in recasting urban-regional spaces and metropolitan governance. Rationales for rescaling urban boundaries and city governance have been hugely influential in shaping policy and practice in cities, and have been taken up by armies of consultants and planning officials ready to assist cities with the reconstruction of their functional geographies. The city-region has assumed a momentum that has made it almost ubiquitous, and too often, it has become a convenient alternative to the status quo.

City-regional planning is guided by core logics of scale, efficiency, globalization, and connectedness (see Harrison, this volume). The

tools of the trade are often familiar across contexts – most promi-
nently involving amalgamation strategies (Sancton 2000), the re-
territorialization of governance (Brenner 1998), and, increasingly,
reputational branding (Ward 2000). For instance, the construction
of city-regions through amalgamation and municipal restructuring
has sought to bring, or even coerce, local communities into line with
a politics of global competitiveness, efficacy, and efficiency (Sancton
2000). Similarly, a recent emphasis on planning for more liveable
and culturally vibrant cities – or, at least, promoting urban spaces
as such – has been presented as a means of achieving economic
development and prosperity. The impetus for planning cosmopoli-
tan, branded, and connected cities is perhaps most clearly seen in
the influence of Florida's (2003) concepts of the creative city and
the re-branding of places to attract the creative classes (Smart and
Tanasescu, this volume).

The attempt to translate an often abstract and desirous concept
into rationalized planning practice – "what we do to become a global
city-region" – unsurprisingly creates contradictions between expectations and outcomes. It is in this sense that, despite its development
in theory and practice, the experience of many municipalities in pursuing city-regional reform has been ambiguous at best. And while
nearly two decades of experimentation have produced a wide range
of contextual experience from which lessons can be learned, the ability to identify unified models of city-regionalism remains out of
reach (Herrschel and Newman 2002; Harrison, this volume).

In summary, understanding the ongoing prospects of city-regionalism
necessitates approaching the city-region at each of the following levels: (i) as the product of global urbanization; (ii) as a concept by
which novel spatial alignments of cities and global networks are
being imagined; and (iii) as a series of ideas motivating practice and
reform. The approach taken in this collection aims to address the
social and political processes of translation, which take place across
these definitions and by the uncertainties and political contestations
inherent in this movement.

FINDING THE CITY-REGION IN PROSPECT?

This book comes at a time when both academics and practitioners
are reflecting on the value and application of the city-region.[2] There
is always an aspect of faddishness in social science research as

disciplines follow the rise of new concepts and key figures. This condition is particularly acute in planning scholarship, where scholarship is mobilized to propel change, either as a means to create new urban forms, or, as in the sense of the city-region, to create new forms of urban governance. City-regionalism has ridden just such a wave of enthusiasm. However, it is pertinent to now raise questions about its value or fit within contemporary contexts, as well as to take account of the ways in which the city-region has evolved in practice. As a concept developed in a context of optimism about the rise of an "urban renaissance" (Scott 2008) in a new global era, it can evoke questions about how well these ideas fit within contemporary contexts characterized by austerity and social and environmental uncertainties. Moreover, the conceptual origins of the term have been stretched and re-adapted to fit across a wide multitude of regional and urban forms and experiences. What was once rooted in discussions about key nodal cities in global networks has been extended to include (or been imposed upon) urban forms of all kinds, and the extension of the logics of the network, competitiveness, and new metropolitanism has been carried with it.

With all of this water having passed under the bridge, it is appropriate to ask the question of where we should look for the city-region after at least two decades of talking about it and experimenting with its form in practice. Each of the authors in this volume was challenged to revisit the conceptual logics and arguments behind the idea of the city-region – or, at least, its emergence as a dominant form of accounting and planning for urban growth and globalization in the past two decades. This makes it possible, or at the very least creates the space, to re-imagine the future of the city-region and open up new conceptual ground for understanding the development of new urban and regional spaces.

John Harrison, in chapter 2, has taken up this challenge directly in the aptly titled "The City-Region: In Retrospect, in Snapshot, in Prospect." For readers coming to the concept of the city-region for the first time, Harrison provides a thorough account of the origins of city-regional thinking, its blossoming as a dominant frame of thinking about the city in the last decade, and the critiques that have grown alongside its conceptualization and practice. Providing much more than an overview of the field, Harrison lays out an argument that city-regionalism can still play a vital role in the future of cities, while also cautioning against its ubiquity. He argues that the value of city-regionalism lies in its properties as what he calls a "chaotic concept." Instead of providing the means for contending with current urban challenges, it is better understood as a series of possibilities. Successful regional planning, Harrison argues, requires looking beyond single models (or, we might add, applying what was successful elsewhere), and finding compatibilities between the city-region and existing state territorializations. In other words, city-regions do not start as blank slates, as Neil Brenner (2003) has noted, but must be responsive to current institutional forms and cultures. A further implication of this responsive approach is that to take this seriously means recognizing when the logics and tools of the city-region are inappropriate to a context. In this sense, Harrison worries that the chaos has "gone too far," and that, too often, the city-region is imposing planning logics in contexts where they do not make sense, and where they potentially burden or hinder successful planning and governance. The implication of Harrison's argument that both the benefits and risks of city-regionalism exist within the chaotic interpretation and extension of the concept is that context matters – that, to be successful, city-regional planning must be actively constructed in relation to local civic and state circumstances, and, by extension, that knowledge of this milieu is essential.

In chapter 3, Rob Shields argues that it is fruitful to extend an analysis of city-regions beyond practice alone, to consider what the growth of city-regional rhetoric tells us about the evolving spatializations of cities. If Harrison can be understood to make an argument for exploring interpretations of city-regional discourse in reconfiguring regional spaces and forms of governance, Shields takes a further step back to understand the attractiveness of the concept, not as a thing in itself, but as a means of making sense of new forms of topography and relational urban framings. Shields views the "city-region" as a reflection of a transitory moment as cities go from defining themselves around regional oppositions (town and country) to an uncertain situation where local identities are now mediated though comparisons with an ill-defined global other. Thus, not purely rhetorical, the fervour surrounding city-regionalism and the political mobilization of this language (see Rees and Lord, this volume) provide an insight into the ways in which cities are being re-imagined, and the types of economic and state relations that frame them. City-regions have been one means of capturing and accounting for these transitions, and the implication is that it is these transitions, and not only the object itself, which should attract analytic attention.

Together, both Harrison and Shields remind us that to identify the city-region and assess its prospects, we must approach it in action. By this, we mean the way in which concepts are mobilized, translated, and applied. This pertains equally to the employment of the concepts of city-regions as a means of rebounding city and regional governance and development, and as a discourse accounting for an urbanizing, global world. In order to obtain an understanding of the city-region in action, it is essential to critically engage the experience of communities, the evolution of city-regional concepts in practice, and the ways in which this range of experience challenge future thinking about the place of urban-regional localities and a global world. It is to the challenge of assessing the prospects of the city-region in the relationships between place, rhetoric, and practice that we now turn our attention.

BETWEEN PLACE, RHETORIC, AND PRACTICE

The chapters comprising the remainder of this collection represent a kind of "typical" experience of city-regions, or, at least, of experiments in city-regionalism. They are typical not in the sense that they represent a uniform pattern of experience; rather, each chapter presents an account of a city-region that has been experimenting with the application of the logics and ambitions of city-regionalism within its individual context.

A great deal of the literature on city-regions, and the core texts from which the key tenets of city-regionalism are derived, are dominated by a relatively narrow range of case studies. Academic scrutiny has followed the continuing domination of older metropolitan centres that still occupy a position of conceptual and material centrality in our society. "World" cities (Friedmann 1986) or "global" cities at the heart of networks of capital and culture (Sassen 2000; 2001) make up the primary lexicon of city-regions, and include cities such as London, Tokyo, New York, Paris, Hong Kong, Singapore, Chicago, Los Angeles, Berlin, and Milan. The result is an academic literature so huge that, in 1995, Friedman sought to take stock of a "decade of world city research" (21). A similar degree of scrutiny has been cast at the other end of the scale of urban fortunes. The collapse of some once-great cities has been considered at length.

Significant population loss, corresponding housing market failure, a sclerotic economy, social distress, and a crumbling downtown have been understood as forming common features of a post-industrial urban landscape. Such characteristics have been found to varying degrees in numerous contexts; however, most attention has been focused on cities of the United States' rustbelt, such as Detroit (Neill 1995), and of Western Europe (Couch et al. 2003; Gospodini 2006), particularly the "shock cities" of the industrial revolution, such as those of Germany's Ruhrgebiet (Almaas 2005; Cooke 1995).

By contrast, many of the cases presented in this volume come from cities mostly outside the mainstream of the discipline. Our cases are drawn from Canada, the United States, and the United Kingdom, and include Ottawa, Montreal, Calgary, Waterloo, Sheffield, Pittsburgh, and Manchester. We caution against referring to these as "a second tier" of cities. To do so may give too much credence to the multitude of ranking systems and metrics used to define the global city while also undermining local and contextual valuations of place (see Smart and Tanasescu, this volume). For the most part, however, it is fair to say that many of our case study examples represent a range of cities which are of moderate population and which do not necessarily house the diversity of economic activity and cultural experience seen to characterize global cities. Our choice of these cases has been conscious. We have not wanted to focus on those totemic cities that are emblematic as city-regions and that dominate the literature. Instead, we wished to focus on cities that are in some way aspirational, and where experiments of city-regionalism have been seen as a means of development and participation in global networks. A subtle shift has taken place in the conversation about city-regions, extending the logic of global city-regions to cities and regions of all sorts. Often this means that cities are involved in shoehorning ideas from elsewhere into local contexts at worst, or applying and adapting ideas to their own situations at best. It is the messy, uncertain, and incomplete nature of these experiments, often taking place over many years, which draws our attention, and which we would argue is typical of the experience of the past two decades.

The approach of the authors to making sense of these experiments is explicitly local. The cases presented are focused on the contextual experiences of places and communities through processes of spatial reform. In this fashion, we have been very much motivated by the perspective of seminal planning scholar Patrick Geddes and the need to understand participation in regional and global networks from a basis of knowledge of one's locality in the first instance. All of the case studies in the second part of this volume explore the fit between city-regional planning models and local places. They address a divergent range of practice and experience, and identify the value communities have found in the concept, but also examine where the ambitions of city-regionalism remain uncertain or fleeting, and what, or even who, is excluded within these processes.

The first three case studies in the book situate city-regionalism within a political understanding of urban development. They question the logics, rhetorics, and discourses of city-regionalism, and seek to address the impacts of city-regionalism on places and communities. In chapter 4, James Rees and Alex Lord ask what a decade of city-regional activity in the United Kingdom has left imprinted upon the nation's conurban spaces. Throughout the 1990s, places such as Manchester were at the locus of city-regional planning discussions; however, the authors argue that city-regionalism is often as much a political project as it is a recognition of existing functional geographies. The origins of the most recent drive for city-regional governance in England, Rees and Lord suggest, are better understood rhetorically – a territorial counterpoint to the then–New Labour government's policy ideologies. While city-regions were supported by Britain's policy elites, their impact on the ground is perceived as halting, incremental, and weak. England's city-regions were not entirely virtual, and spoke to enduring issues about partnership-building and centre-periphery relations. However, the authors conclude that as a radical re-territorialization of urban governance, the project of English city-regionalism has so far not been fully realized.

In chapter 5, Alan Smart and Alina Tanasescu examine recent trends towards global city rankings and the status of cities that aspire to, and act in ways to achieve, positive rankings. Motivated by a Foucauldian analysis of city-regional planning in Calgary, Alberta, the authors argue that ranking systems impose artificial external criteria demarcating the relative value of places. It is not simply that ranking systems fail to capture the multifaceted value of a place, but that they, through systems of metrics and measurement, structure the ways in which wannabe cities act, restructure, and plan in attempting to compete. What is lost is the ability to imagine city-regions in alternative ways, accounting for local inequalities and local development challenges.

David Etherington, drawing on research from Sheffield in the United Kingdom, provides a methodical critique of city-regionalism in chapter 6. The author argues that city-regionalism, far from being neutral, has become a means of extending neoliberal development logics at the scale of the city. While local in name, the city-region for Etherington is better understood as the product of national ideologies that impose discourses of competitiveness and entrepreneurialism onto labour markets. City-regions, in other words, perpetuate structural relations between capital and the state, albeit in novel forms (see, for example, Jonas and Ward 2007a; Ward 2004; Brenner 2003). This language, measured by nationally set targets, forces thinking about development in line with neoliberal development strategies while ignoring the downside of this development and precluding discussion about alternatives. The cost for Etherington is the disguising of the historical continuation of uneven development in the region and the failure to invest in strategies to contend with systemic poverty (see also Etherington and Jones 2009).

Is it possible to think about city-regionalism in different ways? What are the roles of community, identity, and place-making in developing locally robust city-regions? These questions motivate a number of the contributions to this book. Taken together, the remaining five case study chapters make a persuasive argument for the importance of engendering dynamic, flexible, and relational modes of city-regionalism. Such an approach, unfortunately, stands in opposition to much of the experience of city-regions, where large, strategic boundary-drawing and governance exercises are imposed atop a place and its communities.

Caroline Andrew, in chapter 7, contrasts Ottawa's history of a largely bureaucratic regionalization with potential alternate regional narratives explicitly tied to place. Applying recent theoretical work on the role of storytelling and urban place-making, Andrew emphasizes the importance of developing regional identities, and the types of engaged relations and subjective agency necessary to do so. Where, for the most part, city-regional planning in Ottawa has lacked a local political vision or engagement with the wider community, Andrew advocates a connected vision of planning that reflects and respects the city's rich history and diversity of communities. Storytelling, in other words, may be one way of reconnecting local contexts, people, and places to abstract and externally motivated regionalization strategies.

In chapter 8, planning scholar Michael Glass discusses recent experiments in regional planning in Pittsburgh. Glass provides an account of how, on the back of a century of failed regional endeavours and faced with a stagnating economy, the city and its contiguous municipalities in 2008 began a negotiated and partial regional process. Glass argues that the potential success of this process is directly related to its ad-hoc nature. Where previous attempts at imposing new structural boundaries on the city-region, as well as attempts to reconfigure regional governance, failed, the current CONNECT initiative is able to navigate a middle road, creating new relationships between municipalities without getting bogged down in drawing new boundaries or creating new forms of governance. Glass argues that it is the contextual, fluid, and dynamic nature of this process that allows it to succeed where other, more formal, processes have failed.

Political scientist David Wolfe makes a similar argument in chapter 9 for valuing the dynamism of regional relations with his case study of the growth dynamics of Waterloo, Ontario. By reference to the resiliency of city-regions, the author investigates the capacity of regions to cope with shock or to create new development trajectories. In response to the dominance of economic growth models in accounting for resilience, Wolfe argues that consideration should also be given to the makeup of civic institutions and the context of their relations. Resilient city-regions are those where collaboration across both sectors and communities is strong. Where the author sees Waterloo excelling is in its ability to expand these relationships across multiple, targeted initiatives without getting embroiled in the politics of large, strategic restructuring processes.

The resilience or sustainability of cities is, of course, not only about adapting economies. As the final two chapters of this collection remind us, it is also about responding to the pressing social and environmental challenges of our contemporary societies. In chapter 10, Louis Guay and Pierre Hamel consider the ability of cities, such as Montreal, Canada, to respond to these novel challenges. They explore how planning and the creation of regional cooperative networks can provide a means for successfully coming to terms with today's complex and multifaceted hazard scenarios. In other words, the authors ask how an ecological urbanity can be fostered.

In chapter 11, Kyle Whitfield and Allison Williams ask a similar set of questions, investigating the impact of trends towards both regionalization and, more recently, city-regionalism on health service provision in western Canada. The authors chart an evolving rescaling of service delivery that is rationalized as a means of creating greater efficiency, equality, and local autonomy in health services. Yet, despite these compelling logics, the authors argue that often the results are ambiguous: for instance, creating service inequities between regions or increasing service bureaucracy. More concerning, as also noted by Etherington (this volume), the rhetoric of regionalism has the capacity to obscure cuts and declining service provision.

Chapters in this book examine the development of the city-region and present a variety of case studies that prompt both conceptual reflection and the need to better understand the relationship between concepts and practice. Importantly, we have approached this task from a proactively interdisciplinary approach. First, this provides some degree of reflection on the breadth of research and scholarly writing around the city-region. As described above, the challenge of reflecting on the city-region in prospect is picked up by urban planners, political economists, geographers, political scientists, health service planners, and sociologists. There is benefit in sharing this variety with the reader as an objective in and of itself. Moreover, this approach serves a central argument of this collection as a whole – that a key failing to date has been the tendency towards reduction and the dominance of narrow, externally derived logics in the ways we think about and practice city-regionalism (see Conclusion, this volume).

A good example of the value of working across perspectives relates to the close association which has been drawn between city-regionalism and economic development. Cities and regions are rising in prominence as a scale from which economic development is derived, and at which economic policies should therefore be directed. Coinciding with the neoliberal loosening of economic territorial boundaries, urban areas have taken on new roles in seeking to obtain a competitive advantage in national and global economic networks. Municipalities now spend considerable effort in attracting investment and talent, carving out specialist economic niches, and creating the places to support these activities.

Keating (2001), however, noting these changes, cautions against assuming that this emergent political order necessarily defines the city-region as any one thing. This opposes the mainstream of practice, where the tendency has been to adopt overly deterministic views of the politics of re-territorialization, to which cities and regions are expected to adapt. The policy agenda which follows is narrowed to that of "boosterism and growth" (387). What's left out is the diversity (and therefore flexibility) of territorial models; the plurality of what defines a city, a region, or a place; and a politics of development that is open to those wider aspects of prosperity referred to above. Keating states, "As the region or city is reconceptualised as an actor in the global order, there is a reification of what is a complex and plural system and a further closure of political options. Globalization is then brought in to serve what the French call the *pensée unique*, another form of the old 'one best way' philosophy in which political debate about the future of social and economic life is largely precluded" (375).

Opening up the politics of the city-region, maintaining attitudes toward plurality, and supporting the development of diverse institutional forms and engagement are essential to a more robust version of the city-region. Instead of narrow economic policies, *together* our collaborators identify the *interdependent* value of supporting partnerships, innovating governance, engaging community identities, fostering institutional thickness, addressing equity, and building sustainability. Our aim has been to, where possible, integrate perspectives and open up discourse. Where this necessarily exceeds the ability of this single volume, we hope to present a challenge to others to do so.

SUMMARY

By examining the city-region in prospect and in practice, the authors of this volume collectively sketch out new pathways for thinking about and acting upon municipal growth and territorial rescaling of governance. Overall, the book argues that city-regionalism should not be understood either as a static description of a current state of affairs or as a toolkit to be applied to practice. Rather, it involves a range of ideas seeking to account for the growing importance of cities in a global world. Its meanings are neither fully certain nor uncontested, although they often are interpreted as such. Instead, the city-region is best understood as a rallying point around which scholars and communities can come together to reflect upon and negotiate their collective urban futures. This book argues that to make sense of the city-region, and to make it meaningful in practice, it is necessary to understand development from the perspective of local context, to engage communities, and to openly acknowledge its political and contested nature.

This community-centred approach, in its most essential aspect, articulates and makes visible tensions in the normative politics of city-regionalism. Recognition of the value of contingency, and the awareness that city-regions can be adapted, influenced, and debated locally, is a necessary first step to creating smart, locally oriented, and human-centred plans for the future of our urban areas. The challenges of creating economically vibrant, environmentally sustainable, and just urban cities and regions require locally rooted approaches to planning and governance, supported by strong and engaged civic networks. The city-region, as it is currently understood, does not itself provide a clear pathway to achieving these aims. However, opening up the city-region may provide the opportunities to innovate new ways and to think about and develop policy in response to the global urbanization of our societies.

NOTES

1 The three previous paragraphs have been abstracted from an earlier version of Harrison (this voume), with permission of the author.
2 We are not alone in making this observation. A session chaired by John Harrison and Michael Hoyler at a recent annual meeting of the British Royal Geographical Association in London reflected on ten years of city-regional experience in the UK. See Harrison and Hoyler 2014.

REFERENCES

Almaas, I.H. 2005. "Regenerating the Ruhr." *Architectural Review* 205 (1224): 13–14.

Begum, A. 2007. "Urban Housing as an Issue of Redistribution through Planning: The Case of Dhaka City." *Social Policy and Administration* 41 (4): 410–18.

Brenner, N. 1998. "Global Cities, Glocal States: Global City Formation and State Territorial Restructuring in Contemporary Europe." *Review of International Political Economy* 5 (1): 1–37.

– 2003. "Metropolitan Institutional Reform and the Rescaling of State Space in Contemporary Western Europe." *European Urban and Regional Studies* 10 (4): 297–324.

Cohen, J.E. 2003. "Human Population: The Next Half Century." *Science* 302 (5648): 1172–5.

Cooke, P., ed. 1995. *The Rise of the Rustbelt*. New York: St. Martin's Press.

Couch, C., C. Fraser, and S. Percy. 2003. *Urban Regeneration in Europe*. Oxford, UK: Blackwell.

Etherington, D., and M. Jones. 2009. "City Regions and New Geographies of Uneven Development and Inequality." *Regional Studies* 43 (2): 247–65.

Florida, R. 2003. *The Rise of the Creative Class: And How It's Transforming Work, Leisure, Community and Everyday Life*. New York: Basic Books.

Friedmann, J. 1986. "The World City Hypothesis." *Development and Change* 17 (1): 69–83.

– 1995. "Where We Stand: A Decade of World City Research." In *World Cities in a World System*, edited by P.L. Knox and P.J. Taylor, 21–54. Cambridge: Cambridge University Press.

Geddes, P. 1915. *Cities in Evolution*. London: Williams and Margate.

Gospodini, A. 2006. "Portraying, Classifying and Understanding the Emerging Landscapes in the Post-Industrial City." *Cities* 23 (5): 311–30.

Gottman, J. 1961. *Megalopolis: The Urbanized Northeastern Seaboard of the United States*. New York: Twentieth Century Fund.

Harrison, J., and M. Hoyler. 2014. "Governing the New Metropolis." *Urban Studies* 51 (11): 2249–66. DOI: 10.1177/0042098013500699.

Herrschel, T., and P. Newman. 2002. *Governance of Europe's City Regions: Planning, Policy & Politics*. London: Routledge.

Jenkins, P., H. Smith, and Y.P. Wang. 2007. *Planning and Housing in the Rapidly Urbanising World*. London: Routledge.

Jonas, A.E.G., and K. Ward. 2007. "Introduction to Debate on City-Regions: New Geographies of Governance, Democracy and Social Reproduction." *International Journal of Urban and Regional Research* 31 (1): 169–78.

Keating, M. 2001. "Governing Cities and Regions: Territorial Restructuring." In *Global City-Regions: Trends, Theory, Policy*, edited by A.J. Scott. Oxford, UK: Oxford University Press.

Neill, W.J.V. 1995. "Lipstick on the Gorilla: The Failure of Image-Led Planning in Coleman Young's Detroit." *International Journal of Urban and Regional Research* 19 (4): 639–53.

Sancton, A. 2000. *Merger Mania: The Assault on Local Government*. Montreal: McGill-Queen's University Press.

Sassen, S. 2000. *Cities in a World Economy*. Thousand Oaks, CA: Pine Forge Press.

– 2001. *The Global City: New York, London, Tokyo*. Princeton, NJ: Princeton University Press.

Scott, A.J. 2001. *Global City-Regions: Trends, Theory, Policy*. Oxford, UK: Oxford University Press.

– 2008. *The Social Economy of the Modern Metropolis: Cognitive-Cultural Capitalism and the Global Resurgence of Cities*. Oxford, UK: Oxford University Press.

Sudhir, V., G. Srinivasan, and V.R. Muraleedharan. 1998. "Planning for Sustainable Solid Waste Management in Urban India." *System Dynamics Review* 13 (3): 223–46.

Taylor, P.J., G. Catalano, and D.R.F. Walker. 2002. "Measurement of the World City Network." *Urban Studies* 39 (13): 2367–76.

Umali-Deininger, D., and K.W. Deininger. 2001. "Towards Greater Food Security for India's Poor: Balancing Government Intervention and Private Competition." *Agricultural Economics* 25 (2–3): 321–35.

UN Habitat. 2013. *State of the World's Cities 2012/2013, Prosperity of Cities*. New York: UN Habitat.

United Nations Population Division. 2002. *World Urbanization Prospects: The 2001 Revision*. ESA/P/WP.173. New York: United Nations.

Ward, K. 2000. "Front Rentiers to Rantiers: 'Active Entrepreneurs', 'Structural Speculators' and the Politics of Marketing the City." *Urban Studies* 37 (7): 1093–1107.

Yokohari, M., K. Takeuchi, W. Takashi, and S. Yokata. 2000. "Beyond Greenbelts and Zoning: A New Planning Concept for the Environment of Asian Mega-Cities." *Landscape and Urban Planning* 47 (3–4): 159–71.

2

The City-Region: In Retrospect, in Snapshot, in Prospect

JOHN HARRISON

INTRODUCTION: IN WHAT SENSE A *CITY-REGIONAL* WORLD?[1]

The past decade has been dominated by discourses affirming a resurgence of city-regions in globalization. Part and parcel of these discourses is a growing appreciation that city-regions are emerging as the primary spatial scale at which competing political and economic agendas are convened, not least those pertaining to increasing competitiveness while simultaneously tackling entrenched inequalities, encouraging progressive planning, and enabling piecemeal democratic rights. Ever since Allen Scott's (2001a) edited collection *Global City-Regions: Trends, Theory, Policy* conceptually mapped and empirically demonstrated the emergence of "global" city-regions as a new kind of critically important geographical and institutional phenomenon on the world stage, city-regions have been revered as *the* pivotal societal formation in advanced globalization. According to Scott and his acolytes, city-regions represent a new scale of urbanization, and city-regionalism a new phase in capitalist territorial development – a belief fuelled by recognition that while accelerating processes of global economic integration and rapid urbanization are resulting in the resurgence of cities in globalization, substantive expressions of urbanization result in metropolitan landscapes stretching far beyond their traditional territorial boundaries. One only has to look at the exceptional rate of city expansion into larger city-regions comprising multiple functionally interlinked urban settlements in China, for example, to appreciate how "the city" as traditionally conceived no longer adequately reflects the underlying structure of how urban life is being organized in globalization.

Concomitant with this is the recognition that city expansion into globalizing city-regions increasingly challenges existing urban economic infrastructures and urban-regional governance (Harrison 2012a). Reliant as municipalities are on outdated and inadequate institutional structures, infrastructures, territorialities, and statutory frameworks, the requirement for more "appropriate" – generally accepted to mean more flexible, networked, and smart – forms of urban and regional planning and governance arrangements has seen the new city-regionalism mutate over the past ten years to be proxy for the officially institutionalized task of constructing policies, strategies, and institutions at a city-regional scale.[2] Stirred into action by these developments, scholars documenting the rise of city-regions have gone a long way to advance claims of a *city-regional* world (cf. Storper 1997), where cities at the heart of major urban-regional industrial production complexes constitute the "dominant leading edge of contemporary capitalist development" (Scott et al. 2001, 4).

Synonymous with much of this work have been normative claims relating to how city-regions (1) function as the basic motors of the national economies within which they are located, (2) are fundamental to economic and social revitalization, and (3) are vital in establishing effective and progressive planning and policy-making. Moreover, and heavily inscribed in interpretations supporting notions of a city-regional world, there is an idea that city-regions are quasi-autonomous functional economic spaces, increasingly acting and operating across and/or beyond the control of territorial structures formally administered or governed by nation-states. From this perspective, the strategic role and geo-economic power of major city-regions in organizing and structuring globalized forms of capital accumulation have seen key proponents of the new city-regionalism posit how "global" city-regions are superseding national economies as the fundamental unit of capitalist development – a postulation which is doing much to push claims of an advancing city-regional world (Scott 2001a; Ohmae 2001; cf. Storper 1997). Nonetheless, for all these accounts heroically championing the dynamism of city-regions in globalization, the new city-regionalism has not gone unchecked or unchallenged. For critics of the new city-regionalism, concerns have arisen over the theorization of city-regions, as many commentators come to question the capacity of the city-region concept to account for current and future expressions of urban and regional change (Harrison 2007; Jonas and Ward 2007; Ward and Jonas 2004). Away from enthusiastic cheerleading, critics are now quick to point to "the city-region" as having remained a largely Delphian concept.

Placing the city-region concept under the microscope is becoming central to contemporary urban-regional debates, and is the starting point for this chapter. The city-region is not a new concept; what is new is the way the concept is being applied to account for the unprecedented expansion in the size, scale, scope, and reach of the city. Under the umbrella of the new city-regionalism, we have witnessed the production of a renewed spatial vocabulary for conceptualizing cities and regions, urban and regional change. Surveying the literature on the new city-regionalism reveals a proliferation of new terms and concepts conjured up to assist in the theorization of these large-scale and complex urban formations. Included are various derivatives, extensions, and alternatives to the traditional theorization of city-regions, with prominent examples being: global city-region (Scott 2001a); world city-region (Kunzmann 1998); mega-city-region (Xu and Yeh 2010); polycentric mega-city-region (Hall and Pain 2006); mega-region (Florida 2008); metro region (OECD 2007); metropolitan region (Brenner 2002); polycentric metropolis (Hall and Pain 2006); urban region (Meijers 2005); mega urban region (Douglass 2000); polynuclear urban region (Turok and Bailey 2004); super-urban area (Harrison 2015); cross-border metropolitan region (Harrison and Growe 2014); new megalopolis (Knox and Lang 2008); and megapolitan region (Lang and Dhvale 2005).

Now, for an advocate of the new city-regionalism, all of this frantic conceptualization activity may appear to emphasize the rise of city-regions as novel and critically important geographical and institutional phenomena on the world stage (cf. Lovering 1999, endnote 1). Yet for engaged critics, these and other more recent extensions to the city-region concept are doing much to disturb the surety many of us have in writing about and working with city-regions. Failures to adequately outline conceptually or empirically define the "city-region" have led critics to suggest how the city-region has remained an "object of mystery" in many accounts pertaining to a new city-regionalism (Harrison 2007). Nevertheless, we can (broadly speaking) identify three analytical conceptions of the city-region in the new city-regionalism: (1) The *agglomeration* model, inspired by the "new economic geography," where city-regions are conceived as "dense polarised masses of capital, labour, and social life that are bound up in intricate ways in intensifying and far-flung extra-national relationships. As such, they represent an outgrowth of large metropolitan areas – or contiguous sets of metropolitan areas – together with surrounding hinterlands of variable extent which may themselves be sites of scattered urban settlements" (Scott 2001b, 814). (2) A *scale* model rooted in the traditions of political science and public policy, which considers city-regions to be "a strategic and political level of administration and policy-making, extending beyond the administrative boundaries of single urban local government authorities to include urban and/or semi-urban hinterlands" (Tewdwr-Jones and McNeill 2000, 131). (3) A relationally networked *hub and spokes* model which presupposes the city-region to be "a functionally inter-related geographical area comprising a central, or core city, as part of a network of urban centres and rural hinterlands" (UK Government 2005, 1). Indeed it could be usefully argued that two of these conceptual constructs reflect the editors' own understanding of the need to approach the city-region "as the product of global urbanization" (*agglomeration*) and as a concept by which "novel spatial alignments of cities and global networks are being imagined" (*hub and spokes*) (Jones et al., this volume).

The city-region has been actively constructed to be a "chaotic" concept (cf. Sayer 1992), leaving us multiple theorizations of the city-region after ten years of the new city-regionalism. This is not to suggest that having multiple theorizations of the city-region is necessarily problematic; rather, contrasting theorizations of the city-region concept are the result of how city-regions are constructed politically – a direct response to a particular set of challenges, needs, ambitions, and desires which vary across place-specific contexts. This chapter highlights how city-regions and the city-region concept are being actively constructed according to the need to make these new urban economic spaces, with their new governance and planning arrangements, compatible with existing forms of territorially embedded state spatial/scalar organization. The task of making city-regions complementary with existing forms of local, regional, and national state spatial organization requires different constructions of the city-region concept to be developed at different scales, in different places, and at different times to secure the overall coherence of state spatial/scalar organization.

The process by which city-regions are defined, delimited, and designated is a deeply political act – one that is ultimately dependent on the actors involved, the purpose for which the "city-region" concept is mobilized, and the context-specific obstacles posed by this mobilization. Indeed, as the contributions to this collection exemplify, the mobilization of the "city-region" concept as *inter alia* competitive space, planning space, resilient space, functional space, space for place-marketing, or space for political and community engagement highlights the diversity and plurality of approaches to city-regionalism (Jones et al., this volume). It is not surprising to recognize that what we collectively refer to as "city-regionalism" is actually the product of an amalgamation of different disciplinary perspectives (economic geography, planning, political science, sociology) and discursive frames. Capturing a flavour of this, the chapter presents "in retrospect," "in snapshot," and "in prospect" perspectives on theorizing the city-region.

CITY-REGIONS "IN RETROSPECT"

The term "city-region" was first coined at the beginning of the last century. We can trace the city-region concept all the way back to 1905 and the work of Patrick Geddes, a pioneering Scottish planner and a founding father of city and regional planning. Geddes' contribution to developing the city-region concept comes from his studies of Glasgow at the turn of the twentieth century, and his observation that there was an outpouring of population beyond the bounded city such that the city was devouring small towns and boroughs as it went. Geddes' contribution is further indicated by the fact he went on to mint neologisms such as "conurbation" and "megalopolis" to support his recognition that the city should be studied in the context of the region.

The next major advance came in the 1930s, when the German geographer Walter Christaller developed central place theory, advancing understandings of how cities function as systems of cities, rather than as single entities functioning in isolation (Christaller 1933). Like Geddes, Christaller recognized the importance of relationships between cities and their regional hinterlands, albeit this time in the context of predominantly rural southern Germany. For Christaller, it was the economic relationships of cities with their regional hinterlands that proved the foundation for developing the city-region concept in ways which, in part, are consistent with its use today. Furthermore, the model proposed by Christaller reveals the earliest indication of the three different approaches to conceptualizing city-regions evident in the new city-regionalism. *Agglomeration* can be seen in Christaller's recognition that population size is not necessarily synonymous with the importance of a settlement; rather, it is the centrality of place which produces a hierarchy of urban settlements. Conceptualized for Christaller in terms of the settlement's importance in the region around it, the difference some seventy years later is that Scott's (2001a) positioning of global city-regions at the apex of a new global urban hierarchy attaches importance to cities' centrality in global circuits of capital accumulation.

Of particular interest for the present discussion is how Christaller's model is "constructed" thereafter. One of the most striking features of central place theory is Christaller's use of hexagons, as opposed to circles, to enable the inclusion of all areas into his model. At the same time, this removed the challenge of dealing with potential overlap between functional economic areas. Particularly important in Germany, where maintaining territorial equilibrium has been the guiding principle of spatial planning throughout the twentieth century, the use of hexagons gave Christaller's model wide appeal among political elites, for it enabled the production of spatial policies that could be presented as territorially inclusive – indicative of the *scale* model used today (see below in the cases of England and Germany). For this reason, central place theory became a template for post-war national spatial planning in many countries,[3] while the famous layouts it inspired (K = 3 marketing principle, K = 4 transport principle, K = 7 administrative principle) offer the classic example of a *hub and spokes* perspective on city-region relations.

For all this, however, it is the geographer Robert Dickinson who is seen by many to be the founding father of the city-region concept. Inspired by Geddes and Christaller among others, and drawing together evidence from the United States, France, Germany, and Britain, Dickinson's books *The City-Region in Western Europe* (1964) and *City and Region: A Geographical Interpretation* (1967) established the conceptual foundations that enabled the city-region to be presented as a distinct concept. What is most revealing about Dickinson, however, is that despite being the founding father of the city-region concept, he is almost entirely forgotten by both proponents and critics of the new city-regionalism. Why might this be? One major clue lies in the opening statement of *City Region and Regionalism*, where he declares, "This book is not about planning" (1947, xiii). Written at a time when geography produced "town and country planners" (Taylor 1999, 8), Dickinson kicked back against the post-war planning consensus – underpinned by a positivist philosophy asserting how human behaviour could be predicted and therefore planned – choosing instead to pursue a more constructivist approach: what today would amount to an incipient form of the "relational" approach to theorizing the city and region.

Bucking the popular trend of the time left Dickinson somewhat isolated from his peers, which led his contemporaries to contend that "when the great upsurge of interest and work in urban geography began in the 1950s, Dickinson was little more than a footnote to these major shifts in the practice of geography, though his work may have initially influenced (either directly or indirectly) some of the next generation of urban pioneers" (Johnston 2002, 720).[4] Dickinson's two books were universally castigated for being *inter alia* "too long" and "indigestible" (721). It is hardly surprising then that scholars writing about the new city-regionalism some forty years later have been guilty of overlooking Dickinson's contribution, other than the usual perfunctory reference to acknowledge his minting of the term "city-region." But in overlooking Dickinson, today's researchers have neglected his contribution to what remains the cornerstone of our understanding of the concept – namely, that city-regions are socially and politically constructed:

> This concept of the city-region, like all concepts, is a mental construct. It is not, as some planners and scholars seem to think, an area that is presented on a platter to suit their general needs. The extent of the area they need will depend on the specific purpose for which it is required. The concept of the city-region can only be made specific and definable, as a geographic entity, by reference to the precise and areal extent of particular associations with the city. (Dickinson 1967, 227)

Nevertheless, not even the attacks on planning and the assumptions underpinning 1960s spatial science – including work from geographers embracing a humanist perspective to advance ideas on the social construction of place and the emergence of a post-positivist paradigm (e.g. Entrikin 1976) – could rescue Dickinson's ideas and

bring them back into mainstream geography.[5] The city-region concept was to become largely invisible in the lexicon of academics and
policy elites during the 1970s and on into the 1980s, due in large
part to the rise of globalization and a consensus suggesting how
advances in technology and communication would induce an era of
global deconcentration and deterritorialization, characterized by a
diminishing role for cities. Furthermore, the rapid decline of those
major industrial cities that had benefited most from the Fordist
growth dynamic (for example, Dortmund and Essen in the Ruhr
district of Germany, the "snowbelt" cities of Detroit and Pittsburgh
in the northeastern United States, and Liverpool and Manchester in
the north of England), resulting in mass unemployment, unprecedented levels of social upheaval, and general urban decay, saw the
attention of academics and policy elites switch from the regional
relations and functionality of these once-great industrial cities to the
crises unfolding in their inner cores.

CITY-REGIONS "IN SNAPSHOT"

By the year 2000 there may well be as many as 500 cities with more than
a million inhabitants while the largest of them, Tokyo, Sao Paulo,
Mumbai and possibly Shanghai (though the list is perpetually being
revised both upwards and downwards), will perhaps boast populations of
more than twenty million trailed by a score of cities, mostly in the
so-called developing countries, with upwards of ten million. Sometime
early [in the twenty-first] century, if present trends continue, more than
half of the world's population will be classified as urban rather than rural.
(Harvey 2000, 38)

Here Harvey neatly contextualizes how the resurgence of interest in
city-regions owes much to the changing fortune of cities in globalization. For one, the predicted decline of cities never materialized; in
fact, quite the opposite happened. Certainly globalization has rendered distance less of a barrier to exchange, and thereby extended
our capacity to interact across space more freely and frequently; but
as globalization has advanced, the propensity for economic activity
to cluster in dense agglomerations has delivered overwhelming evidence affirming how a select group of "global" cities (e.g. London,
New York, Tokyo) and "metropolitan" regions (e.g. Silicon Valley,
Baden-Württemberg, South East England) bucked the trend of

national economic decline to emerge as strategic territorial platforms for post-Fordist capital accumulation. Their recognition gave rise to the dominant "global city" (Sassen 1991) and "new regionalist" (Scott 1998; Storper 1997) discourses of the 1990s, and fuelled accelerated urbanization. Less than a decade into this century, Harvey's prediction that more than fifty percent of the world's population would live in cities became reality. Rather more startling is the current forecast that this will rise to seventy percent by 2050, when the world population is estimated to exceed nine billion (UNFPA 2007).

While it is not possible here to go into depth about the drivers underpinning this wider context of accelerating processes of global economic integration and urbanization, it is necessary to emphasize three related points. First, cities and metropolitan regions have emerged as foci for globalized capital accumulation insofar as localized agglomeration economies foster and harbour the conditions, assets, and capacities upon which transnational capital depends. Second, claims that globalization is fuelling a resurgence of cities as drivers of competitiveness and affluence entice more and more people to become urban dwellers, meaning that globalizing cities are spilling over their traditional "city limits." And third, the recognition that a globalizing city's development is less linked to its nearby *regional* "hinterland" than to a far-reaching *global* "hinterworld" (Taylor 2001) ensures the resurgence of the city-region concept to map and conceptualize the transforming metropolitan economic, political, and social landscape at the beginning of the twenty-first century; but this definition of the city-region cannot be equated with that minted by Dickinson, and used by others throughout the second half of the twentieth century, as the regional relations of the city. Reflecting on this, Kathy Pain usefully surmises how "confusion arises concerning what functional expansion means in theorizing this *new* city-region scale" (2011a, 84; emphasis added).

It is precisely this confusion which prompted Allen Scott and colleagues to develop the concept of the "global" city-region (Scott 2001a). In an extension of the logic that saw global cities defined by their external linkages during the 1900s (Sassen 1991), global city-regions are defined in this century by the external. *and* internal dynamics that shape them (Hall 2001). From this perspective, it could be suggested that the defining feature of theorizing the global city-region is actually the return of Dickinson's ideas on the regional

relations of the city to contemporary studies of cities in globalization. Adding weight to this argument is the recognition that much
work on the theorization of these spatial formations is being led by
a group of predominantly British geographers who advocate the
need for a more radically "relational" approach to the conception of
cities and regions (Allen and Cochrane 2007, 2011; Allen et al.
1998; Amin 2004; Massey 2007). Here Allen et al. echo Dickinson's
much earlier observations:

> [Regional] studies are always done for a purpose, with a specific
> view. Whether territorial, political, cultural or whatever, there is
> always a specific focus. One cannot study everything, and there
> are multiple ways of seeing a place: there is no complete 'portrait
> of a region'. Moreover ... 'regions' only exist in relation to par-
> ticular criteria. They are not 'out there' waiting to be discovered;
> they are our (and others') constructions. (Allen et al. 1998, 2)

Unlike Dickinson, though, Allen et al.'s (1998) book *Rethinking the
Region* was very well received, with the above quote often cited in
contemporary urban and regional studies as signifying a substantive
expression of the underlying mantra of a reconstructed and re-theorized
late-twentieth-century regional geography centred on regions (and
regional space) as the outcome of social relations/processes.[6] What
makes Allen et al.'s contribution all the more important in this discussion is the overall aim "to *conceptualize* the geography of growth ...
and in so doing review how regions are made and remade over space
and time" (viii–ix, original emphasis).

Analyzing the dynamics and geography of growth within South
East England – pivotal region of the 1980s Thatcherite "neoliberal
growth project," and England's only authentic "global" city-region
– Allen et al.'s study revealed how regions and regional space are the
product of "stretched out" social relations/processes. By comparing
maps illustrating the distribution of different socio-economic indicators (e.g. earnings, income, house prices, employment, national
government spending, trade, and investment flows), Allen et al.
demonstrated how social relations/processes do not easily equate
with an "area," making it a challenge to map them, and have their
own "regional" geography, making the task of pinning down "the
region" incredibly difficult. Their analysis went on to show that
the boundaries of a region change depending on which social

relations/processes are the focus of attention, and rarely coincide with the actual politico-administrative unit of regional government. Moreover, where the process of city expansion into globalizing city-regions is occurring, networks of social relations/processes stretch across and beyond the boundaries of sub-national political and administrative units.

Relating this back to the city-region concept, the intellectual lineage taking us from Allen et al.'s exposition of the dynamics and geography of growth to Scott's development of the global city-region concept is clearly not a big leap. Whereas Allen et al. were concerned with analyzing accelerating processes of global economic integration with geographic differentiation (e.g. uneven development in relation to class, labour, ethnic, and gender dimensions), in order to understand the dynamics and geography of (urban-regional) growth, Scott's endeavour to develop the concept of the "global city-region" derived from his motivation to (1) promote the "new regionalism" as an alternative to the hyper-globalist view of the world as a borderless space of flows, and (2) put "global city-regions firmly on the analytical and policy agendas" as exemplars of regional socio-economic formations that are less subservient to the dictates of the central state than older regionalisms (Scott 2001a, xiv). The latter point is particularly revealing. On the one hand, it revealed the rationale behind the claim that city-regionalism is a new phase of post-national capitalist territorial development. Yet on the other hand, it exposed to critics how Scott's motivations led him and his followers to overstate the decline in the power of the nation-state vis-à-vis the emergent power structures of globalizing city-regions, and to overplay the "smooth transition" to a city-regional world implied in much work on the new city-regionalism (see Ward and Jonas 2004).

Although there is much to admire in the new city-regionalism, in the first instance critics have been able to demonstrate how in all but a select few truly "global" city-regions the state retains the propensity to remain orchestrator-in-chief, shaping city-regions – their policies, governance and planning arrangements, powers, and functions – in ways that enable it to protect its own legitimacy for maintaining regulatory control and management of the economy. Moreover, state theorists have demonstrated how new urban and regional spaces of planning and governance are emerging alongside, rather than replacing, extant territorial units of state spatial/scalar organization in globalization. As Neil Brenner advances: "The rescaling of state power never entails the creation of a 'blank slate' on which totally new scalar arrangements could be established, but occurs through a conflictual 'layering' process in which emergent rescaling strategies collide with, and only partially rework inherited landscapes of state scalar organization" (2009a, 134).[7]

Despite all the bravado of city-regions being competitive territories *par excellence*, free from the shackles of regulatory control, city-regions and their more networked planning and governance arrangements have to be constructed to "fit" extant structures of state spatial/scalar organization, which are historically and territorially articulated and embedded. Current debate therefore centres on understanding the space-times in which these new networked forms of urban-regional governance complement, contradict, overlap, or compete with inherited patterns and structures of sociospatial organization (Harrison 2013). What this research is beginning to show is how different constructions of the "city-region" concept are being mobilized in different places, at different scales, and at different times to make more networked urban-regional planning and governance arrangements compatible with extant forms of territorial state spatial/scalar organization. Illustrative of this is how distinct brands of city-regionalism have evolved over the past ten years, with the contrasting evolution of city-regionalism in England and Germany offering one such illustration.

The Evolution of City-Regionalism in England

England was thrust to the forefront of attempts to construct more flexible and networked forms of urban-regional governance following the collapse of plans to establish elected regional government in 2004. In vogue among policy elites, city-regions emerged to fill the resulting policy gap, with the outcome being a series of initiatives designed to operate across a variously defined city-region scale (Harrison 2012b; see also Rees and Lord, this volume). England's love affair with all things city-regional is perhaps best evidenced by *The Northern Way*, a highly ambitious growth strategy stretching across three administrative regions, centred on eight hierarchically differentiated but functionally connected city-regions in the north of England. The Northern Way Growth Strategy saw city-regions constructed according to Scott's *agglomeration* model, presented as competitive territories, free from all regulatory constraint, *par excellence*; this strategy purported a smooth transition, with city-regions (networked governance) replacing regions (territorial governance). The spatial map of the Northern Way illustrates this, including the disappearance of extant regions (Figure 2.1). These points were reinforced when regional institutions, themselves swept up by the city-regionalism hype, began producing individual regional spatial strategies privileging networks as the most appropriate perspective for regional economic development (see Harrison 2010).

Nonetheless, the can-do bravado of the new city-regionalism experienced a very short honeymoon period in England. Scott's *agglomeration* model was jettisoned in favour of the *scale* model,[8] with new initiatives (e.g. City Development / Economic Development Companies and Multi-Area Agreements – both launched in 2006) framed as mechanisms by which to increase cross-territorial and inter-territorial alliances, and thereby extend planning and governance arrangements beyond the administrative boundaries of single local government authorities. In the case of the Northern Way, responsibility for the program was devolved in a matter of weeks from the central state to a steering group led by institutions from each of the three regions – a move that tasked regional institutions with the challenge of how to make compatible their day-to-day statutory responsibilities for delivering effective regional governance across their territorially defined region whilst at the same time developing new networked governance and planning arrangements that transcended regional and sub-regional boundaries. Regional institutions quickly realized that, although they were able to retain the agglomeration model when working together on the "pan-regional" vision of eight functionally related city-regions operating across their three regions, the agglomeration model is not, when it comes to working as individual regions, compatible with delivery of their statutory responsibilities of coordinating economic development to make regions more competitive while spreading economic prosperity and opportunity to everyone. This is evidenced by the individual regional spatial strategies produced during this period.

If we take the North West region as our example, at the zenith of city-region orthodoxy in England, the Regional Spatial Strategy produced in 2006 had all the hallmarks of the new city-regionalism. The agglomeration model was deployed to spatially select the three Northern Way city-regions as pivotal societal and political-economic

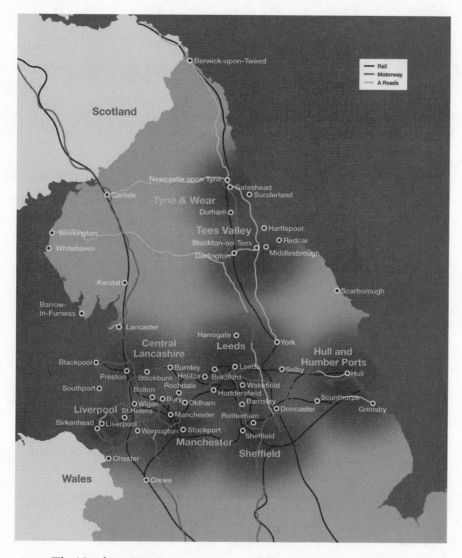

2.1 *The Northern Way*

formations; lines demarcating existing forms of territorial organization were airbrushed out, networked forms of regional governance did not conform to any known political or administrative unit, and the concept of fuzzy boundaries was promoted, as no line on the map reflected any known politico-administrative unit, with the most prominent lines on the map referring to international, national, and regional connectivity. In short, the North West was now represented and defined as a relationally networked space of flows, a reflection on how networks of social relations/processes stretch across and beyond the boundaries of the region as a political and administrative unit (cf. Allen et al. 1998). Nevertheless, by the time of the 2008 Regional Spatial Strategy, conceptualizing the region as a networked space had been jettisoned. The three Northern Way city-regions were now defined by hard, unambiguous lines and mapped directly onto known politico-administrative units with no gaps or overlaps – the most prominent line on the map was now the regional boundary, while connections beyond the region were downplayed in favour of inter- and intra-regional connections. The agglomeration model for conceptualizing city-regions had clearly been jettisoned in favour of the scale model – a reflection of the process that has taken place in the North West, and England as a whole, to try to make more net-worked governance spaces compatible with extant territorial struc-tures of state spatial organization.

To understand how and why different conceptions of the city-region have been employed across different spaces, at different scales, and at different times in England, we need to reflect how: (1) the theoretical rationale for city-regions lends itself to the agglomeration model, but the political rationale for city-regions – particularly in England where city-region policies were aimed at rectifying weak cross-boundary urban governance, poor horizontal coordination, and a lack of policy integration across local govern-ment authorities – lends itself to the scale model; (2) city-regions are initially designated according to an economic logic (the agglomera-tion model); however, the marking out of city-regions as spaces of governance and/or planning is determined more by local territorial politics (the scale model) than any relationally networked economic rationale (Harrison 2010); (3) the agglomeration model produces overlaps and gaps that prove politically sensitive – particularly where areas fall in the gaps; (4) many of these new networked spaces of urban-regional planning and governance are in fact a scalar amplification or contraction of previous territorial forms of state scalar organization; they are therefore neither as "new" nor as "net-worked" as many proponents of city-regions would have us believe (Lord 2009); and (5) regional institutions, under the direct super-vision of the central state, have played a pivotal role in orchestrating city-region development in ways that maintained their role as coordinators of regional economic development while at the same time protecting the state's legitimacy for maintaining regulatory control and management of the economy (Harrison 2012b).

With this in mind, the next "city-region" initiative to be launched was specifically designed to overcome many of these barriers. Launched in June 2010 amid a crescendo of enthusiastic grandstanding, Local Enterprise Partnerships (LEPs) are designed to operate across a functional, rather than administrative, geography in England. Signalling the 2010 Conservative–Liberal Democrat Coalition Government's preferred model for sub-national economic development, planning, and governance, LEPs are significant in that alongside their launch, the UK government has dismantled aspects of the inherited landscape of state scalar organization by airbrushing out regions from policy and abolishing the regional tier of planning and governance in England (see also Rees and Lord, this volume). Amounting to a deliberate attempt to remove some of the command-and-control apparatus of the centralizing state, LEPs were framed as part of a wider "localist agenda" designed to present local areas with more of a blank piece of paper on which to inscribe proposals for urban-regional governance that "better reflect the natural economic geography of the areas they serve" and can "differ across the country in both form and functions" (Department of Communities and Local Government 2010, 13–14). Nonetheless, a year after LEPs were first announced, the facts did not reflect a city-regionalism that proponents thereof would instantly recognize. Of England's thirty-nine LEPs, only three have a core geography that is cross-regional; only four identify as being explicitly city-regional (a further fifteen are based on a city or cities, while seventeen identify with country and county structures – an even more historically embedded territorial unit). Average population is a mere 1.5 million, the smallest being 0.5 million (Cumbria), the largest 8.0 million (Pan London), and the largest outside London 3.4 million (South East). And, of 326 local authorities in England, over ninety percent are wholly within a single LEP.

A number of important points can be distilled from this. First, the legacy of inherited structures of state scalar organization is such that despite the UK government's attempt to airbrush regions from policy and abolish the regional tier of planning and governance, past and present territorial units formally administered or governed by the state remain "active progenitors" in the form and function of new,

more flexible and networked governance and planning arrangements (cf. Smith 1992). From this perspective, city-regions are not
the quasi-autonomous political-economic spaces many proponents
of the new city-regionalism would have us believe. Second, the lack
of overlap runs counter to evidence showing how expansion in the
size, scale, scope, and reach of city-regions in globalization means
there are fewer clean breaks to separate one functional economic
area from another one nearby.[9] This suggests that although city-
regions are designated according to their economic competitiveness
– not unlike Christaller's rationale for using hexagons to avoid overlap and gaps in his development of central place theory – policy
elites are acutely aware of the need, where possible, to avoid the
politically thorny issue of areas falling in the gaps, particularly when
it comes to institutionalizing structures and practices of city-region
governance and/or planning. The result is what we might call "compromised city-regionalism" (Harrison 2010), with LEPS exemplify-
ing how the tension, struggle, and resulting compromise between the
economic logic for constructing new urban-regional governance and
planning arrangements to fit functional economic areas and political
claims to territory have produced a geography of territorially defined
sub-regional, as opposed to city-regional, functional economic areas
(Figure 2.2). Or, to put it another way, LEPS represent a new form of
territorially organizing sub-national economic development that
operates within, not beyond, central state control.

What the enduring role of the state – manifest in compromised
city-regionalism – alerts us to is the critique of forced amalgamation
as ill-suited to the endogenous social, political, and economic
development of city-regions that has been developed by, among
others, Andrew Sancton. With particular reference to the Canadian
context, Sancton argues that highly autonomous city-regions only
exist in unusual circumstances (e.g. sovereign city-states), with the
broader recognition being that in modern liberal democracies, city-
regions "will not and cannot be self-governing ... [because] boundaries will never be static, will never be acceptable to all, and will
always be contested" (Sancton 2008, 3). In short, the argument is
that the territory over which city-region governance is to be enacted
struggles to keep pace with the rate of urban expansion. From this
perspective, it appears there is little room for manoeuvring, but
recent analysis by Jen Nelles has taken to invoking the concept of
the "imagined metropolis" to present a counterpoint to Sancton's

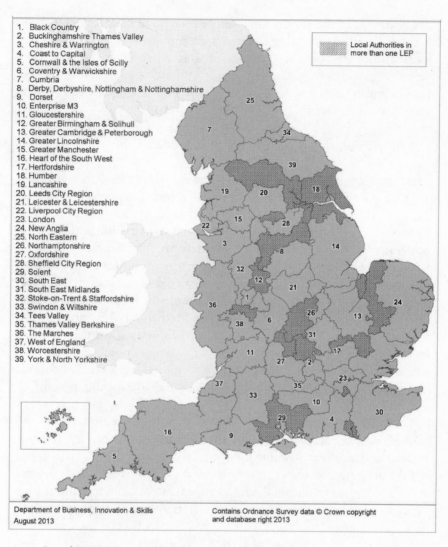

1. Black Country
2. Buckinghamshire Thames Valley
3. Cheshire & Warrington
4. Coast to Capital
5. Cornwall & the Isles of Scilly
6. Coventry & Warwickshire
7. Cumbria
8. Derby, Derbyshire, Nottingham & Nottinghamshire
9. Dorset
10. Enterprise M3
11. Gloucestershire
12. Greater Birmingham & Solihull
13. Greater Cambridge & Peterborough
14. Greater Lincolnshire
15. Greater Manchester
16. Heart of the South West
17. Hertfordshire
18. Humber
19. Lancashire
20. Leeds City Region
21. Leicester & Leicestershire
22. Liverpool City Region
23. London
24. New Anglia
25. North Eastern
26. Northamptonshire
27. Oxfordshire
28. Sheffield City Region
29. Solent
30. South East
31. South East Midlands
32. Stoke-on-Trent & Staffordshire
33. Swindon & Wiltshire
34. Tees Valley
35. Thames Valley Berkshire
36. The Marches
37. West of England
38. Worcestershire
39. York & North Yorkshire

Local Authorities in more than one LEP

Department of Business, Innovation & Skills
August 2013

Contains Ordnance Survey data © Crown copyright
and database right 2013

2.2 Local Enterprise Partnerships

argument – namely that "the central feature of city-region governance networks is that they are products of cooperation" (Nelles 2012, 7). Again drawing heavily on the Canadian case (but referring to Germany also), Nelles advances the argument that where actors have a shared image of the metropolis (or city-region) and engage at that scale, the willingness and capacity of local municipalities to coordinate policy and politics in pursuit of the collective territorial

development of the region can overcome some of the barriers identified by Sancton. In other words, fostering relationships between
local authorities can be achieved if and when formally defining,
delimiting, and designating city-regions is debunked in favour of less
formal, more dynamic and fluid governance arrangements (Glass
and Wolfe, this volume).

The Evolution of Metropolitan Regionalism in Germany

Metropolitan regionalism in Germany can be traced to the early
1990s and the global city discourse. Unlike England, which has
London, Germany does not possess a global city. Rather it operates
a polycentric "horizontal" urban system comprising cities well-
positioned within national and European circuits of capital accumulation.[10] Responding to the growing rhetoric around the importance
of cities and major urban regions in organizing and structuring
globalized forms of capital accumulation, the federal government
introduced the concept of the European Metropolitan Region (EMR)
in 1993. Between 1993 and 2005, eleven EMRs were approved
incorporating 57.98 million inhabitants – an acknowledgment that
while Germany does not have an *a priori* global city such as London
or Paris, it could identify what might amount to aspiring, potential,
or emerging global cities.

The importance attached to the EMR is that a new "discursive
frame" was constructed around the agglomeration model of city-
region development. Establishing EMRs created a new urban hierarchy in Germany, which (despite not having formal powers) was
able to lobby state, national, and European actors and institutions to
recognize their superior strategic importance within spatial planning
and development policies. This and other factors – for example,
greater European integration – saw Germany's EMRs significantly
expand their functional role, importance, and influence through the
1990s and 2000s. Yet EMRs also led to the exacerbation of already
strikingly uneven spatial development in Germany. Also, the emergence of a metropolitan region discourse as a challenge to dominant
ideas of development – based on regions as political-administrative
territorial units – was fraught with contradictions, overlaps, and
competing tendencies. Just as had been the case in England, new
forms of more networked urban-regional planning and governance
(EMRs) sat uneasily alongside existing forms of state scalar organization – namely, the regional *Länder*.

In June 2006, following a two-year technical and political process, the federal government and federal state ministers responsible for spatial planning (*Landesplanung*) published and adopted "Concepts and Strategies for Spatial Development in Germany" (*Leitbilder und Handlungsstrategien für die Raumentwicklung in Deutschland*) as their new national spatial plan for urban and regional development (BMBVS/BBR 2006). The aim was simple: to advance the importance of a network-driven approach to conceptualizing regional growth and competitiveness in a way that can "relate to all types of area – from rural-peripheral areas to metropolitan areas" to ensure spatial inclusivity (BMVBS/BBR 2006, 5). But whereas in England the task of ensuring spatial inclusivity has seen the agglomeration model jettisoned in favour of the scale model, the *Leitbilder* retains the eleven EMRs as its starting point but identifies for the first time two other types of networked space: (i) *growth regions outside metropolitan regions*, predominantly rural areas accounting for a substantial share of overall economic growth due to the presence of dynamic clusters, medium-sized cities, and important regional centres of innovation and specialized technology; and (ii) *stabilization areas*, primarily rural or old industrial areas in peripheral locations or located close to borders characterized by below-average development due to falling between areas of growth. The result is a city-regional world where trans-region boundary lines remain ambiguous and do not correspond to units formally administered or governed by the central state.

What marks Germany out as a pertinent case study is how policy elites responded to the challenges posed by establishing EMRs in the period leading up to 2006 by simultaneously employing all three approaches to conceptualizing city-regions: *agglomeration* to identify the eleven EMRs as dense nodes of economic and social activity; *scale* to enable all areas to be included in what now amounts to an embryonic national spatial plan based on trans-regional networked forms of governance; and *hub and spokes* to, first, connect metropolitan regions to other significant regional foci, and second, identify places that have some functional role in national circuits of capital accumulation but find themselves marginalized from European and global circuits of capital accumulation because they lack a larger core. The importance of this is how each conceptualization of the city-region is constructed to serve a political purpose: *agglomeration* to re-emphasize the superior strategic importance of the EMR for growth and competitiveness in global capital accumulation; *scale* to alleviate some of the political angst caused by the spatially selective discursive frame of the EMR (a case of "picking winners"); and *hub and spokes* to visually capture the importance of cooperation, collaboration, and exchange necessitated by both the city-region as agglomeration and the city-region as scale partitioning state space into a mosaic of regional spaces, often construed as leading to unfettered interregional competition.

What does this tell us about the city-region concept? First, it reinforces the point about the city-region concept being bent and shaped to fit particular political agendas. We see in the German example how once more the starting point for city-regions is definitively economic and neatly conceptualized by the construction of the city-region as an agglomeration. Yet to sustain city-regionalism as a political project requires compromise – compromise to ensure spatial inclusivity, and compromise to make these networked spaces of governance compatible with extant territorial structures of state spatial organization. On the former point, whereas the England example showed how this compromise has seen the agglomeration model jettisoned in favour of the scale model, Germany is currently experimenting with the idea that political compromise can be achieved in and through the perceived complementarities of the three different approaches to conceptualizing city-regions. On the latter, what we do not see in the *Leitbilder* is the compromise to make networked spaces of governance compatible with extant territorial structures of state spatial organization. On first viewing, the *Leitbilder* present these new networked spaces as emerging onto a "blank slate" (cf. Brenner 2009). Although this appears to amount to an embryonic national spatial plan based on more networked and flexible urban and regional spaces, it is important to note that EMRs and their derivatives remain discursive frames. Planning competencies remain ostensibly at the federal level, with any ceding of powers to EMRs tightly regulated by the *Länder*. Following on from this, although important territorial units such as the *Länder* are noticeably absent in the *Leitbilder*, one territorial unit remains very prominent – *Bundesrepublik Deutschland*: the Federal Republic of Germany. What this amounts to is that "although the Federal State are accepting of the need to think beyond the narrow confines of territorial bound politico-administrative units *within* the national context ... there is an unwillingness at this point to consider such practices when it involves collaboration with areas that lie *beyond* the national border" (Harrison and Growe 2014, 34, original emphasis).

All of this points to a corollary, which is that contra Scott and key proponents of the new city-regionalism more generally, city-regions are not as free from the regulatory supervision of the central state as many would have us believe (see also Guay and Hamel, this volume). The state remains *the* orchestrator of city-region development, and any claims toward a city-regional world should not be seen as manifesting at the expense of the nation-state, but rather as a conduit of a state manoeuvring its activities in order to maintain regulatory control and management over the economy under globalizing conditions.

CITY-REGIONS "IN PROSPECT"

When Allen Scott minted the global city-region concept, he identified cities with more than one million inhabitants as his starting point. Quick to admit the inadequacy of this approach to defining global city-regions, he did deem it sufficient for identifying which cities were worthy of consideration as being of superior strategic importance in advanced globalization. This now seems remarkably outdated. A further billion people have been added to the world population; where there were only 272 cities with a population over one million in 1990, there are now 479, while China alone will have 219 cities with populations more than one million in less than fifteen years. Add to this the fact there will be twenty-seven megacities – defined as cities with populations over ten million – by 2025, of which twenty-one will be in the Global South, and the future of the city-region is never more important than currently.

This raises a number of important points when considering the future of the city-region concept. First, although at one level we can say super-urban areas reinforce the trend of city-regions increasing in size, number, scale, scope, reach, influence, and importance in globalization, the reality is that recognition of this very point is serving to fuel the search for these larger configurations in the belief *pace* Florida (2008, 42) that "bigger and more competitive economic units … [are] the real engines of the global economy." What we have witnessed over the past decade is a search for city-regionality on an even greater scale (Hall and Pain 2006; Knox and Lang 2008; Ross 2009; Harrison and Hoyler, 2015). From Scott's (2001) initial identification of global city-regions ranging from 1 to 27.9 million people, we have seen the OECD (2007) refine this to seventy-eight metro-regions ranging from 1.5 to 35 million, Florida (2008) constructing forty mega-regions ranging from 3.7 to 121.6 million, and most recently, UN-HABITAT identifying super-urban areas in the range of 20 to 120 million, but inferring a future where the Pearl River Delta, for example, may exceed 260 million. The reason for suggesting this to be a search for city-regionality is precisely because constructing large-scale multi-nodal urban complexes is nothing new. Let us not forget Europe's "blue banana," the discontinuous urban corridor of industrial growth stretching from North West England to northern Italy constructed in the late 1980s to showcase the economically advantageous position of major urban regions within national and European circuits of capital accumulation. We can point to other long-standing examples (e.g. Europe's "golden banana," an urban corridor stretching along the Mediterranean coast from Valencia [Spain] in the west to Genoa [Italy] in the east, and the Singapore-Johor-Riau growth triangle in south-east Asia) of politically constructed economic spaces that transcend national boundaries, as well as numerous examples of large urban complexes identified as being of superior strategic importance within individual national contexts.

The simple point here is that many of these *new* economic spaces that have emerged over the past decade are only new in their identification – each, constructed as a smaller grouping of urban economic spaces, seeks to be presented as being at the apex of a new global urban hierarchy of "bigger and more competitive economic units" (Florida 2008). The trend is one of conjoining neighbouring urban configurations to form a larger configuration, irrespective of whether they are real or imagined geo-economic spaces. Little thought is given to the coherence of these large urban complexes, in particular to whether new forms of territorial cooperation and/or conflict bind or otherwise coalesce this purported geo-economic space into a coherent unit (Jonas 2012). Moreover, the city-region, as a captured concept, is used to legitimize and publicize certain decisions, actions, and agendas. But, beyond these purely discursive frames, it remains to be seen if anything more concrete will emerge.

Meanwhile, the search for city-regionality is also extending to the opposite end of the spectrum. For such is the political appeal of city-regions that smaller areas (that is, those which fall outside the scope of city-region policy because they do not have sufficient critical mass to be captured as an important agglomeration) are so desperate to be included in this policy sphere that they actively search for city-regionality (see Smart and Tanasescu, this volume). Local Enterprise Partnerships in England once more prove to be a useful example of this. Launched with the explicit intention to establish new flexible, smart, and networked forms of urban-regional governance across a functional rather than administrative geography, one criterion imposed by government was that it would only grant approval for LEPs to be established in areas where there was a convincing argument that the LEP reflected a "real" functional economic area. Nevertheless, the starting point for most LEPs was political, not economic, reflecting the real sense of territorial dependence among key stakeholders in establishing LEPs. For this was a process dominated by territorial interest groups who began searching for evidence of functionality/city-regionality that fit the territory unit over which they exercised some power. No more is this exemplified than when seventeen out of the thirty-nine LEPs approved by government mapped directly onto historically embedded county structures.

What can we take from this? First, it provides further evidence that making networked spaces of urban-regional governance compatible with embedded territorial forms of state spatial organization is being achieved by thinking relationally within, much more than across, territorial units. Second, it reinforces how overcoming the politically thorny issue of ensuring spatial inclusivity is best achieved by adopting the scale model of city-region development, albeit always with the rhetoric of the agglomeration model very much to the fore in policy discourse. Third, as Brenner (2009b, 30) rightly surmises, city-regions are not simply the outcome of capital accumulation strategies but are "mediated through large-scale institutional forms (e.g. the modern state) and diverse social forces (e.g. ... place- or territory-based social movements)." And fourth, it re-emphasizes the spatial and scalar flexibility of the new networked spaces of governance and planning being constructed under the auspices of the new city-regionalism. The agglomeration model is still being invoked to construct even bigger urban-regional complexes. Yet where other constructions of city-region development are being mobilized, these new networked spaces remain relatively small.

Expanding the city-region concept to account for all expressions of urban and regional change leads us to a fundamental question: do we now need new and more appropriate vocabularies for mapping and conceptualizing the transforming metropolitan economic, political, and social landscape?

CONCLUDING COMMENTS:
THE CITY-REGION AS A CAPTURED CONCEPT

While no one can deny that city-regions are a critically important geographical and institutional phenomenon on the world stage, important questions are beginning to be raised as to the way(s) in which the city-region concept is being constructed politically to take account of, and in many cases fuel, changes to urban-regional governance and planning arrangements. This chapter has attempted to shed light on some of the unanswered questions surrounding the new city-regionalism and the foundations upon which it has been/is being constructed, namely: why are different constructions of the city-region concept in use? What purpose(s) do different constructs of the city-region have? Why are different conceptions of the city-region dominant, emerging, or residual in different space-time configurations? What are the roles of individual and collective agents, organizations, and institutions in orchestrating and steering contemporary urban and regional development through public policy and city-region strategies? What is the impact of their constructions of city-regions and city-region development? Who stands to gain/lose from different constructions of city-regions? Is what we have witnessed over the past decade tantamount to a city-regional world, or even a world of city-regions?

These are all important questions and require much greater attention than is available in this chapter. However, in this final section, I want to briefly reflect on a few of the key points that have emerged above. The first point to emphasize is that there are multiple ways of engaging with and constructing city-regions (cf. Allen et al. 1998). Indeed, much of the popular appeal of the city-region is precisely because it is this chaotic concept. Certainly the longevity of the city-region as a policy tool owes much to the fact that it can be bent and shaped to fit place-specific challenges, most particularly the challenge of making these new networked spaces of governance and planning compatible with existing forms of state spatial/scalar organization, which are historically and territorially embedded. It is fundamental therefore that in our research and work with city-regions we do not simply assume the city-region with which we work but engage with it, either by outlining conceptually or empirically defining the space over which political and economic power is being exercised. To reiterate, choosing which city-region geography and city-region concept to adopt and apply is a deeply political act.

Derived from this, second, the pendulum has swung too far in the trial-and-error search for city-regionality. Ever since the city-region concept punctuated the popular "global city" and "new regionalism" discourses to emerge dominant at the beginning of this century, the seemingly endless search for city-regionality has stretched the city-region concept above and below the spatial scale of the "global city-region" originally minted by Scott as being at the heart of the new city-regionalism. On the one hand, the past decade has seen a mantra of "onwards and upwards" as the search for bigger economic units has been dominant. But where does this search stop? Have we already reached the apex with UN-HABITAT's super-urban areas? Where do we go next? On the other hand, it has been shown how the past decade has also seen a search for city-regionality in spaces that initially fell outside the scope of being city-regional in public policy. This is exemplified by England and Germany, where all areas/spaces are now included within the scope of city-region policy, irrespective of whether they are urban/rural, central/peripheral, or growing/lagging. How many of the spaces identified as city-regions today would Allen Scott recognize as city-regions vis-à-vis the original theoretical rationale for city-regions functioning as pivotal societal and political-economic formations in globalization? Contrast this with another question: how many of these "city-regional" spaces have been constructed for other purposes (e.g. spatial inclusivity)? As we look back on a decade of city-regionalism, the evidence clearly favours the latter, and by some distance, if the examples of England and Germany are anything to go by. Moreover, it raises the question of whether anything concrete will ever emerge. Or will many of these spaces of city-regionalism remain purely discursive frames and abstract spaces?

As a direct result of this, third, we are now witness to a multiplicity of city-regions, from the real to the imagined, from the large to the small. A defining feature of the new city-regionalism promoted by Allen Scott was the incredible spatial and scalar flexibility of the city-region concept; this flexibility has only increased over the past decade. The key question therefore is which city-region to choose. For what we have seen with the emergence of city-regions is not just a multiplication of scales (as the city-regional becomes a new strategic level alongside the local, urban, regional, national, supranational, etc.) but a multiplication of city-region scales (from local to global). Deciding which city-region to choose is therefore a deeply political act, one that requires us to critically interrogate why some city-regional spaces are prioritized over others, considering all the time by whom they are constructed, and more important than this, for whom they are constructed.

As Kathy Pain correctly emphasizes in her account of the changing realms of globalizing cities (Pain 2011b), this incredible spatial and scalar flexibility also poses problems for the planning of the mega (or global) city-region. Taking London as her example, Pain emphasizes how the construction of LEPS as a localist approach to city-region development poses major headaches for city-region development at a scale more akin to Scott's global city-region. Whereas previously the global city-region of London was administered by two Regional Development Agencies – South East Development Agency and East of England Development Agency – working alongside the London Assembly and Mayor's Office to provide oversight across the functional economic geography of London, the abolition of the regional tier of governance in England leaves a large gap between centrally orchestrated national planning and the twelve LEPS operating at a more local/subregional level across this bigger and more competitive city-regional space. Stated bluntly, and indicative of a much general issue resulting from the incredible spatial and scalar flexibility of city-regions, Pain concludes that arrangements for bigger and more competitive city-region spaces "will be weaker," not stronger, with these politically orchestrated transformations to the planning and governance of globalizing cities (Pain 2011b).

To briefly conclude, all spatial configurations display some degree of city-regionality, but whether this degree of city-regionalism is sufficient to warrant city-region status in public policy – widely accepted to mean of superior strategic importance – is highly debatable. For this reason, although a new urban landscape is clearly emerging in globalization – which city-regionality plays a key role in forming – this does not constitute a city-regional world. Nevertheless, that city-region research has remained vibrant over the past decade does suggest the city-region concept remains a useful tool for mapping and conceptualizing the transforming metropolitan economic, political, and social landscape of globalizing cities. We just need to remember to adequately outline conceptually or empirically define the "city-region" at the heart of our inquiries.

NOTES

1 The subtitle is an adaptation of Gordon MacLeod and Martin Jones' (2007) article, which asks "In what sense a regional world?"

2 Enthusiasm from policy elites the world over to design and build new urban and regional governance and planning arrangements over the past ten years has led to the argument that city-regions represent a new scale of urbanization, and city-regionalism a new phase in capitalist territorial development, becoming almost self-perpetuating. To borrow Lovering's (1999) terminology, the policy tail can be seen wagging the analytical dog: that is, the accepted wisdom of the construction of tiers of city-regional governance has been used as further evidence of city-regions acting as autonomous political and economic spaces, elevating city-regionalism to a position of orthodoxy among academics and policy elites, which in turn fuels further rounds of policy intervention, all to then be used by those advocating a *new* city-regionalism as further evidence of city-regions being this new scale of urbanization and city-regionalism a new phase in capitalist territorial development (see Harrison 2007 for more on this in the context of new city-regionalism).

3 Most famously, Christaller himself was to move into government service during the Second World War to work in the SS–Planning and Soil Office, where he had responsibility for reconfiguring the economic geography of Germany's eastern conquests – notably occupied Poland and Czechoslovakia, and plans for Russia – which he planned using central place theory. Christaller's model is still clearly evident in aspects of German spatial planning, and also played a role, for example, in the UK Government's 1946 New Towns Act.

4 It is worth remembering that *The City Region in Western Europe* (1964) and *City and Region: A Geographical Interpretation* (1967) were published at the same time as the much more revered *Locational Analysis in Human Geography* (1965) by Peter Haggett, *Models in Geography* (1967) by Richard Chorley and Peter Haggett, and *The Geography of Market Centers and Retail Distribution* (1967) by Brian Berry. Unlike these books,

Dickinson's books "promoted neither the hypothetico-deductive approach to [cities'] development that attracted many new students nor the mathematical and statistical methodologies which they adopted" (Johnston 2002, 726).

5 See Johnston (2002) for a fascinating and revealing insight into why Dickinson's innovative research on urban geography was not taken up by other scholars to the extent it might reasonably have been expected to.

6 Two points: (1) I am aware that both books are much more than just the one quote referred to in this chapter, and that it would be an easy and obvious critique to highlight the many differences between them. However, I feel the point raised here remains a valid one in the context of this chapter. (2) Just as the city-region concept endured a period of dormancy, so the regional concept came under attack during the 1970s, hence the reference to the *new* regional geography of the 1980s and 1990s, to which John Allen, Doreen Massey, and Allan Cochrane were all major contributors.

7 See Brenner (2004) for a masterful account of governmentalized remappings of state space in globalization.

8 That is, in all but public policy discourse, where it remained an important tool for policy elites looking to promote new urban-regional initiatives by tapping into the discourse on city-region competitiveness.

9 The original proposals had over seventy local authorities (c. 22 percent) located in at least two LEP areas; by the time thirty-nine LEPs were approved, this number was thirty-five.

10 In the latest rankings of global network connectivity produced by the Globalization and World Cities (GaWC) research group, the situation in England is that London remains the most globally connected city in the world, but the next English city in the ranking (Manchester) is 113th with a connectivity 22 percent that of London. If you contrast this with Germany, Frankfurt is the most connected city (38th) with a connectivity half that of London; but Germany has a further five cities that rank in the top one hundred (Berlin 55th, Hamburg 60th, Munich 67th, Dusseldorf 76th, and Stuttgart 91st) (Taylor et al. 2010).

REFERENCES

Allen, J., and A. Cochrane. 2007. "Beyond the Territorial Fix: Regional Assemblages, Politics and Power." *Regional Studies* 41 (9): 1161–75.

– 2010. "Assemblages of State Power: Topological Shifts in the Organization of Government and Politics." *Antipode* 42 (5): 1071–89.

Allen, J., D. Massey, and A. Cochrane. 1998. *Rethinking the Region*. London: Routledge.

Amin, A. 2004. "Regions Unbound: Towards a New Politics of Place." *Geografiska Annaler* 86B (1): 33–44.

BMVBS/BBR (Bundesministerium für Verkehr, Bau-und Stadtentwicklung/ Bundesamt für Bauwesen und Raumordnung). 2006. *Leitbilder und Handlungsstrategien für die Raumentwicklung in Deutschland*. Berlin: BMVBS/BBR.

Brenner, N. 2002. "Decoding the Newest 'Metropolitan Regionalism' in the USA: A Critical Overview." *Cities* 19 (1): 3–21.

– 2009a. "Open Questions on State Rescaling." *Cambridge Journal of Regions, Economy and Society* 2 (1): 123–39.

– 2009b. "A Thousand Leaves: Notes on the Geographies of Uneven Spatial Development." In *Leviathan Undone? Towards a Political Economy of Scale*, edited by R. Keil and R. Mahon, 27–50. Vancouver, BC: UBC Press.

Christaller, W. 1933. *Die Zentralen Orte in Suddeutschland*. Jena, Germany: Gustav Fischer.

Department of Communities and Local Government. 2010. *Local Growth: Realising Every Place's Potential*. London: DCLG.

Dickinson, R.E. 1964. *The City Region in Western Europe*. London: Routledge & Kegan Paul.

– 1967. *City and Region: A Geographical Interpretation*. London: Routledge & Kegan Paul.

Douglass, M. 2000. "Mega-Urban Regions and World City Formation: Globalisation, the Economic Crisis and Urban Policy Issues in Pacific Asia." *Urban Studies* 37 (12) 2315–35.

Entrikin, N. 1976. "Contemporary Humanism in Geography." *Annals of the Association of American Geographers* 66 (4): 615–32.

Florida, R. 2008. *Who's Your City? How the Creative Economy Is Making Where to Live the Most Important Decision of Your Life*. New York: Basic Books.

Geddes, P. 1905. "Civics: As Applied Sociology." *Sociological Papers* 1, 104–44, reprinted in *The Ideal City*, edited by H.E. Meller, 75–122. Leicester, UK: Leicester University Press.

Hall, P., and K. Pain, eds. 2006. *The Polycentric Metropolis – Learning from Mega-City Regions in Europe*. London: Earthscan.

Harrison, J. 2007. "From Competitive Regions to Competitive City-Regions: A New Orthodoxy, but Some Old Mistakes." *Journal of Economic Geography* 7 (3): 311–32.

– 2010. "Networks of Connectivity, Territorial Fragmentation, Uneven Development: The New Politics of City-Regionalism." *Political Geography* 29 (1): 17–27.

– 2012a. "Global City-Region Governance, Ten Years On." In *International Handbook of Globalization and World Cities*, edited by P.J. Taylor, M. Hoyler, B. Derudder, and F. Witlox, 309–17. London: Elgar.

– 2012b. "Life after Regions? The Evolution of City-Regionalism in England." *Regional Studies* 46: 1243–59.

– 2013. "Configuring the New 'Regional World': On Being Caught between Territory and Networks." *Regional Studies* 47 (1): 55–74.

– 2015. "Cities and Rescaling." In *Cities and Economic Change*, edited by R. Paddison and T. Hutton, 38–56. London: Sage.

Harrison, J., and A. Growe. 2014. "From Places to Flows? Planning for the New 'Regional World' in Germany." *European Urban and Regional Studies* 21 (1): 21–41.

Harrison, J., and M. Hoyler, eds. 2015. *Megaregions: Globalization's New Urban Form?* Cheltenham, UK: Edward Elgar.

Harvey, D. 2008. "Cities or Urbanization?" *City* 1 (1): 38–61.

Jonas, A.E.G. 2012. "City-Regionalism: Questions of Distribution and Politics." *Progress in Human Geography* 36 (6): 822–9.

Jonas, A.E.G., and K. Ward. 2007. "An Introduction to a Debate on City-Regions: New Geographies of Governance, Democracy and Social Reproduction." *International Journal of Urban and Regional Research* 31 (1): 169–78.

Kunzmann, K. 1998. "World City Region in Europe: Structural Change and Future Challenges." In *Globalization and the World of Large Cities*, edited by F.C. Lo and Y.M. Yeung, 37–75. Tokyo: United Nations University Press.

Lang, R., and D. Dhvale. 2005. "Beyond Megalopolis: Exploring America's New 'Megapolitan' Geography." *Metropolitan Institute Census Report Series Number 05:01*. http://america2050.org/pdf/beyondmegalopolislang.pdf. Accessed March 2012.

Lord, A. 2009. "Mind the Gap. The Theory and Practice of State Rescaling: Institutional Morphology and the 'New' City-Regionalism." *Space and Polity* 13 (2): 77–92.

Lovering, J. 1999. "Theory Led by Policy: The Inadequacies of the New Regionalism (Illustrated from the Case of Wales)." *International Journal of Urban and Regional Research* 23 (2): 379–95.

MacLeod, G., and M. Jones. 2007. "Territorial, Scalar, Networked, Connected: In What Sense a 'Regional World'?" *Regional Studies* 41 (9): 1177–91.

Massey, D. 2007. *World City*. Cambridge: Polity Press.

McKinsey Global Institute. 2008. *Preparing for China's Urban Billion – Summary of Findings*. New York: McKinsey & Company.

Meijers, E. 2005. "Polycentric Urban Regions and the Quest for Synergy: Is a Network of Cities More than the Sum of the Parts?" *Urban Studies* 42 (4): 4765–81.

Moore, M., and P. Foster. 2011. "China to Create Largest Mega City in the World with 42 Million People." London: *The Telegraph*, 24 January.

Nelles, J. 2012. *Comparative Metropolitan Policy: Governing Beyond Local Boundaries in the Imagined Metropolis*. London: Routledge.

Northern Way Steering Group. 2005. *The Northern Way: Growth Strategy*. Newcastle, UK: The Northern Way.

OECD. 2007. *Competitive Cities in the Global Economy*. Paris: OECD Territorial Review.

Ohmae, K. 2001. "How to Invite Prosperity from the Global Economy into a Region." In *Global City-Regions: Trends, Theory, Policy*, edited by A.J. Scott, 33–43. Oxford, UK: Oxford University Press.

Pain, K. 2011a. "Spatial Transformations of Cities: Global City-Region? Mega City-Region?" In *International Handbook of Globalization and World Cities*, edited by P.J. Taylor, M. Hoyler, B. Derudder, and F. Witlox, 83–93. London: Elgar.

– 2011b. "Cities in Transformation – What Role for the State?" *GaWC Research Bulletin 384*. http://www.lboro.ac.uk/gawc/rb/rb384.html. Accessed March 2012.

Regional Plan Association. 2006. *America 2050 – A Prospectus*. New York: Regional Plan Association.

Ross, C. 2009. *Megaregions – Planning for Global Competitiveness*. Washington, DC: Island Press.

Sancton, A. 2008. *The Limits of Boundaries: Why City-Regions Cannot Be Self-Governing*. Montreal: McGill-Queen's University Press.

Sassen, S. 1991. *The Global City – London, Tokyo, New York*. Princeton, NJ: Princeton University Press.

Scott, A.J. 1998. *Regions and the World Economy – The Coming Shape of Global Production, Competition, and Political Order*. Oxford, UK: Oxford University Press.

– ed. 2001a. *Global City-Regions: Trends, Theory, Policy*. Oxford, UK: Oxford University Press.

– 2001b. "Globalization and the Rise of City-Regions." *European Planning Studies* 9 (7): 813–26.

Smith, N. 1992. "Contours of a Spatialized Politics: Homeless Vehicles and the Production of Geographical Scale." *Social Text* 33: 54–81.

Storper, M. 1997. *The Regional World – Territorial Development in a Global Economy*. New York: Guildford Press.

Taylor, P.J. 1999. "Place, Spaces and Macy's: Place-Space Tensions in the Political Geography of Modernities." *Progress in Human Geography* 23 (1): 7–26.

– 2001. "Urban Hinterworlds: Geographies of Corporate Service Provision under Conditions of Contemporary Globalization." *Geography* 86 (1): 51–60.

Taylor, P.J., P. Ni, B. Derudder, M. Hoyler, J. Huang, and F. Witlox, eds. 2010. *Global Urban Analysis – A Survey of Cities in Globalization*. London: Earthscan.

Tewdwr-Jones, M., and D. McNeill. 2000. "The Politics of City-Region Planning and Governance." *European Urban and Regional Studies* 7 (2): 119–34.

Turok, I., and N. Bailey. 2004. "The Theory of Polynuclear Urban Regions and Its Application to Central Scotland." *European Planning Studies* 12 (3): 371–89.

UK Government. 2005. *Planning Glossary*. London: Office of the Deputy Prime Minister.

United Nations Population Fund (UNFPA). 2007. *State of the World Population*. New York: UNFPA.

United Nations Human Settlements Programme (UN-HABITAT). 2011. *State of the World's Cities Report 2010/11*. New York: UN-HABITAT.

Ward, K., and A.E.G. Jonas. 2004. "Competitive City-Regionalism as a Politics of Space: A Critical Reinterpretation of the New Regionalism." *Environment and Planning A* 36 (12): 2119–39.

Xu, J., and A.G.O. Yeh. 2010. *Governance and Planning of Mega-City Regions: An International Comparative Perspective*. London: Routledge.

3

Re-spatializing the City as the City-Region?

ROB SHIELDS

All territories are regions but not all regions are territories ...

(Paasi 2009, 124)

This chapter considers the notion of the city-region from the bottom up, as an experience and representation of the way major cities have grown and sprawled into each other, presenting opportunities and challenges; and from the top down, as municipal political projects to amalgamate towns and recapture suburban edge-cities, and as an overall re-centring of major regions on key central cities in ways that clarify the roles of some and boost the status of pretenders to global city status.

"City-region" is a term that attempts to capture and convey the idea that "cities" have changed in their significance, powers, and reach. The new term is part of attempts to describe and understand the increased role that urban populations and governments are playing globally, in both cultural and economic terms. It is a response to the lived experience of the way that cities such as Baltimore and Washington have grown together, or of the urbanization of larger regions such as the Zhujiang (Pearl River) Delta of Guangdong, now one of the most urbanized regions of the world.[1] The term is also used more rhetorically, puffing up the importance of such regions in political-economic and academic visions of the importance of the urban. As Smart and Tanasescu (this volume) note, such visions themselves inform policy logics through self-reinforcing relationships between rhetoric and action. Nations in this view are held to be assemblages of urban economies, and contemporary culture is held to be defined within cities and by the events therein. Indeed, as factory and other urban economic activity has long surpassed the wealth generated by rural agricultural works, this difference in per capita economic productivity has meant that the accumulation of wealth and consumption opportunities are strongly urban, and cities have been seen as engines of economic growth. As Harrison also discusses in this volume: "The existing literature on knowledge-intensive and creative city-regions can be read in two ways: as suggesting that an exclusive club of city-regions with new economies will emerge, or as meaning that all city-regions could create conditions favourable for developing new industrial activity" (Bontje et al. 2011, 98).

The city-region reflects the way in which cities have grown by sprawling into other centres, becoming multi-nodal regions that no longer have a single downtown or focus of activity. Rather than concentric rings of growth out from a core, multiple centres grow to diffract with each other. Rather than a single peak of any one quality, of a defining variable or place, that would form the heart of "the" city, multiple foci are spread across a region, distracting from any given identity but also levelling regional differences under the guise of a single place-image. What is lost is the precise sense of cities defined by a place such as downtown. Yet the tendency is to continue to refer to these city-regions as "places"; clearly the precision of the concept of "place" has also been lost in what amounts to a social change that is both cultural and economic. Dispersion and diversity have become not just a social fact but an economic strategy. This has brought with it visibility, roles such as airline and shipping hubs, and travel connections to other major centres. However, it has also brought quality issues: environmental challenges, and the risk that sprawl will amount to a mediocre urban life experience and to identity challenges. Every city-region suffers to some extent from Gertrude Stein's comment about how estranged she was by the growth of her birthplace, Oakland, California: "It was not natural ... not there: there is no there there" (Stein 1937, 289).

Late-twentieth-century spatial structures of distribution, infrastructure, distance, national regulatory reach, and regional trade blocs came to be seen as generating both leading and lagging regions. In this context, economic clusters, industrial districts, and regional agglomeration economies are all examples of attempts to investigate and encourage synergies that are the result of spatial proximity, zoning, social interaction, and information flows. That is, as Huxham

(1996) put it, a shift occurred in scale from international comparative advantage to regional competitive advantage to the sectoral collaborative advantage of clusters within cities. The concentration of production and power in mega city-regions, and the importance of metropolises with sufficient scale to ensure a diversity of labour, talent, and initiative as "creative cities," shifted the stress toward regional development strategies and integrated environmental planning for sustainable growth. City-regionalism allowed smaller global cities such as Toronto and Montreal to re-present themselves as larger and more diverse entities, which efficiently offered both a breadth and depth of people with skills, understandings, and outlooks.

Scott (2006) has argued that city-regions with self-motivating creative sectors – from artisanal manufacturing to media and cultural production, financial services, and high-tech innovation – have grown strongly because they benefit from four aspects of globalization: 1) the expansion of markets and the higher profits from increased output; 2) distinctive, hard-to-replicate products (such as Hollywood movies); 3) the ability of leading firms in these centres to draw on global networks of talent and resources; and 4) the ability to profit locally from outsourcing routine production to lower-cost centres. To these four, we can add 5) the significance of these places themselves as established crucibles where labour forces meet talent, resources, and production (Hollywood, Silicon Valley, and so on). That is, places and local social life act as vehicles and reasons for local firms to collaborate (Ganne 1983). Shenzen (one of China's largest emerging economic city-regions contiguous with the northern border of Hong Kong), for example, began as a place to manufacture things cheaply; it became a local economic environment that was difficult to compete with because of the confluence of low-cost labour, logistical links and facilities such as ports, and factory managers' experience with manufacturing for export to demanding consumers globally.

For municipalities, interest in their surrounding region and in defining or promoting themselves as "city-regions" reflects a convergence of factors pushing rural municipalities to collaborate in the delivery of services, and to amalgamate to achieve economies of scale. They compete to attract business activity by producing coherent and powerful place-brands, by tightening the identity and competitive, pro-business policies of regulators in these areas. It also reflects political ambition and an interest amongst elites in importing the latest urban economic planning fashions purveyed by consultants. While Scott (2001) emphasizes urban growth factors controlled by firms, much of the city-region literature shifts to issues of planning policy (Corey and Wilson 2006; Blakley 2010) and municipal governance (Boudreau 2006; Brenner 2002; 2003) – especially infrastructure and economic development (Jonas 2007; Bristow 2009; 2010). In practice, these may involve the same urban elites, but they act, ally with one another, and are organized in different ways to pursue a collective urban project, as opposed to individually pursuing specific business ventures. This is an important shift. Furthermore, even as municipal governments are generally creatures of national policy, created by and dependent on the policies of the nation-state, there has been enormous faith placed in local, endogenous growth factors that contrast with the more traditional neo-classical emphasis on economy-wide factors that are exogenous to regions, such as exchange rates, international trade regimes, or national labour standards, amongst others (Storey 2009; Simmie 2010; Wolfe and Bramwell 2008; Johansson et al. 2001, in Stough et al. 2011).

DRAWING THE BOUNDARIES
OF THE CITY-REGION

Where and how does one draw the boundaries or cast the scale of analysis of city-regions that are also tied to global trade? Where does the city-region end, and on what basis should it be defined? There is no universal definition. Travel-to-work areas, for example, vary widely with commuter workforces. Cities that are developing rapidly or depend on very specific skills, such as in the oil-drilling industry, may have global commuters (as do Aberdeen and Fort McMurray). In addition, the ways geographic boundaries are drawn around any region can arbitrarily change the statistical qualities found inside its boundaries dramatically. The definition of cities' and of regions' boundaries is not based on standardized criteria, meaning that what exactly falls within and outside of a city, a region, or a "city-region" varies from metropolis to metropolis.

Annsi Paasi (2009, 121) notes that city-regions gain their boundaries, symbols, and governing organizations in a process of institutionalization. He traces the assumptions of both academic and political "regionalisms" since the early 1990s and their component elements such as boundaries and identity. Following the work of many others, Paasi foregrounds the distinction between regional identification and its institutional identity that is blurred in the discourses of some planning documents. An identification with a region and as a region is assumed to pre-exist as a normative framework or habitus of everyday life. This local or regional "affect" (Davidson, Park, and Shields 2011)[2] is then deployed rhetorically as an ideology justifying the construction and expansion of a region as an institutional identity and power in a "region building project" concerned with economic and social development (ibid., 137–45; Jones 2004).

City-regional research has come late to this power of place and has come to it "from above." It involves the capacity of cultural and sacred sites and heartlands to inspire us to feel loyalty or recall emotions such as pride. These affects are as real as pain or joy, even if they are not tangible objects. In their novel ways of freshly representing areas and geographically located groups of people and firms, city-regions harness affect. Whether rising or falling in popularity, the notion of the city-region is one way of nourishing a sense of economic possibility based on a sense of the region, or of "place" in its expanded sense, as potential. Institutional region-building involves sharing similar affects across the citizenry, such as identifying with the city-region or taking on the qualities said to characterize an area.

The lack of strict comparability between city-regions makes it difficult to apply lessons learnt in one place to other places without careful analysis of both the internal and external forces and qualities operating in both places (see Glass, this volume). What is needed is to harness the virtuosity of groups in accomplishing things that cannot easily be replicated, and to generalize them based on a shared access to the advantages in the city-region environment. Thus successful firms attempt to spin off subsidiary ventures. These attributes or talents of social collectives are more easily marshalled and coordinated by collecting them together in organized places – in this case, the city-region. "A globalised world is a marketplace where country has to compete with country – and region with region, city with city – for its share of attention, of reputation, of spend, of goodwill, of trust. That places should look to the disciplines of the marketplace for inspiration about how to prosper in this world is entirely logical" (Anholt 2004, 119). A city-region's uniqueness, its difference from other city-regions, is the basis of not only its identity, but its competitiveness. Simply put, people in other places look to a given city-region for things they do not have locally. Looking to what is unique locally and avoiding copying is thus an important rule of thumb often violated in the haste to declare a city-region.

THE POLITICAL RHETORIC OF CITY-REGIONS

Other researchers recognize regions as based in rhetorical practices of representation: that is, as discursive constructions that particular proponents such as groups of elites promote to increase local economic efficiencies or to attract and coordinate state subsidies. The contrast between the emphasis on the institutionalization of an identity and the construction of a branded economic development region is the contrast between the intangible but nonetheless real qualities of regions ("virtualities") and the attempt to construct new representations (abstractions, fictions, and ideologies). On the one hand, city-regions are representations or discourses on space; on the other hand, they are examples of space as a container and framework for both everyday and industrial activity: they are spaces of representation, to use Lefebvre's critical language (1991; Shields 1991b). "Social constructionist" approaches have led to a growing emphasis on the creation of new identities via branding exercises in the media. The most successful of these endeavours draw on local narratives and stories of place and identity (see Andrew, this volume). However, when narrowly interpreted in terms of branding, a naïve constructionism can often downplay the power of place and the resulting legal and institutional arrangements that are entered into

> global capitalism, which, instead of homogenizing the world, is producing increasing polarization and uneven development at all spatial scales from local neighbourhoods to global networks. This is inevitably transforming the current spatializations of power and forcing researchers to map the emerging socio-spatial shapes. Discourses for interpreting these tendencies ... have mainly been concerned with the economic aspects of globalization, less with politics and governance, and least with the cultural aspects. Additionally, they rarely touch at all upon the everyday lives of the ordinary people who produce and reproduce the 'real' processes of globalization. (Paasi 2003b, 960)

City-regions are a novel spatial form that has arisen in this process (for a history and definitions, see Harrison, this volume). However, this form has intangible (virtual) and tangible aspects. City-regions have appeared to be territorial in the sense of being governed – and developed and branded – by local municipal and economic administrations, and have also been regions ascribed to physical areas (such as a river valley or a plain) on the basis of some analytical similarity. If these are merely administrative arrangements, or if the region is too abstract and without affect, it may bewilder residents and internal authorities, who may perceive themselves more dissimilar to than like their city-regional neighbours. Consider Shenzen, a creation of the Chinese Communist Party as part of a foreign-trade zone, and clearly developed as part of a profitable real estate plan by local authorities who transformed villages and rice fields into a city of offices and factories, but also part of a broader region with a long and deep history of centuries of import and export shipping.

Naïve social constructionist approaches lend themselves well to media-based and advertising approaches grounded in language and ideas, rather than social activity and contested interaction. They carry the temptation that regions can easily be built by promoting and manipulating a popular imaginary of region-images to reconstruct a region as a discursive and spatial myth. For example, there have been a number of mis-steps based on the constructivist approach, particularly in attempts to "brand" places and regions artificially via media images, with little relation to local reality. This applies as much to industrial development as to tourism promotion campaigns (Ashworth and Kavaratzis 2009; Govers and Go 2009; Bianchini and Ghilardi 2007). An example was the $25 million tourism advertising campaign for landlocked Alberta, Canada, that used a photo of Beadnell Beach in Northumberland, England, in 2009. Communications firm Calder Bateman and the Alberta Public Affairs Bureau defended the choice as it "fitted the mood and tone of what [they] were trying to do."[3] Media-aware and visually attuned publics pride themselves on spotting such mismatches between image and place. These cases of inauthentic images reveal the importance of respecting the linkages between abstract representations, virtualities such as regional affect and culture, and actual materialities, despite the apparent opportunity offered by digital media to separate them, to magically graft an idealized image onto the actual topography or the population of a place.

Most analysis has understood city-regions as the result of devolved power and responsibility for regional development from national or state governments to new institutions. Their mandates are defined in terms of new spatial areas that embrace existing political-administrative units. These "new state spaces" (Brenner 2004) respond to urban boosterism and locational politics. In some cases, they allow new actors to join existing elites, reshaping local orders and governance. The root of the word "region" is the Latin *regio* ("line, direction, area") from *regere* ("to direct"). If Paasi (2003a) notes that region is fundamentally about institutional boundary drawing, Ulrich Beck (2003) notes that, today, this is a process that is nonetheless "fraught" and contested because regions are more than ever obviously related to economic and identity projects, which means that they appear inauthentic and instrumental. This suggests a more sophisticated view that promotes spatializations or brands city-regions only if they can be derived from a tangible, actual reality. The reality has to be in place, both tangible and intangible, before the stories are told about identity.

Particularly when seen from an international economic context, city-regions as contiguous sets of metropolitan areas (cf. Scott 2001), such as the Toronto-Hamilton conurbation or the Lower Vancouver Mainland, are the spatial face of global networks of production, consumption, and control that provide a contemporary glimpse of the effects of accumulation and globalization. Seen from such analytical heights, city-regions are diagrams of culture and economy mapped onto municipal and metropolitan landscapes. Previous representations – all slightly different in scope and intent – include 1970s "mega-cities," 1980s "localities" (Cooke 1989), and 1990s "clusters" (Cumbers 2004). But seen from below, city-regions are the range of everyday life from home to work and recreation (cf. Lefebvre 1992). They are the economic working units of identification for most people. This equivocal quality of city-regions – Harrison (this volume) calls them a "chaotic concept" – suggests a pragmatic and strategic aspect to the use of this label by political and economic actors. In particular, one finds it used to capture suburban municipalities and rural counties that, since the 1950s, have competed with central cities, drawing away higher socio-economic strata and highly valued economic activities – and thus reducing the tax base of the core. At the same time, the political institution of a city-region may amount to a "capture" of downtowns by suburban voters opposed to urbanization. Any deployment of the concept of "region" relates to defining and fixing in place "demarcated zones and co-ordinates.

It is the topography of the social in terms of differentiated systems, or fields based on territorialized and non-transformable objects" (Diken 2011, 96). City-regionalism restages the tension between centre and core while it attempts to return the metropolitan cores that are the "headline" of identities such as "greater Montreal" to a privileged position as the metropolitan "heart," to re-inscribe that urban identity on suburban residents and an urban taxation regime on suburban edge-cities and rural hinterlands.

CRITICAL GEOGRAPHICAL APPROACHES: SPATIALIZATION AND CITY-REGIONS

Instead of a rhetorical and media-driven approach or a reduction to merely an economic strategy, geographical approaches recognize that place-images are both physically grounded in location and relationally grounded in the relative status of each place compared to other places. These are understood as a geopolitical system. Changing place-images or regional identities requires not only a campaign that focuses on the local, but a broader approach that changes the position of a place vis-à-vis other places in a network of identities. Such spatial identity regimes linked to practices are *social spatializations* in which leading and lagging places are linked, not only in terms of material and economic flows, but in terms of *relative differences* that are informational, material, and affective. Changing the identity of a place or region involves recasting it in relation to the places or regions to which it is tied. These relationships may be as part of a mosaic (for example, of states or provinces), part of a dualism (north versus south), or part of a hierarchy (journalistic rankings of cities). Spatialization is a way of looking at processes, practices, and identities as they are woven together to produce places that then act back on humans by framing behaviour. It takes us beyond looking for the city-region as a "thing" sitting out in the landscape on one hand, and thinking of the city-region as just a fable or an image-making exercise on the other.

Social spatialization is the ongoing process of allocating behaviour and meaning to networks of places and spaces. Although they are outcomes of social action, as a created "second nature," they have an ecosystem-like influence on further action (Lefebvre 1991). To be from "the right side of town" or "the wrong side of the tracks" still communicates good and bad character, even in an era when the placement of railroads is no longer a defining feature of cities. Senses of place and region transcend the purely "natural" and material, and we must look beyond the environment of an area – and even beyond the region itself – to properly understand this within the ways that regions themselves are understood to exist as idealizations. Spatially, any site or area is obviously interconnected with others. Temporally, historical patterns may extend into the future as projected trends. However, we can go further to say that these relationships in time and space are part of overall relational networks of similar as well as contrasting, adjacent as well as distant sites and regions in which each is distinguished not only by images proper to itself, but by its distinctiveness or similarity, and its juxtaposed status to other sites. This cultural formation is socially constructed over the long term, and constitutes a spatialization of places and regions as "places-for-this" and/or "places-for-that." That is, each site or area is construed as appropriate for certain social activities and behaviours – and this is central to its identity. Places and regions are cast (or spatialized) as certain types of place: romantic, harsh, warm, boring, polluted, foreign, and so on. Lefebvre argues that such spatial regimes are grounded in modes of production on a grand, epochal scale with little explanation of how change comes about. Place is not just a matter of real estate or landed property; it is intellectual property, cultural property. What might merely be notable or strategically advantageous land is only the geological foundation of a mythic landscape of historic national events or nationalistic memories, not to mention advertising images. Visual representations, literature, and folk tales – small and tall – are aspects of the spatialization of a site or region. This is hardly a fixed system of coordinates; rather, it is a relational network of differences that provides the principle and rationale for movement between places and regions.

Social spatializations are relational, and span scales and link together domains, tying language and literature to place and landscape, the global to the local, and the conceptual to gesture and behaviour. Dominant social spatializations are encountered when we face the injunction to act in specific ways in different locations, separating "places for this" from "places for that" (Shields 1991b). This disciplining of comportment extends to affect and is an important aspect of public governmentality and power (Shields 2011). The essential relevance to city-regions is that these are not neutral settings but milieux which work to accomplish or frustrate courses of action. As social spatializations change – for example, linking the local to the global – life chances in each specific location are restructured.

With the experience of two decades of city-region talk and policy experimentation, spatialization makes sense of the city-region phenomenon in several ways. First, it directs attention to how city-regions are related to local activities, such as boosterism, place-marketing, and the institutionalization of specific practices of territorial governance in relation to local resources and geographies. It draws attention to not only the ascribed identities of areas but also their relation to a wider context; the deployment of power, effort, and force to achieve and maintain specific spatial identities at the expense of others; and the enhancement of dominant social actors to the detriment of others. City-regions are thus not only new spatial forms, but articulate power to places in novel ways that are historically contingent upon globalization. They selectively direct attention to state projects at specific scales and away from the tensions of other projects and manifestations of the restructuring of social spatializations. In this wider context, spatialization directs attention to how city-regions respond to understandings of the world as a theatre of operations where certain kinds of relations are possible to other places – whether peripheral hinterlands, other city-regions, or global "megapolitan" regions, such as the Pearl River Delta area around Shanghai.

Perhaps Paasi's separation of aspects of regions in general – the way it plays on affective identification and the boundary-drawing and identities of region-building projects – is a clue to the way forward. What spatialization is implied when city-regions are studied empirically in relation to other city-regions? To its credit, the city-region literature describes the interdependent aspects of regional identification, identity, and institutionalization (Scott 2001; Ward 2004; Jonas 2007; Paasi 2009). In the global city networks literature (Taylor 2004), on the basis of economic, transport, and travel flows between them, many of the same areas are hypothesized to be linked in a topological arrangement as a set of cities rather than city-regions (see Smith 2003 for an innovative example). As Lai (2009, 1277) outlines:

Since the early 1980s, urban scholars have systematically explored the interplay between globalisation and urban development, relating dominant socioeconomic trends within cities (such as industrial restructuring, labour market changes and social

polarisation) to the emergence of a global urban hierarchy ...
This hierarchy divides cities into different tiers of importance
according to their degree of integration into the global economy
(mainly according to transnational corporation (TNC) activities),
and their roles as basing points of global capital in the spatialisa-
tion and articulation of global production and markets.

Global cities are ranked in diagrammatic representations that place
and spatialize the cities into regional hierarchies that look a bit like
the mid-game of pieces in Scrabble or dominoes, where each city is a
piece. Usually, these are mapped in a way that flattens the layers of
relations between city-regions down to levels of economic predomi-
nance. This does not do justice to the role and visibility of cultural
capitals as sites where global cultural and ethical trends and predispo-
sitions around regimes of value are legitimized, if only intermittently.
For example, consider the social role of the Edinburgh Festival, the
Venice Biennale, or the Cannes Festival and their economic impacts
that are registered elsewhere, such as in London theatres, designers'
contracts for construction shaping the skyline of Shanghai, or the box
office receipts of Hollywood or other film production centres.

Quite distant centres are intimately linked on multiple registers, creating a spatialization that embraces a "second nature" separate from
the physical geography and distances. These linkages constitute the
field, medium, or space that is as cultural and economic as any goods
that actually flow through it. Rather than an interval that must be
traversed, it is more akin to a "spacing" in that it has structuring effects
on relations and shaping effects on objects as well as on the city-
regions and other spatial forms within its field. Visualizations of a set
of relative intensities of relatedness are produced and can be diagram-
matically laid out in a two-dimensional representation of the global
city and city-region network space. However, this division of labour
between studies of cities and studies of networks has limited the extent
to which city-regions are understood as an aspect of globalization.
Although they may appear to be local initiatives rather than national
creations, city-regions are creatures of a global spatialization.

CITY-REGION AS A NEW "SYNOPSIS" OF CITY AND COUNTRY

Perhaps the main function of the "city-region" is as an equivocal,
"chaotic" concept: breaking an existing spatialization of national

urban hierarchies or a regime of territorial governance. We can easily recall from their persisting elements that earlier spatializations emphasized divisions between town and countryside (Williams 1973), centres and hinterlands on the scale of no more than a few hundred kilometres at most, with peripheral areas consigned to wilderness status a bit like the colonial cartographers' unmapped "white" zones in their Atlases. Suburbia already blurred this divide, and thus was treated as an anomalous category, and even as monstrous "sprawl." Displacing an earlier modernist fascination with the contrast between the town and the country with a synoptic term of "city-region" marks an important shift in the spatial forms in which regional economies are envisioned to work. This has implications for the governance of economic activities ("rural" versus "urban" land uses and industrial activities) and the ways in which life is understood to be lived, although the weekly routines of most everyday lives are spatialized at a smaller scale than the city-region. The hypothesis that city-regions are one aspect and effect of a broader regime of spacing and placing suggests that the debates on this term may signal attempts to shift social spatializations toward, or to recognize new relationships between, the city and countryside, as well as toward more frequent discussions of the relationship between local and global scales that are entangled in each other in the form of the city-region.

In conclusion, "city-regions" are not just chatter, but neither are they a panacea. Instead, they problematize old boundaries. They represent a redrawing of lines on the "playing field" for cities vis-à-vis other cities in a global, not national, context in which they must find their niche. They also redraw the line between city and country and thus are highly significant for the rural areas and small urban centres surrounding metropolitan cores.

By blurring what seems natural to distinguish, "city-region" merges the idea of a city as a site or node versus region as a container. The term seems to converge the pair in a kind of synoptic spatial form, a bit like bringing the left and right sides of a stereoscopic image together into a simulated 3D projection. It is not a synthesis of city and country, but rather, a synoptic combination. The effect of "city-region" as synopsis is to operationalize new spatial forms and to extend what Allen and Cochrane (2010) refer to as the "reach" of governance to the scale of economic activities and local labour markets. Many of these were attempts to either work around or supplement the state as an awkwardly slow regulator, or as raising impediments to production and markets, which were particularly a feature of the economic cycle that ended with the 2008 housing market crash and subsequent great recession.

City-regions as an element in a new social spatialization might thus address the fraught relationship between cities and peri-urban developments such as suburbs and shopping malls (see Patchett and Shields 2012). Core and suburban edge-city can be reconciled in ways that fit, at least for the current moment in many cities, the spatial scale of accumulation to neoliberal governmental regimes. As a practice of space, city-regions have been widely studied as administrative projects. As an identity project that expands the urban municipality to the region, they re-present the city as covering a region. They thus re-centre citizens' identification on the city core and away from the plethora of polycentric "edge-cities" that characterized a certain type of urban vision of the late twentieth century (for example, Mississauga, Ontario, on the western border of Toronto). One might hypothesize that this is one shift in an ongoing struggle to consolidate the symbolic value attached to real estate into a clear hierarchy with the city core, the traditional downtown, as the most symbolically significant focus, as opposed to the outlying, rival edge-cities. Amidst notable increases in land value, the downtown cores are then opened to redevelopment as time-spaces that surpass the 9-to-5 Central Business District concept in terms of the diversity of activities and architectural and infrastructural investment. This might be one aspect of the logic that sees new downtown investments for after-hours and weekend social activity, wherein stadiums and sports arenas, opera houses, and civic assembly spaces are built in downtowns (often requiring upgrading of transportation). Significantly, these spaces involve commodified crowd-practices of mass consumption that fit poorly with the niche-consumption often supposed to define the era of online shopping.

Identification with city-regions requires an affective alignment with an intangible and complex spatial form. Like the city, a city-region can be "all that surrounds me" but at the same time, it is even more intangible, lacking in physical edges (rivers, greenbelts, agricultural fields, and so on that are utterly "outside" the city), and the city-region itself cannot be touched directly. City-regions and large cities that extend "over the horizon" are thus totalities that are always, to an extent, objects of faith.[4] I am not referring to the city-region as a representation or idea, but rather, to its reality as a lived space of representations. As such, the city-region becomes a frame for everything we can imagine happens within it, a "space of representations."

While they do not exclude other traditional notions of region, city-regions are primarily competitive socio-economic units imposed on geographies and communities rather than organic to everyday experiential milieux. City-regions allow us to rethink our relation not just to "the city" and its core, but also to distant places in more narrowly competitive economic terms. We can hypothesize that this has the effect of increasing the abstractness of spatialization even as neoliberal globalization interpolates individuals and communities to global supply chains and production circuits as residents within "city-regions." While they may allow people to understand their connection to others in distant labour markets (to which jobs might have been outsourced, for example, or where poor labour standards reign) and thus to mobilize jointly, the city-region is worrying in that it does not have a clear relationship to citizens, populations, or citizenship. This conceptual underdevelopment is in part related to the economic focus of the city-region research as well as the mismatch between the scale of the city-region and the municipal administrative areas and political units through which citizenship is exercised and democracy realized.

As noted above, city-regions are also projects to re-present space. As urban representations, they engage the abstract quality of place-images and brands in attempts to selectively unbind these from (negative) past images, and to develop novel, marketable images for city-regions. The significance of the "city-region" as an intangible entity known only piecemeal through its effects heightens the importance of cultural and affective elements such as place images, identification with the city-region, and branding. Regions are cast, spatialized as appropriate crucibles of innovation, as "places-for" innovation, risk, and experiment, rather than received ideas and the equilibrium of community cycles. This has led to an increased role for regional institutions concerned with cultures, lifestyles, and images. Narratives of competitiveness in turn legitimize planning interventions that concretize the "city-region." This takes the form of not only infrastructure, but the revitalization of downtowns with signature architectural projects such as concert halls and stadiums. The "city-region" becomes a self-fulfilling prophecy, despite its chaotic qualities. It competes to attract not just business activity, but innovators and entrepreneurs specifically. Ironically, the players that create the attractiveness of the area may be forgotten in this process, leading to the impoverishment of not just neighbourhoods, but also cities and regions. The virtualities of urban economic development are thus embedded in local institutions and places as forms of cultural infrastructure, in part through the channel of representations and discourses on a city-region. The ability of city-regions to adapt to demands, stresses, and opportunities has also led to an interest in resilience, and to an interest in "learning regions" as social innovation communities and technology complexes (Morgan 1997).

This chapter has foregrounded the competing aspects of the city-region to unpack the contents of this "chaotic" spatial concept. It argues that city-regions represent a significant new geographical concept, but one which is part and parcel of a changing social spatialization of cities. The city-region appears as an analytical concept imposed on urban regions, as a political and economic project to recapture suburbs and redefine our relation to the city as well as our expectations and understanding of our place in it. It integrates rural hinterlands with the sprawling megalopolises that major global cities have become, while providing an increasingly stereotyped model for aspiring peripheral cities. It integrates practice with perception, affect, and representation. City-regions constitute one aspect of not only the lived experience of globalization, but a novel spatial entity that has become the face of an ever more abstract social spatialization.

NOTES

1 NASA's Visible Earth gallery of Landsat 3 and 7+ satellite imagery offers a comparison of the urbanization of the Pearl River Delta between 1979 and 2003 online at http://visibleearth.nasa.gov/view.php?id=7949.

2 "Affect" is meant here in the Deleuzian and Spinozist sense of the capacity of a site or of spatial areas to affect us beyond offering functional affordances (such as the general flatness of a beach that might allow the laying out of nets or use as a playing field, or the view offered by a commanding height), but still providing a kernel around which both individuals and groups can coordinate and mobilize concerted action.

3 http://forums.canadiancontent.net/news/83749-canada-promotes-landlocked-province-alberta.html.

4 Such "virtualities" are known through their actual effects but exceed any given instance or "bit" of the reality of the city-region – they extend into the past and are forcefully "mythic."

REFERENCES

Allen, J., and A. Cochrane. 2010. "Assemblages of State Power: Topological Shifts in the Organization of Government and Politics." *Antipode* 42 (5): 1071–89.

Anderson, B. 1983. *Imagined Communities*. London: Verso.

Anholt, S. 2004. "Some Important Distinctions in Place Branding." *Place Branding and Public Diplomacy* 1 (2): 116–21.

Ashworth, G., and M. Kavaratzis. 2009. "Beyond the Logo: Brand Management for Cities." *Journal of Brand Management* 16 (July–August): 520–31.

Beck, G. 2003. "Signs of Life: A New Lesson from Las Vegas – A Souped-up Shopping Center on the Strip Uses Technology to Announce Itself as a Retail, Cultural, and Civic Destination. Mediated Architecture Can Finally Make a Public Place." *Architectural Record* 191 (6): 199.

Bianchini, F., and L. Ghilardi. 2007. "Thinking Culturally about Place." *Place Branding and Public Diplomacy* 3 (4): 280–6.

Bontje, M., S. Musterd, Z. Kovacs, and A. Murie. 2011. "Pathways toward European Creative-Knowledge City-Regions." *Urban Geography* 32 (1): 80–104.

Boudreau, J.A., P. Hamel, et al. 2006. "Comparing Metropolitan Governance: The Cases of Montreal and Toronto." *Progress in Planning* 66: 7–59.

Brenner, N. 2002. "Decoding the Newest 'Metropolitan Regionalism' in the USA: A Critical Overview." *Cities* 19 (1): 3–21.

– 2004. *New State Spaces: Urban Governance and the Rescaling of Statehood*. Oxford, UK: Oxford University Press.

Bristow, G. 2009. *Critical Reflections on Regional Competitiveness: Theory, Policy and Practice*. New York: Routledge.

– 2010. "Resilient Regions: Re-'place'ing Regional Competitiveness." *Cambridge Journal of Regions, Economy and Society* 3 (1): 153–67.

Cohen, A.P., ed. 1982. *Belonging: Identity and Social Organization in British Rural Cultures*. St. John's: Institute of Social and Economic Research.

Cooke, P., ed. 1989. *Localities; The Changing Face of Urban Britain*. London: Unwin Hyman.

Corey, K.E., and M.I. Wilson. 2006. *Urban and Regional Technology Planning: Planning Practice in the Global Knowledge Economy*. New York: Taylor & Francis.

Cumbers, A., and D. MacKinnon. 2004. "Introduction: Clusters in Urban and Regional Development." *Urban Studies* 41 (5–6): 959–69.

Davidson, T., O. Park, and R. Shields, eds. 2011. *Ecologies of Affect.* Waterloo, ON: Wilfrid Laurier University Press.

Diken, B. 2011. "Fire as a Metaphor of (Im)Mobility." *Mobilities* 6 (1): 95–102.

Ganne, B. 1983. *Gens du Cuir, Gens du Papier, Transformations d'Annonay depuis les années 1920.* Paris: CNRS.

Govers, R., and F.M. Go. 2009. *Place Branding. Glocal, Virtual and Physical Identities, Constructed, Imagined and Experienced.* London: Palgrave.

Herrschel, T. 2010. *Cities, State and Globalization: City-Regional Governance in Europe and North America.* New York: Taylor & Francis.

Jameson, F. 1984. "Postmodernism, or the Cultural Logic of Late Capitalism." *New Left Review* I/146.

Jonas, A.E.G., and K. Ward. 2007. "Introduction to a Debate on City-Regions: New Geographies of Governance, Democracy and Social Reproduction." *International Journal of Urban and Regional Research* 31 (1): 169–78.

Jones, A. 2004. "Narrative-Based Production of State Spaces for International Region-Building: Europeanization and the Mediterranian." *Annals of the Association of American Geographers* 96 (2): 415–31.

Lai, K.P.Y. 2009. "Global Cities in Competition? A Qualitative Analysis of Shanghai, Beijing and Hong Kong as Financial Centres." *GaWC Research Bulletin* 313 (A). http://www.lboro.ac.uk/gawc/publicat.html. Accessed 9 May 2012.

Lefebvre, H. 1991. *The Production of Space*, translated by N. Donaldson-Smith. Oxford, UK: Basil Blackwell.

– 1992. *Critique of Everyday Life.* London: Pion.

Malecki, E.J. 2000. "Knowledge and Regional Competitiveness." *Erdkunde* 54: 334–51.

McGuirk, P. 2007. "The Political Construction of the City-Region: Notes from Sydney." *International Journal of Urban and Regional Research* 31 (1): 179–87.

Morgan, K. 1997. "The Learning Region: Institutions, Innovation and Regional Renewal." *Regional Studies* 31 (5): 491–503.

Paasi, A. 2003a. "Boundaries in a Globalizing World." In *Handbook of Cultural Geography*, edited by K. Anderson, M. Domosh, S. Pile, and N. Thrift, 464–72. London: Sage.

– 2003b. "Global Times and Emerging Socio-Spatial Shapes." *International Journal of Urban and Regional Research* 27 (4): 960–3.

– 2009. "The Resurgence of the 'Region' and 'Regional Identity': Theoretical Perspectives and Empirical Observations on Regional Dynamics in Europe." *Review of International Studies* 35 (S1): 121–46.

Patchett, M., and R. Shields, eds. 2012. *Strip Appeal: Reinventing the Strip Mall*. Edmonton: Space and Culture Publications.

Scott, A.J., ed. 2001. *Global City-Regions: Trends, Theory, Policy*. Oxford, UK: Oxford University Press.

– 2006. "Creative Cities: Conception Issues and Policy Questions." *Journal of Urban Affairs* 28 (1): 1–17.

Shields, R. 1991a. "Imaginary Sites." In *Between Views*, edited by S. Gilbert, 22–6. Banff, AB: Walter Phillips Gallery, Banff Centre for the Arts.

– 1991b. *Places on the Margin: Alternative Geographies of Modernity*. London: Routledge Chapman Hall.

– 2011. "The Tourist Affect: Escape and Syncresis on the Las Vegas Strip." In *Ecologies of Affect: Placing Nostalgia, Desire and Hope*, edited by T. Davidson, O. Park, and R. Shields, 103–24. Waterloo, ON: Wilfrid Laurier University Press.

Simmie, J., J. Sennet, P. Wood, and D. Hart. 2002. "Innovation in Europe: A Tale of Networks, Knowledge and Trade in Five Cities." *Regional Studies* (UK) 36 (1): 47–64.

Simmie, J., and R. Martin. 2010. "The Economic Resilience of Regions: Towards an Evolutionary Approach." *Cambridge Journal of Regions, Economy and Society* 3 (1): 27–43.

Smith, R.G. 2003. "World City Topologies." *Progress in Human Geography* 27 (5): 561–82.

Stein, G. 1937. *Everybody's Autobiography*. New York: Random House.

Storey, D.J. 2009. *Small Firms in Regional Economic Development: Britain, Ireland and the United States*. Cambridge: Cambridge University Press.

Stough, R., R. Stimson, and P. Nijkamp. 2011. "An Endogenous Perspective on Regional Development and Growth." In *Drivers of Innovation, Entrepreneurship and Regional Dynamics*, edited by K. Kourtit et al., 3–20. Berlin: Springer-Verlag.

Taylor, P.J. 2004. *World City Network: A Global Urban Analysis*. New York: Routledge.

Ward, K., and A.E.G. Jonas. 2004. "Competitive City-Regionalism as a Politics of Space: A Critical Reinterpretation of the New Regionalism." *Environment and Planning A* 36 (12): 2119–39.

Williams, R. 1973. *The Country and the City*. London: Chatto and Windus.

Wolfe, D., and A. Bramwell. 2008. "Innovation, Creativity and
    Governance: Social Dynamics of Economic Performance in City-
    Regions." *Innovation-Management Policy & Practice* 10 (2–3): 170–82.

4

Leaving the City-Region Behind?
The Growth and Decline of Metropolitan
Rescaling in Manchester, England

JAMES REES AND ALEX LORD

INTRODUCTION

For many academics and commentators, city-regions have become a subject of great interest over the first decade of the twenty-first century. Prompted by both popular treatments that imagine the new urban territories of the coming years (Florida 2008) and the agglomeration school's account of the economic variables that are driving this reconfiguration of metropolitan geographies, a great deal of academic effort has been expended thinking about how a state-institutional counterpart might be incorporated to provide formal recognition of what are said to be functional spaces. The result is a body of literature that is now replete with both theoretical and empirical work on the origins and application of the city-regional concept (Gonzales, Tomaney, and Ward 2007; Harding 2007; Harrison 2007; Jonas and Ward 2002; McGuirk 2007; John, Tickell, and Musson 2005; Jonas, Gibbs, and While 2005; Pain 2008). One of the results of the sheer size of this corpus is an impression felt in some quarters that finding, or perhaps sometimes *creating*, city-regions should be an end in itself. Best indicated by a policy discourse that has heralded the birth of a "new city-regionalism" (SURF 2004) – presumably in contrast to the "old" city-regionalism of, for example, Patrick Geddes – many cities have sought to reconsider their administrative boundary settlements and devise an institutional apparatus of formal or semi-formal standing to match analyses of what the "true" extent of their city has become.

This close proximity between policy-makers, eager to devise an evidence-based justification for their institutional manoeuvrings, and a waiting and willing academic community keen to provide purportedly objective accounts of what state rescaling "should" look like based on the mapping of various socio-economic data, has given rise to a post-hoc impression that, in some places, city-regions have come to be *actually existing* entities as both functional and administrative spaces. This, we argue, has resulted in a misreading of the recent trajectory of the most recent city-regional project in the United Kingdom. Crucially, understanding this misrepresentation helps make sense of the ease with which the city-region policy discourse has been almost completely eradicated following the formation in 2010 of a Conservative–Liberal Democrat coalition, which has instead pursued a "localist" agenda and replaced city-regions with poorly institutionalized and funded Local Enterprise Partnerships (LEPS).

In England, the part of the UK on which this chapter focuses, the rise of the city-region dates to the early 2000s and the second administration of Prime Minister Tony Blair. The city-region, so this policy narrative ran, would be more aligned with the realities of a functional economic space, and more conducive to the promotion of economic growth (Harding et al. 2006). Recognizing and sharing in this argument, the government responded with statutory support for the identification of city-regions and corresponding City Regional Development Programmes for the eight largest conurbations in the North of the country – Liverpool, Manchester, Central Lancashire, Sheffield, Leeds, Hull and Humber Ports, Tees Valley, and Tyne and Wear – the so-called "Northern Way" (see Figure 2.1 in chapter 2 above; Goodchild and Hickman 2006).

At its most successful, this approach to city-region construction was said to be simply a legitimization of long-established informal working arrangements. For an example, central government often pointed to the experiences of the city of Manchester, where a series of institutions of varying configuration had filled the vacuum left by the abolition of Greater Manchester County Council, a previous attempt at metropolitan government that had operated from 1974 to 1986. However, in citing Manchester's desire to retain some form of metropolitan governance to support the logic that other cities should be encouraged to do the same, officials never fully explored some important questions, for instance: (1) was there one clear and mutually held interpretation amongst the shadow city-region institutions of their territorial reach; (2) what was the extent of their political power and legitimacy; and (3) what degree of democratic support (tacit or otherwise) did the creation of city-regional policy enjoy? The most obvious and straightforward way to answer these separate questions is to point out that, in general, the emergent mode of city-regional governance in England was never about the dissolution of existing local authority boundaries, and, despite a growing consensus regarding the benefits of cross-boundary working, the council and the town hall have remained the key locus of local identity and democratic control. This is not to say that the city-regional project did not take seriously the need to "get governance arrangements right," most especially tying city-regional organizations into the traditional mechanisms of scrutiny and accountability, but instead that city-regional institutional development was a largely elite project that was rarely the subject of public debate. We return to this in more detail later in the chapter.

In what follows, we consider the emergence and development of English city-regionalism before discussing a more in-depth case study of Manchester – often regarded to be the metropolitan area with the most highly evolved city-regional governance in the country. Both sections are based on a series of interviews with city-regional officials and politicians in the period 2008–11, as well as attendance at private and public seminars and conferences connected to English city-regional policy-making, both in "provincial" England and in London.

THE NATIONAL POLICY CONTEXT FOR ENGLISH CITY-REGIONALISM

The proposal for (and subsequent rejection of) a formal, elected tier of regional government in England following a resounding "no" vote in a referendum held in the North East of England in 2004 has been well documented (Harrison 2007). However, the subsequent rethink of England's sub-national governance architecture, conducted largely within the confines of the Westminster-Whitehall village at the centre of the British state, has received considerably less attention (see Ayres and Stafford 2009). Growing out of the recognition that some sub-national scale of governance was desirable to act as a strategic platform for planning and investment decisions, the argument emerged in the wake of the democratic rejection of formal regionalism that informally constituted city-regions represented a more appropriate geography to capture the functional extent of cities. As a result, the early invigoration of the UK city-region discussion focused on better understanding large cities as catchments and containers of flows of various sorts (Harding et al. 2006; Turok and Robson 2007). In this period, a lobby for the city-regional scale emerged linking policy-engaged academics, think-tanks, and local government, augmented by a range of research sponsored by the Northern Way,[1] resulting in early expressions of city-regional policy as City Regional Development Plans, published in 2005 (Northern Way 2005). As well as exploring issues of city-regional reach and footprint, these documents focused on economic development, defined as actions to improve connectivity, higher education, science and research, and business growth, particularly in aspects of the local economy envisaged as representing exposure to high-growth sectors of the global economy.

In 2006 the replacement of the previous attempt at democratic regionalism with this more instrumental approach to city-regionalism became a formal government intention when the relevant government department, Communities and Local Government (CLG), published a White Paper that indicated the government's preference for policy that enabled "bottom up," voluntary arrangements between local authorities to facilitate the creation of policy for, and in, city-regions. To enable the degree of cooperation and coordination between neighbouring local authorities necessitated by this policy, Multi-Area Agreements (MAAS) were introduced to allow local authorities to assemble themselves into voluntary contractual partnerships across geographies that approximated to city-regions (CLG 2006).

Further clarity on the direction the city-regional project would take in England came with the emergence of proposals emanating from other government departments – most significantly, the holder of the national purse strings, HM Treasury. The *Sub-National Review* (HM Treasury 2007) endorsed the relatively decentralist and permissive approach taken towards the development of city-regions around the already emerging MAA partnerships, but qualified with the caveat that economic development and urban regeneration interventions must be delivered and managed at the "right" spatial scale. Moreover, the *Sub-National Review* endorsed the widely held view amongst local authorities that further upheavals in local government were undesirable, and that city-regions should be organically formed across and between existing lines of local authority control without contemplation of boundary changes or new tiers of government (HM Treasury 2007).

This focus on voluntary arrangements and organic city-region formation was shot through with political tension in two significant ways. First, debates over city-regionalism had, until the *Sub-National Review*, been dominated by the local authorities comprising the Core Cities group – the most significant urban centres in Britain outside London. However, in the wake of the *Sub-National Review*, increased involvement of non-metropolitan local authorities was stimulated – possibly as a natural check to the perception that the amplification of already dominant metropolitan areas into even larger city-regions would see a concentration of even greater power in city hall and the corresponding threat of a loss of identity for more "peripheral" local authorities. Concerted engagement by these non-metropolitan areas saw them successfully change the terms of the debate so that a wider variety of city-regional configurations came to be discussed as just one, albeit still a dominant, form of "sub-regional space." Second, the spatial politics of this tension between often neighbouring local authorities became increasingly important in shaping the debate around how the purported benefits said to stem from instituting a form of city-regional governance should be shared. Collectives of smaller local authorities argued that decision-making should proceed on the basis of a more even pattern of development in which the payback to city-regionalism was shared across the territory as evenly as possible. This case was aided by the need for the ministry, CLG, to be seen to treat all local authorities equally in the creation of policy. However, in endorsing and adopting this approach, government signalled a rejection of the spatially selective approach that analyses of city-regions as well-defined spaces of flows and activities implied in favour of a political accommodation with the idea that endogenous benefits would flow from the enhancement of cross-boundary governance arrangements per se.

Nevertheless, in a partial acceptance of a more selective approach benefiting those areas that had already gone further in developing policy, institutions, and governance arrangements, and in response to lobbying from the same actors for a statutory basis to their city-region arrangements, the central government confirmed in 2008 that it would select from bidding cities two that would "pilot" more formal city-region arrangements. The two cities successful in gaining

this pilot status were Manchester and Leeds, and Manchester continued to press ahead more rapidly than other cities as it submitted
a proposal for a "Combined Authority" just before the national election in May 2010. However, following the election of a Conservative–
Liberal Democrat coalition, the city-regional governance policy
agenda changed rapidly with the demolition of the sub-national
architecture that had been built during the successive Labour administrations of the previous thirteen years. The Regional Development
Agencies were wound up, as was the archipelago of interconnected
city-regions known as the Northern Way. In parallel, the logic and
rationale for the two successive attempts at sub-national governance
were also jettisoned and replaced with a new territorial scale – "new
localism" (DCLG 2012). The result is that English city-regionalism
can now be understood in retrospect as a particular moment in time
sandwiched between the regionalism of the late 1990s and the
Coalition's localism from 2010 onwards. So what should we make
of the English experiment with city-regionalism?

THE POLITICS OF THE CENTRAL-LOCAL CONSTRUCTION OF CITY-REGIONS

Dating the English city-regional movement to the period 2005–10
illustrates that it was a relatively short-lived reality. The project was
always weakly embedded as an institutional construct, halting in its
progress, and ultimately, following the formation of a national coalition government that was strongly opposed to any "regional" governance level, easy to sweep off the map. In general, rather than
city-regionalism being driven solely by bottom-up demands (and
there was geographical variance in the extent to which it was led by
the assertion of local pressures for autonomy and belief in the need
for cross-boundary working), the evidence from the eight city-
regions of the Northern Way shows that outcomes depended on
the influence of central government policy – and more pressingly, the
local expectation of access to funding streams associated with the
"city-regional agenda" – as well as the ability and willingness of
central government spending departments to negotiate with the
emerging city-regions. If we add in the diverse histories of the extent
to which a metropolitan decision-making body had existed or been
retained for the city-regional area, it is very clear that no one model
of the city-region existed, even within the North of England. Finally,

city-regions were never a populist or democratic project (although concerns to demonstrate accountability and governance were prominent), and yet they were encumbered with the territorial politics inherent in attempts to create cross-boundary governance projects, as well as other inter-scalar tensions. Two of the most prominent axes of political tension, as we shall see, were centre-periphery (urban-rural) and ambitious urban areas versus their regions.

Analytically, English city-regionalism has to be understood as developing within a political space of negotiation constructed between the central and local. This reflects the reality of the relatively centralized (and, despite the short-lived regional experiment, unitary) English state, and the relative lack of autonomy of local government institutions and actors. Nevertheless, even in this constrained system, levels of effective or "earned" autonomy were still highly variable. Some city-regional spaces became relevant sites of intelligence deployment and claim-making, resulting in self-assertions of city-regional identity and a corresponding position in national debate. Others were much slower to "find" such an identity and to develop a politically unified voice with which to speak to either the unofficial channels of political decision-making or, crucially, the formal process of legislative reform necessary to allow city-regions to actually take shape.

What was on offer to city-regions was primarily the chance to govern a metropolitan area in a more coherent and streamlined manner and to claim greater powers in relation to planning, economic development, and growth – powers in Britain primarily wielded by central government departments. Hence the underpinning principle of much central government policy and legislation was devolutionary (HM Government 2006; HM Treasury 2007). The quid pro quo for what was always a relatively cautious devolution of powers was evidence of more robust governance structures for and within the city-regions themselves.

But the appetite and capacity to respond to this agenda at the local level was highly variable. At one end of the spectrum, Greater Manchester, discussed in more detail below, was exerting considerable political capacity and will to shape the options being discussed at the centre, and then adopting those that suited its aims. City-regions that encompassed former metropolitan counties (including, for example, cities such as Liverpool and Leeds) had the advantages of a clearer functional-geographical rationale, a greater degree of institutional thickness, and an institutional memory of the political and practical challenges of cross-boundary working. At the other end of the spectrum, smaller, more peripheral, or fragmented urban areas appeared more reactive and cautious. For those with weaker capacity, caution was understandable given the intrinsic moral hazard in investing in costly (in financial and political terms) city-regional governance arrangements that might or might not have resulted in genuine changes that allowed local politicians and officers to have claimed a "prize" that satisfied local political stakeholders. Hence different putative city-regional or metropolitan spaces proceeded at very different speeds with projects that, if they had anything in common, involved forms of spatial envisioning based on the reality or "logic" of their spaces, all the while reflecting the political-territorial realities lying below the surface. Local political tensions, or a more prosaic scepticism or reluctance to get involved, were counterbalanced in many cases by a reluctance to be seen to be left behind and fail to "get in on the act." Thus there was a very evident multi-speed process of development with successive waves of activity designed to manufacture city-regional configurations. The best metric for this is the very slow rate at which Multi-Area Agreements (MAAS) – the formal contracts designed to underpin local authority cooperation – were signed between the central government and local areas between 2007 and 2009.

We turn now to the experience, from a Northern city-region perspective, of the central-local negotiation process. This started "optimistically" with non-prescriptive guidance for MAAS and support for a process of negotiated devolution of powers, but ended in a "realist" position of watching and waiting from the local perspective. As noted, city-regions were initially looking for greater autonomy to promote economic growth and an accompanying delegation of powers and funding – from Regional Development Agencies (RDAS) and national quangos – although this ultimately became bogged down in shifting national priorities. In the early stages, it was possible to discern growing local capacity and confidence, while local authority officers engaged in MAA negotiations were encouraged by CLG in particular to be "radical" and challenging in their "asks" that generally requested reforms within particular policy fields or the ceding of control to the city-region. Yet many MAA actors soon became disillusioned with Whitehall: "the negotiation process was really tortuous, I had to negotiate with BERR, Treasury, CLG, DfT, DIUS, and then their agencies Hefce[2] and Network Rail

... you'd end up falling out over one word! Inevitably the [asks] have been watered down!" (MAA representative in the North West).

Following the completion and sign-off of the MAAs, it became apparent that turning what were essentially aspirations into concrete policy depended on the government's commitment to actually make real devolutionary concessions: "There is a sense of frustration here that we've produced authoritative cases that these 'asks' should just *happen*, yet certain parts of government, whether LSC[3] national office or Hefce or DIUS, are either stonewalling or just finding it all too difficult" (MAA representative in the North East).

Hence the MAA process exposed a number of cleavages and tensions within Whitehall. First, there was the willingness or ability of parent departments to steer their quangos (for example, those responsible for higher education, skills policy, and rail transport) to recognize and negotiate with MAAs, but furthermore, to engage constructively with devolutionary intent, particularly as most quangos have a national purview. Moreover, the extent of cross-departmental collaboration and "buy in" was questionable, especially from those such as the Treasury and Business departments, which have a national spatial-economic outlook, or those like the Department for Work and Pensions (DWP), with strong hierarchical, aspatial, and silo-based delivery arms. CLG drove the development of sub-national policy, was responsible for MAAs, and was the standard-bearer for devolution, yet the city-region process exposed once again its weakness against the much larger departments.

More ambitious city-regions viewed the process as a precursor to longer-term ambitions to form more robust and autonomous city-regional institutions, and played on their already strong channels into ministerial and Whitehall decision-making (Rees and Harding 2010). Others saw it as a way to get a seat at the table of central government, not least because more peripheral and declining areas felt overshadowed by larger cities, even to the extent that Whitehall civil servants could be hazy about their exact locations and characteristics: "The MAA gives you the ability to talk to [government spending departments], it raises your profile. For us [as a non-major city] to be able to talk to Whitehall – you *can* do that at a district level – but it gives us more credibility as an emerging sub-region, it's about profile and direct conversations with central government. Government already comes to Manchester, it doesn't come to us" (MAA representative in the North West).

For others, the impetus for the difficult work of building capacity and knowledge in which to ground city-regional institutional development came from higher up the scalar hierarchy, rooted in the concern not to "lose out" in the latest agenda: "There was a drive from within [NE] Government Office, that the city region put in an MAA ... yes, it is partly about developing strategy but just as important was providing momentum to bind the partnership ... there was a feeling that if you don't get it right in this part of the region, the whole region is stuffed!" (MAA representative in the North East).

In this case, the important dynamic was the sense that an asymmetry was developing where a smaller and weaker economy was forging ahead with, at least, stronger governance arrangements. Or for some, particularly those in the South and East of England, where there was a sense of grievance based on a perception of being disfavoured in New Labour's public spending decisions, the spatial project of city-regionalism offered a means of insertion into and a higher profile in national dynamics: "We saw it as getting into the Labour dominated centre, getting something more for our area which had lost out to the Northern cities" (MAA representative in the South East).

The development of the city-region agenda in the post-SNR period was a form of *weakly* centrally-orchestrated city-regionalism, with very variable outcomes. The initial policy logic behind city-regions, which subsequently influenced the design of the MAAS as an instrument of city-regionalism, was based on the large urban areas that approximated to functional economic spaces. This reflected the roots of the concept within the Core Cities Group and the Northern Way – acting essentially as a sub-national lobby. Yet CLG soon found that the "agenderization" of city-regions – accompanied by a perception that national funding might flow at some point – meant that other places wanted a piece of the action. This was reflected in a gradual shift in emphasis towards generic cross-boundary working and a language of "sub-regionalism," and the application of MAAs in the free-standing Midlands cities, across London boroughs, and in other multi-nodal portions of the urban South East. Ultimately, devolutionary progress was painfully slow, with central government and regional institutions unwilling to relinquish control or devolve budgets. Consequently, evidence-based practices and economic claim-making were deployed to win support from central government, and most particularly the Treasury, who remained sceptical throughout about the scope for sub-national actors to boost growth or rebalance the national economy away from the South East (Burch et al. 2009). The following section explores this process in much more detail through the case of Greater Manchester. Always a "front-runner" in the city-regional movement, Manchester made far more progress than other city-regions in developing genuine institutional capacity and policy-making scope, at least up until 2010.

CITY-REGION IMAGINEERING:
THE CASE OF GREATER MANCHESTER

Manchester's modern governance and political economy has already been the subject of much discussion (Cochrane et al. 1996; Deas and Ward 2000), yet some history is critical for understanding the more recent period of strengthened articulation of a specifically city-regional agenda. The abolition of the Greater Manchester County Council (GMCC) in 1986 marked the nadir of central-local relations in the Thatcher period, but the Association of Greater Manchester Authorities (AGMA), created as a metropolitan political-administrative successor body, was unusual in the UK in being politically coherent and stable, providing a forum for metropolitan cooperation when needed (Hebbert and Deas 2000). Actual institutional capacity remained fragmented, weak, and low-profile, and collaboration was built slowly, largely as a by-product of Manchester City Council's (MCC) increasingly entrepreneurial approach to "post-industrial" economic development, which focused on partnership with the private sector, particularly following the collapse of any collective resistance to national government after the third Conservative win in 1987 (Quilley 2000). The bids to host the Olympics and Commonwealth Games, the completion of major infrastructure projects, and efforts to market the city-region internationally demanded greater cross-district cooperation, and the 1990s saw the creation of an inward investment agency (MIDAS), an international marketing body, and, by 2003, a strategic economic development body, Manchester Enterprises, encompassing the metropolitan area (Rees and Harding 2010). These economic development–focused, metropolitan institutions are small in budgetary terms in relation to their constituent local authorities, yet their combined financial executive strength eclipses that assembled in any metropolitan area outside of London.

Since the turn of the century, the evolution of city-regional governance had involved a higher level of institutionalization and the
articulation of a more distinctively metropolitan strategy and vision.
The collapse of English regionalism, and emerging policy associated
with the *Sub-National Review*, presented Manchester with an
opportunity. Manchester's political elite had been vocal critics of the
RDA and resumed a campaign of more assertive involvement in the
London-based national policy-making process, aimed at establishing
a policy and legislative environment favourable to its city-regional
aspirations. Lobbying was facilitated by the favourable access of
senior Manchester politicians and officers to ministers and Whitehall
more generally, underpinned by the city's favourable reputation with
national Labour politicians (Harding et al. 2010). But equally it
reflected the internal capacity and "institutional thickness" (see also
Jones et al. [Conclusion] and Whitfield and Williams, this volume) to
create new city-regional arrangements in advance of settled national
policy. In the early negotiations around the MAA, Manchester demonstrated its confidence to set the terms of the debate, demanding
access to senior civil servants and eschewing the timorous language
of "asks." Rather than the MAA being viewed as an end in itself,
Manchester used the succession of government city-regional policy
tools – first the MAA, then the "city-region pilot" concept, and finally
the Combined Authority model that emerged from the eventual legislative outcome of the SNR: the Local Democracy, Economic
Development and Construction Act.

Manchester's rapid reconfiguration of existing metropolitan institutions and capacity-building in this short period – notably the creation
of seven thematic "commissions," and in particular the Commission
for the New Economy – was one source of pressure to reform metro-
politan-level governance arrangements. The period of negotiation
around the city-region pilot exercise (2008–09) in particular was one
in which central government expressed concerns about the transpar-
ency and democratic accountability of the arrangements for Greater
Manchester. These had been stretched to the breaking point by the very
public failure to secure agreement over a congestion-charging scheme
in 2008, leading to central government doubts over the credibility of
city-regional executive arrangements, and it was clear that evidence of
robust accountability and decision-making arrangements would be
needed before the government was willing to delegate further powers
and permit enhanced local autonomy. AGMA's constitution was revised

to enable majority voting and delegation to the Commissions, placing the AGMA Executive Board at the heart of metropolitan arrangements. The Combined Authority proposal finally agreed to just before the 2010 national election, and ratified early in the Coalition era, sought to bring together significant powers and pooled resources for metropolitan transport, economic development, and regeneration.

The undoubted importance of institutional reconfiguration and governance reform tended to obscure the parallel development of distinctively *city-regional* policy and powers; after all, establishing *autonomy to do* begs the question of *autonomy to do what?* (Jonas and Ward 2007). Manchester's MAA, in common with others being developed across England, focused on complex reforms to the delivery of skills and training, as well as administrative reforms related to economic development functions on a more coherently metropolitan footprint. Ultimately, Greater Manchester designated the Commission for the New Economy as its statutory Employment and Skills Board, with powers to control public spending on adult skills, as well as control over post-age-16 training provisions. To this was added a range of transport governance issues that reflected Manchester's frustration over its lack of control over key transport and infrastructure decisions made by executive agencies such as Network Rail, or higher tiers of government. In Manchester's view, the failure to solve key transport bottlenecks – perceived to be holding back economic development – was a function of a lack of prioritization of the city's needs by these agencies. Transport reforms revolved around detailed protocols with these other agencies, and ultimately plans within the Combined Authority proposal to create a more powerful Transport for Manchester body modelled on London's arrangements.

Finally, a key policy theme led by the Commission for the New Economy has been a distinctively Mancunian approach to restructuring the economy and reshaping the supply of skilled labour. The Manchester Independent Economic Review (MIER) provided a bleak assessment of Manchester's productivity lag: "The challenge is to increase the skill level of those already resident in Manchester City Region. This is absolutely vital for sustainability and the future prospects of those parts of the city-region which are relatively deprived ... It is clear that this needs to start with children in their early years, when their cognitive abilities are mainly being shaped" (MIER 2009, 23). Consequently, policies have been developed that, although they have continuities with earlier national regeneration

programs, appear to represent bespoke social policies for the city-
region. They focus on reforms to existing public services, in particular making them better integrated and more effective at intervening
to "tackle deprivation," deal with long-term unemployment, and
deliver services for pre-school children ("early years"), as the quote
above suggests. As an example, Manchester City Council controls
around 15 percent of the annual £22 billion public spending in the
city, and a central aim is to extend the authority's influence over the
commissioning of the relevant services in the expectation that they
can be better tailored at the local level: notably health, Sure Start,
and unemployment supports that determine key outcomes for
labour market engagement. Greater Manchester has been trialling
and evaluating these reformed approaches within geographically
defined pilot areas in the metropolitan area. Such new approaches
have been influenced by increasing interest (both before and after
the arrival of the new government) in the UK in quantifying expenditure on social problems, and attempting to identify and quantify
where long-term savings to the public purse can be made by judi-
cious investment in preventative approaches. It is clear that Greater
Manchester hopes such home-grown "reformed" approaches can be
successful in the post-2010 context of deep public spending cuts,
particularly to local government, and the new Coalition Government's
localism rhetoric.

As previously noted, much of this in-depth policy development and
governance reform occurred in the absence of public debate, and real
political tensions only erupted into the open occasionally. Perhaps
the spat most visible to citizens, as briefly noted above, was the
"debacle" of the attempt to introduce congestion charging in order
to unlock a package of central government funding for a major transport infrastructure upgrade. Unable to secure elite consensus through
the established AGMA metropolitan decision-making structure –
because a small number of (again, peripheral, and relatively wealthy)
constituent authorities were fully cognizant of the latent opposition
of their own local constituents – the stage was set for a Greater
Manchester–wide plebiscite. To the surprise of few, a vocal and effective opposition campaign ensured a resounding rejection of the proposed charge. This was a major setback for Greater Manchester's
image in the eyes of central government, and hence for its city-
regional ambitions. Two years later, after the lengthy and careful process of elite negotiation of the Combined Authority deal, two of the

peripheral local authorities, with a different political complexion from the majority of local authorities, played brinksmanship in a successful effort to secure concessions from the group. Nevertheless, there was enough collective commitment to the project for it to secure consent in the national Parliament in 2010, and Greater Manchester continues to develop its governing capacity and policy reach, albeit in a much less fertile national context.

CONCLUSION

The starting point for this chapter was the sense gained from some of the academic and policy literature that in the case of England, as elsewhere in the developed world, city-regions have become actually existing functional spaces with coherent governance institutions to match. Academic analysts can indeed be forgiven for making this link, given that policy-makers and politicians have been keen to bolster the impression that the two are commensurable. However, by contrast, this chapter has shown that, whatever the merits of the socio-economic and demographic analyses behind the city-regional cheerleading, attempts to match functional space with an administrative counterpart have often been frustrated. Ultimately, the real character of English city-regionalism – halting, incremental, and weakly institutionally and legislatively rooted – was perhaps most starkly highlighted when the new Coalition Government from 2010 was able to virtually erase city-regionalism from the policy landscape.

Even in Manchester, though, the political-institutional apparatus that exists and has been used to create the impression of "metropolitan Manchester" as an actually existing entity is in reality a mixture of artefacts from the previous Greater Manchester County Council and newer agencies, the creation of which has been justified by sometimes contrasting interpretations of the city-region's extent. In contrast to the supposed ideal of formal city-regional governance, the result is a much weaker formulation based on negotiated bespoke cross-boundary cooperation to address specific issues, and piecemeal partnerships where economic inter-linkages are most clearly present. Often the best examples of collaboration have been the result of entirely contingent factors, such as personal ties and cordial relationships between senior local authority personnel.

However well-established this ad-hoc cross-boundary working may have become, the formal declaration of actually existing city-regions that some policy-makers have felt moved to make is something of a logical leap: English city-regions have probably never existed in the way that the term is most commonly understood by an international academic community. Instead, English city-regions were always almost virtual – or soft – spaces, more akin to policy development bodies, or cross-boundary secretariats (Allmendinger and Haughton 2010). Indeed, in many cases, city-regional agencies, such as they existed, were expanded from existing limited-life agencies morphed to speak to the in-vogue spatial scale. Moreover, many of these agencies have a larger nominal presence than their under-resourced nature could justify: in reality, they are often relatively powerless and fundamentally reliant for their ongoing operation on the consent and good will of local authorities, from which they are usually staffed through secondments.

The degree to which this peculiarly English form of city-regionalism actually constituted progress towards the realization of a more substantive form of city-regionalism, recognizable to an international audience, was inevitably conditional on the patronage of much more powerful local authority chief executives and (political) leaders. Where the most progress was seen to be made was in metropolitan areas such as Manchester, with a tradition of relatively settled intra-metropolitan relations; even in these cases, however, core-periphery relations have always been strained due to the political differences between inner city and suburban/rural hinterlands – hence the likelihood that city-regional "reach" was often sacrificed in favour of a more congenial "metropolitanism" (Rees and Harding 2010).

Instead, as this chapter has charted, city-regions in England were created from a complex interplay of central-local relations in a particular political-economic era that reached its apogee in the last years of the Labour government. One of the first acts of the new Conservative-led Coalition Government was to carry out "linguistic cleansing" that expunged anything "regional" from the spatial governance lexicon. The 2004 referendum rejection of a regional assembly for the North East of England was widely seen as the death knell of the "new regionalism" (Harrison 2008), but this was nothing compared to the ease with which government ignored, and then reversed, the whole direction of late New Labour policy on urban regeneration, economic development, and sub-national governance as set out in the SNR. Yet, as our analysis makes clear, the new government accepted the argument for the existence of "functional economic areas" (see also BIS 2010), and perhaps ironically, its answer to the vacuum created by the abolition of

Regional Development Agencies (closed down in March 2012) was a more ostensibly *city-regional* solution of Local Enterprise Partnerships (LEPS) covering every patch of England by requiring every local authority to enter into cross-boundary partnerships with its neighbours in an approximation of their aforementioned functional areas. To be led by private sector chairpersons, they have been set the task of "rebalancing" the economy back toward private sector–led growth.

Given this set of apparently conflicting observations, it would take a brave academic to attempt to predict even the near-term future. As noted, LEPS are now the only institutional vehicle sitting between local authorities and the national level in England – it just so happens they approximate to a functional definition of the city-regions that had been developing – but they will not be substantially resourced, and it is not entirely clear what functions they will have. On the one hand, one would assume that there are opportunities for LEPS in the current political climate. The Coalition Government is pursuing an overarching "localism" policy of decentralizing decision-making to the lowest possible level, and in promoting more balanced (i.e. less London-centric) growth.[4] But the problem is that the overriding priority is the reduction of the deficit, and this inevitably means that resources to promote economic growth are extremely scarce, with attendant job losses in the public sector meaning that capacity and expertise are likely to dwindle. Given that the UK is currently hovering in and out of recession, and that austerity conditions are predicted to exist well into the new Parliament after 2015, the opportunities to further tinker with city-regional governance look constricted. In Manchester, every effort is being made to retain capacity for when economic conditions improve, but again the mood music is austerity. If one thing *is* clear, it is that in England, with its patchwork of rigidly defined local authority boundaries, there will always remain a strong rationale for cross-boundary working, including, but not limited to, those spaces that look most like city-regions – whatever the prevailing political complexion of the central government. The ideas underpinning English city-regionalism, while currently lying dormant, are unlikely to die out entirely.

NOTES

1 The Core Cities Group is a lobbying organization representing the interests of eight of England's larger cities outside of London (not all of which are in the North of England; see http://www.corecities.com). The Northern

Way was established in 2004 across the three Northern regions that aimed to improve economic development, mainly through compiling evidence and developing strategy, as well as influencing central government. With its parent regional development agencies, it closed in March 2012. See http://www.thenorthernway.co.uk.

2 A mixture of central government departments and executive agencies. Explanation of acronyms not previously used: BERR: Department for Business, Enterprise and Regulatory Reform; DfT: Department for Transport; DIUS: Department for Innovation, Universities and Skills; Hefce: Higher Education Funding Council for England.

3 LSC: Learning and Skills Council, responsible for funding and planning education and training for over-16-year-olds in England.

4 One wonders whether this aim, ostensibly the same as the previous government's, can be achieved in an era of austerity.

REFERENCES

Allmendinger, P., and G. Haughton. 2009. "Soft Spaces, Fuzzy Boundaries, and Metagovernance: The New Spatial Planning in the Thames Gateway." *Environment and Planning A* 41 (3): 617–33.

Ayres, S., and I. Stafford. 2009. "Deal-Making in Whitehall: Competing and Complementary Motives Behind the Review of Sub-National Economic Development and Regeneration." *International Journal of Public Sector Management* 22 (7): 605–22.

Burch, M., A. Harding, and J. Rees. 2009. "Having It Both Ways: Explaining the Contradiction in English Spatial Development Policy." *International Journal of Public Sector Management* 22 (7): 587–604.

Castells, M. 1996. *The Rise of the Network Society*. Oxford, UK: Blackwell.

Cochrane, A., J. Peck, and A. Tickell. 1996. "Manchester Plays Games: Exploring the Local Politics of Globalisation." *Urban Studies* 33 (8): 1319–36.

Davies, J. 2008. "Double-Devolution or Double-Dealing? The Local Government White Paper and the Lyons Review." *Local Government Studies* 34 (1): 3–22.

Deas, I., and K. Ward. 2000. "From the New Localism to the 'New Regionalism': The Implications of Regional Development Agencies for City Regional Relations." *Political Geography* 19 (3): 273–92.

Department for Business, Innovation and Skills (BIS). 2010. *Understanding Local Growth*. BIS Economics Paper No. 7. London: BIS.

Department for Communitites and Local Government (DCLG). 2012. *Localism Act: Power Shift to Communities Charges On.* http://www. communities.gov.uk/news/communities/2126308. Accessed 9 July 2012.

Florida, R. 2008. *Who's Your City?* New York: Basic Books.

Geddes, P. 1915. *Cities in Evolution.* London: Williams and Margate.

Gonzalez, S., J. Tomaney, and N. Ward. 2006. "Faith in the City-Region?" *Town and Country Planning* 75 (November): 315–17.

Goodchild, B., and P. Hickman. 2006. "Towards a Regional Strategy for the North of England? An Assessment of the 'Northern Way.'" *Regional Studies* 40 (1): 121–33.

Harding, A. 2007. "Taking City Regions Seriously? Response to Debate on 'City-Regions: New Geographies of Governance, Democracy and Social Reproduction.'" *International Journal of Urban and Regional Research* 31 (2): 443–58.

Harding, A., M. Harloe, and J. Rees. 2010. "Manchester's Bust Regime?" *International Journal of Urban and Regional Research* 34 (4): 981–91.

Harding, A., S. Marvin, and B. Robson. 2006. *A Framework for City-Regions.* London: Office for the Deputy Prime Minister.

Harrison, J. 2007. "From Competitive Regions to Competitive City-Regions: A New Orthodoxy, but Some Old Mistakes." *Journal of Economic Geography* 7 (3): 311–32.

– 2010. "Networks of Connectivity, Territorial Fragmentation, Uneven Development: The New Politics of City Regionalism." *Political Geography* 29 (1): 17–27.

Hebbert, M., and I. Deas. 2000. "Greater Manchester – 'Up and Going'?" *Policy and Politics* 28 (1): 79–92.

HM Treasury, Department for Business Enterprise and Regulatory Reform and Department for Communities and Local Government. 2007. *Review of Sub-National Economic Development and Regeneration.* London: HMSO.

John, P., A. Tickell, and S. Musson. 2005. "Governing the Mega-Region: Governance and Networks across London and the South East of England." *New Political Economy* 10 (1): 91–106.

Jonas, A.E.G., and K. Ward. 2002. "A World of Regionalisms? Towards a US–UK Urban and Regional Policy Framework Comparison." *Journal of Urban Affairs* 24 (4): 377–401.

– 2007a. "Introduction to Debate on City-Regions: New Geographies of Governance, Democracy and Social Reproduction." *International Journal of Urban and Regional Research* 31 (1): 169–78.

– 2007b. "There's More Than One Way to Be 'Serious, About City-Regions.'" *International Journal of Urban and Regional Research* 31 (3): 647–56.

Jonas, A.E.G., D.C. Gibbs, and A. While. 2005. "Uneven Development, Sustainability and City-Regionalism Contested: English City-Regions in the European Context." In *Regionalism Contested: Institution, Society and Territorial Governance*, edited by I. Sagan and H. Halkier, 223–46. Aldershot, UK: Ashgate.

McGuirk, P. 2007. "The Political Construction of the City-Region: Notes from Sydney." *International Journal of Urban and Regional Research* 31 (1): 179–87.

MIER. 2009. *Manchester Independent Economic Review: Reviewer's Report*. http://www.manchester-review.org.uk. Accessed 9 November 2011.

Northern Way. 2004. *Moving Forward: The Northern Way First Growth Strategy Report: Summary*. Newcastle-upon-Tyne, UK: Northern Way Steering Group.

Pain, K. 2008. "Examining 'Core-Periphery' Relationships in a Global City-Region: The Case of London and South East England." *Regional Studies* 42 (8): 1161–72.

Quilley, S. 2000. "Manchester First: From Municipal Socialism to the Entrepreneurial City." *International Journal of Urban and Regional Research* 24 (3): 601–15.

Rees, J., and A. Harding. 2010. "Greater Manchester Case Study. Appendix C2." In *The Case for Agglomeration Economies in Europe, Final Report*. Luxembourg: ESPON.

SURF. 2004. *Releasing the National Economic Potential of Provincial City-Regions: The Rationale for and Implications of a 'Northern Way' Growth Strategy*. Salford, UK: Centre for Sustainable Urban and Regional Futures.

Turok, I., and B. Robson. 2007. "Linking Neighbourhood Regeneration to City-Region Growth: Why and How?" *Journal of Urban Regeneration and Renewal* 1 (1): 44–54.

Ward, K., and A. Jonas. 2004. "Competitive City-Regionalism as a Politics of Space: A Critical Reinterpretation of the New Regionalism." *Environment and Planning A* 36 (12): 2119–39.

5

On Wanting to Be a Global City: Global Rankings and Urban Governance in Calgary

ALAN SMART AND ALINA TANASESCU

INTRODUCTION

In recent years, academic work on global and creative cities has had a substantial impact on urban governance in cities around the world, particularly in the many cities with aspirations of becoming "global" or "world class." One of the consequences of widespread popular and policy uptake of the global cities discourse is that many cities are devoting significant resources to finding ways to increase their standing on global cities ranking lists or to make their cities more attractive to the "creative class" and economic investment. This phenomenon should remind us that by studying, indexing, classifying, and counting, we are in fact producing and reproducing fields of knowledge with "real" impacts on social structures and subjects. It is not simply that cities want to become more "global" in the sense of attracting a larger proportion of the world's investment capital or head offices, or becoming better connected through airport hubs, intermodal ports, and fibre-optic backbones. These are the elements of what we refer to as *direct* characteristics of urban "global-ness." Rather, what we want to concentrate on in this chapter is the *indirect* influence of the desire for global city status. Many cities are trying to develop or market characteristics that make them appear more global, believing that higher global ranking will in itself attract more of the direct features of global status. A better position in the hierarchy of global cities is widely believed to facilitate the relocation or in-situ development of the resources and features that lead a city to be more global. It is for this reason that many cities adopt development strategies to re-brand, place-market, or re-scale. Many sponsor "iconic" buildings, other features, or events that will attract wider attention and resources. Lui Tai-lok writes that iconic buildings, mega-events, and mega-projects are "becoming contagious through intense inter-city competition under globalization" (2008, 215).

In this chapter, we will first build on ideas from Michel Foucault and some Foucauldians to explore these dynamics and consider the implications for secondary city governance of "wannabe" global cities or creative city policy initiatives (Peck 2005). Our analysis will explore the ways in which global city discourses and their focus on ranking and indexing are producing and reproducing cities as social facts, or "truths," that enable particular governmental projects. By employing Foucault's analysis of the subject and the role of knowledge in micro-strategies involved in governmentality, we examine the impact of global cities discourse in everyday practice. Rather than taking for granted that projects of governmentality succeed in their goals, as the Foucauldian tradition generally assumes, our research suggests that we must consider failures and unintended consequences as well (Smart 2006). A case study of Calgary will be used to explore these processes, focusing on the policy agendas of the City of Calgary's Calgary Economic Development Agency, the Calgary Chamber of Commerce, ideas about the Calgary-Edmonton Corridor, and the redevelopment of East Village. As the Introduction and Harrison (this volume) make clear, ideas about globalization and efforts to better position them-selves are having pervasive effects on city-regions around the world. Calgary's dynamics are somewhat distinct in that the vast majority of the regional population is contained within the unified political frame of the City of Calgary, although growth outside its boundaries has been accelerating in recent years. This situation means that it is easier for Calgary to adopt coherent growth strategies than it is for many other fragmented urban regions, and that the primary political con-straints have been at the provincial rather than the regional scale.

POWER AND KNOWLEDGE
IN GLOBAL CITIES DISCOURSE

Since the mid-1990s, a surge of research has focused on the rescaling of urban organization and agendas, with global cities being an important element of these economic, political, and cultural projects. Attention to scale is related to the prominence of political projects that change the scale at which activities had previously been routinized (Smith 1996; Leitner et al. 2002; Herod and Wright 2002). As part of these "massive upheavals of entrenched interscalar relations," local spaces have been increasingly seen as "key institutional arenas for a wide range of policy experiments and political strategies" (Brenner and Theodore 2002, 341). Supranational transformations limit the ability of national institutions to provide adequate "regulatory fixes" to resolve crises. By pushing issues either upward or downward from the scale at which regulation was formerly achieved (e.g. the nation), new actions can be facilitated, or other claims delegitimized (Miller 1997).

Ash Amin (2002) suggests that rescaling should not be seen as simply a change in the forms of territoriality without questioning the boundedness of processes. A scalar analysis finds that cities are "localised economic systems, now facing perforation ... through their integration into a wider territorial space," whereas Amin's non-scalar or topological approach sees "local economic activity as part of, and inseparable from, proximate and distanciated transactions" (395). A locality is not a bounded region so much as a "contingent and ever-shifting mesh of interactive processes" (Olds and Yeung 1999, 535). Many rescaling projects involve the bricolage of rags and patches, with breaks and gaps held together by projective imaginaries more than concrete lineaments (Smart and Lin 2007). Many elements are virtual in the sense that their very existence is uncertain. In the analysis that follows, we find that the desire by "secondary" cities to acquire higher positions on global city rankings fits with this analysis. Urban political projects to repackage and market their resources to attain higher positions on global city league tables (or their creative, liveability, etc. equivalents) are not just about becoming more global, nor are they just a top-down transformation of urban places by neoliberal globalization. Instead, the pursuit of higher ranking itself is hoped to attract outside attention and interest.

Since the 1970s, research on "global" or "world" cities has probed the mechanisms and dynamics driving increasingly interconnected "world-city nodes" (Friedmann 2002, 9) in the global economy (Brenner and Keil 2006). This concern with the socio-economic and political implications of capitalism on cities drove a research agenda focused on exploring the impact of global flows of capital, information, and people on city life and spatial configurations, particularly for those who failed to benefit. The conclusions reached by many theorists (notably, Sassen 2002; Castells 1998; Friedmann 1986; King 2006) converged on the emergence of a hierarchy of global cities with strategic functions in the world system. Their conceptualization of world city hierarchy prioritized those acting as command and control centres coordinating transnational production and exchange. Neil Smith (2002, 85) stresses that since commodity trade and finance were already significantly globalized in the nineteenth century, the novel feature of global cities must be seen as the globalization of economic production. Global cities are the places where transnational corporations (TNCs) interact with global finance to coordinate an ever more fragmented and complexly integrated global production system.

Dissenting voices point out that global capital is only one element of the globalized production system, and that centres such as Dhaka and Manila, where the global supplies of migrant labour are coordinated, should also be recognized as key command hubs for global production (Tyner 2000). More generally, the broad issues raised by the intersection between urbanization and globalization may be missed by emphasis on only command and control centres. Arguably all cities are globalizing in one way or another, if only through decline due to the loss of their traditional economic functions to other production zones. Broadening the conceptualization of a "global city" to recognize these factors, however, would reduce its utility in the construction of clear ranking systems.

One factor in the growth of global city analysis has been that researchers have gained access to data and technologies that enable increasingly sophisticated analyses of cities' levels of centrality in the global economy. Indices have been constructed to determine the power level of a particular city based on the number of TNC headquarters and the degree of foreign investment present (Friedmann and Wolff 1982; Sassen 2001). The aim of these city typologies and hierarchies was to uncover the network of relationships that constituted the flows of capital, people, and commodities on a global scale, as well as their function and structuration.

More recently, a city's position on global rankings has come to influence urban governance and economic development strategies. The movement of global city rank construction from academic to policy circles illustrates this shift. For example, the management consulting firm A.T. Kearney teamed up with the Chicago Council on Global Affairs and *Foreign Policy* magazine to create the Global Cities Index, a composite measure that included areas of business activity, human capital, information exchange, cultural experience, and political engagement.

This index is only one example of such attempts at classifying urban centres according to their relative ranking and function in the global economy. A few other well-known classifications and rankings of cities include: the Mercer Quality of Living Global City Ranking, the Innovation Cities Index, the Global Power City Index, the Most Liveable Cities Index, and the Global Financial Centre Index (Mercer 2007; Ni and Kresl 2010).

Generally, the critical side of the global cities literature fails to make it into such mainstream reports, articles, and governmental usage, neglecting issues such as growing inequality, political repression, declining welfare provision, and transfers to advance the interests of powerful corporations and urban elites (Douglass 2001; Flusty 2006; Jonas and Wilson 1999; Keil and Ronneberger 2000). The concept of the hierarchy of global cities has become a means of boosting images, benchmarking attractiveness for investment against competitor cities. Contemporary discourse on global cities plays a key role in policy-making for state agents seeking investment, a competitive edge, labour, "brand" recognition, and citizen commitment. Social movements also use global city discourse to make claims for more progressive projects and initiatives, as we examine below.

The aim of this chapter is to examine ways in which global city discourses affect more than the overt relative classification or ranking that they offer. By studying, indexing, classifying, counting, and auditing, we are in fact producing and reproducing fields of knowledge with "real" impacts on social structures and subjects (Foucault 1980, 1991). Discourses on global cities reproduce both the "city" and its global context as social facts or "truths," and in so doing, encourage and facilitate certain types of governmental projects. Foucault gave primacy to the analysis of discourse in social analysis by emphasizing how people write or speak about a subject or a body of knowledge. In doing so, he aimed to destabilize the assumed structures of power (Barnard 2000). By "discourse," Foucault meant ways of referring to and constructing knowledge about a particular topic/practice, and examining the effects and consequences of representation. His concern was to understand production of knowledge by analyzing discourses of "the social, the embodied individual and shared meanings" (Hall 2002, 43). Foucault asserted that subjects such as "madness" or "sexuality" can only meaningfully exist within discourses about them (45). The subjects who personify the discourse, such as the prisoner, the madman, or the "city," are historically contingent; different *epistemes* arise to displace their predecessors and open new discursive formations with authority to determine what is considered "truth." This emphasis on the historical context is critical: "it was only within a definitive discursive formation that the object could appear at all as a meaningful or intelligible construct" (46). But it is not just knowledge; it is also power to use the construct to transform the world. Even more importantly, it is knowledge that can make the citizenry consent to the need for its world to be transformed, as when we accept the inevitability of "going global."

The strength of the Foucauldian approach is that it takes seriously minute details of apparently mundane administrative practices. For example, Miller and Rose note how, over the course of the twentieth century, "new indexes of economic activity were invented that would render the economy amenable to management, and new technologies of macro-economic regulation were brought into being" (2008, 95–6). Once the desirability of the attachment of a "global" adjective to a city becomes accepted, operational choices of what is measured, indexed, and ranked have considerable implications for governmental strategies and tactics. If air travel connections are a key element in the index, it may be worthwhile to increase the incentives provided to airlines to make your centre into a "hub" for their operations, even above the inherent attraction of connectedness for corporate locational choices.

How did academic attempts to measure and rank the degree of global-ness of urban centres come to influence urban governance? The liberalization of cross-border flows of manufactured goods and capital (but not of most people) since the mid-1970s has certainly been a key factor. During the last few decades, the economic embeddedness of cities in their hinterlands has become seriously challenged and transformed (see Conclusion, this volume). A small city can no longer assume that rural residents will market through it, nor that its own residents will buy goods from its merchants, as online shopping and Walmarts, stuffed with low-cost global goods, challenge their economic niches. Increasingly, cities are being "globalized" in the sense that if they do not forge new economic roles in which they can compete regionally or globally, they seem destined to decline; this is particularly so for industrial centres in the rustbelts of the rich countries. The hyper-mobility of TNCs has increased their bargaining power against nations and localities (Castells 1998; Harvey 2005).

One result is the rise of urban entrepreneurialism, where cities compete for economic growth, and reconstruct growth machines to enhance their competitive edge and defend old niches from global challenges, or craft new opportunities from globalized markets. In some ways, this can be seen as little more than an updating of old-fashioned boosterism or place-marketing (Rutheiser 1996). Still, inter-urban competition does seem to have increased, enhancing the importance of turning place-in-itself into place-for-itself, particularly for middle-ranking cities, with an opportunity to improve their salience for outside investors. As the Introduction indicates, this requires, for many cities, a restructuring of city-region governance to facilitate the political agency necessary to play such games.

The adoption of neoliberal philosophies by government leaders has resulted in a downloading of costs and obligations to cities that forces them to look farther afield for their economic futures (LeSage Jr. and McMillan 2006). Ranked lists of cities are only one element of this inter-urban competition and place-marketing, but they are often of distinctive importance because of their apparent concreteness. As the new public managerialism has emphasized benchmarking and performance measurement (Clarke et al. 2007), external rankings fit with the general governmental ethos. As well as consuming rankings, cities and other governments often commission their own rankings, as we describe below, allowing them to select measures that give them some edge.

The classic global city or world city rankings are inherently weighted to emphasize the largest cities of the rich countries. As a result, while smaller cities might dream of playing in those leagues, such aspirations are usually unrealistic. Consequently, alternative ranking systems that are in one way or another related to global "beauty contests" are more likely to appeal to smaller cities. Smaller cities often do much better on rankings based on "liveability" or "cost of doing business." Richard Florida's (2002) rankings of "creative cities" have been particularly successful and influential. Florida's system is based on an alternative theory of urban economic growth. He argues that there has been a systemic shift from a situation where the location of large corporations, pursued by labour seeking jobs and careers, was the central dynamic, to one in which corporations are likely to move to places where the "creative class," as the key scarce factor in the "contemporary knowledge economy," wants to live. Cities must make efforts to establish the right climate for the creative class "or they will wither and die" (13).

Jamie Peck (2005, 740) sees Florida's speaking engagements as attempts to convince civic leaders of the necessity of commissioning a report on their creative situation and potentiality. Peck is particularly scathing about how uncreative these consulting reports are, largely consisting of boilerplate spiked with occasional references to local musicians or artists. Unfortunately, deficit-ridden states such as Michigan have bought into these ideas with its "Cool Cities" program. Aspirant, and often suffering, cities are "Florida's audience, and his market. And a large number have been ready, willing and able to join the new market for hipsterization strategies" (747), which recycle a "narrow repertoire of newly legitimized regeneration strategies" (752). Because of the emphasis on trying to attract people over which a city has no control, Peck compares creative city strategies to Melanesian "cargo cults, in which airstrips were laid out in the jungle in the forlorn hope of luring a passing aircraft to earth" (762). In the meantime, cities throughout North America are remade to fit the fantasies of upper-middle classes, resulting in urban regeneration/gentrification being seen as a solution for the city, rather than as the displacement of an underprivileged group by a more privileged one with many detrimental consequences (Smith 2002). Wilson and Keil (2008, 846) argue that Florida's creative class is really about "finding another rationale to privilege in public policy the desires and aspirations of capital and the affluent."

Reflecting on governmentality, Michel Foucault describes the latter as an "ensemble formed by the institutions, procedures, analyses and reflections, the calculations and tactics that allow the exercise of this ... complex form of power" (1991, 142). This process has led to governmentalities that rely on disciplines and specific bodies of knowledge which shape government apparatuses and the conduct of conduct. Foucault uses the idea of governmentality to delineate the transition from repressive sovereign power concerned with territory to a form of power concerned with the population, whose security and well-being comes to require government intervention. In this vein, our efforts should focus on understanding the effect of everyday practices, discourses, and forms of power (Sharma and Gupta 2008).

From an anthropological perspective, the Foucauldian approach is incomplete. It generally provides a detailed reading and interpretation of governmental projects, but very little information on what happens when those projects are implemented, which usually is very different from the objectives asserted by the reformers who initiate the new projects. The ethnography of government and policy has usually emphasized why governing initiatives do not have the effects intended, and how their targets manoeuvre to evade or undermine the government's goals. As Foucault also notes, "one cannot confine oneself to analyzing government alone if one wants to grasp the mechanisms of power in their detail and complexity" (1980, 72, in Mitchell 1999, 169). Anthropology offers methods to understand these multi-layered, contradictory, and fluid processes of governance and diffuse workings of power. Ethnography can probe everyday bureaucratic practices and discursive constructions, and shed light on the practice of rule (Sharma and Gupta 2008). We can examine how power works in disaggregated manners (Foucault 1991) through dispersed institutional and social networks, and consider the role of individuals, groups, and communities in the governance process. Our case study of Calgary begins from a Foucauldian analysis of global city measurement and aspiration, but also attempts to consider the complex array of outcomes of such projects, and how various groups try to turn the technologies of ranking and "world classing" to their own advantage.

CALGARY AS A WANNABE GLOBAL CITY

Calgary is a young city that grew through rather arbitrary decisions about the location of the Canadian Pacific Railway. Calgary is a classic boosterist city, inventing itself through the hosting of events such as the Calgary Stampede and the Olympics, and with aggressive real estate promotion producing booms and busts at regular intervals from at least 1914 (Foran 2009). Even by the standards of Canadian urban politics, which Magnusson and Sancton (1983) suggested were distinctively about boosterism, Calgary has always been "on the make." As a result, Calgary is often seen as the most "American" of Canadian cities, where growth trumps all else (Smart 2001). It has been the fastest-growing large Canadian city for most of the last fifteen years (Ghitter and Smart 2009; Miller and Smart 2012).

Calgary is a regional centre that grew quickly in most of the twentieth century through its role in the extraction of natural resources,

particularly wheat, ranching, coal, and especially oil and gas, from
the southern Alberta hinterland. Now, a case can be made for its
emergence as a global city, if a small one with only 1.1 million people. While the literature on global cities has emphasized metropolises that are also the most important financial centres, the basic
definition focuses on cities that serve as "command and control centres" for transnational corporations and nexuses of global decision-
making. London, New York, and Tokyo clearly serve these roles, but
why not Houston as well, with its concentration of big oil firms?
Calgary serves a similar role in Canada as Houston does in the
United States, but has increasingly become less a centre for regional
operations of American companies, or even as head office for companies that concentrate on domestic petroleum operations, and more
a centre with many rapidly globalizing corporations. As early as
1979, Richards and Pratt (1979, 172) could state that Calgary
ranked "only behind Houston and London as a world capital for oil
finance." One indicator of Calgary's global influence has been the
worldwide controversy about the oilsands/tarsands and their contribution to global warming and other forms of environmental dete-
rioration. While the oilsands are located far to the north of Alberta,
Calgary's head offices are where most decisions are made about their
exploitation. Calgary is fast becoming the wealthy controller of the
second largest pool of oil after Saudi Arabia.

Even in the conventional global city terms of a command and control centre, Calgary makes a reasonable case for being included as at
least a modest global city. The 2010 Global Urban Competitiveness
ranking places Calgary at sixty-first out of five hundred cities.
Calgary ranks quite well in a number of benchmarks, once measures
that are biased towards large populations are converted to per capita measurements (Ni and Kresl 2010). According to a recent report
by Calgary Economic Development, Calgary ranks first among large
Canadian cities "in head office concentration and employment"
(2010, 2). This metric is cunningly chosen, since Calgary still greatly
trails Toronto in absolute numbers of head offices. Measured by
head offices per 100,000 population, however, Calgary heads the list
at 9.3 head offices per 100,000 compared to 4.7 for Toronto (ibid.,
10). In 2009, there were 114 head offices in Calgary, up from only
78 in 2000, a growth rate of 46.2 percent over the decade. Calgary
is "now home to approximately one in seven of Canada's major
corporate headquarters and as such is now Western Canada's head

office capital" (ibid., 2). Of those head offices, 84 percent are in the energy sector.

Still, size usually matters for most exercises in urban ranking, and Calgarians took with some alacrity to the Toronto Dominion Bank's 2003 coining of the concept of the Calgary-Edmonton Corridor in a report on what it called the "western tiger." Its description of the region between and including Alberta's two main cities as "the only urban agglomeration to enjoy a US-style standard of living with a Canadian style quality of life" attracted national and some international attention. Their reassessment of this report in 2007 states that they actually underestimated the economic expansion that would occur, and the potential in the rest of the province (TD Economics 2007). As impressive as those figures are, they remain an artificial construct based on statistics and stretched over several hundred kilometres; they fail to create a memorable image for a city, and do not answer the question for others of what Calgary is, beyond being rich. As an example of imagineering city-regions, it is probably a stretch too far, at least for now, and certainly has no capacity as a place-for-itself, and at most, a modest reality as a place-in-itself.

As a result of the expansion of well-remunerated employment, per capita income in Calgary rose to $47,178 in 2006, the highest in the country and substantially above that of Toronto, which weighed in at $35,774. Calgary's growth in per capita income has been rapid: a 25.2 percent increase between 2002 and 2006 (Calgary Economic Development 2007). Calgary Economic Development and the Calgary Chamber of Commerce both have stated that attracting talented workers is among the most important factors for continued growth and prosperity. Even the economic downturn since 2008 is seen as only delaying a return of pressing general labour shortages and intensified competition for scarce highly-skilled personnel, increasingly discussed again in 2012.

Richard Florida's ideas have influenced economic development strategies in Calgary. During his second visit to Calgary, Florida reported that Calgary ranked fairly high among Canadian cities in attracting the creative class, saying, "You're a very good talent magnet ... Number two in the country," and that "compared to other similar sized cities, you would rank highly in North America" (*Calgary Herald* 2008).

The Calgary Chamber of Commerce weighed in on this issue by issuing a call for the city to make itself into "Renaissance Calgary."

Its "blueprint for a 21st century world-leading capital" notes that eighty percent of the Chamber's members feel that the overall quality of life had declined in the three years before 2007, and proposes measures to capture "the spirit of creativity, innovation, competitiveness and cultural vibrancy," and translate it into "practical actions that enable the city to achieve its potential as a global leader" (Calgary Chamber of Commerce 2007).

Many reports produced by agencies in Calgary, such as the City of Calgary itself, the Chamber of Commerce, the Calgary Foundation, and Sustainable Calgary, concentrate on producing various benchmarks, report cards, and rankings. A substantial section of Calgary Economic Development's website is devoted to rankings. Table 5.1 shows some rankings they chose to highlight.

One can also locate other lists where Calgary did not receive such high grades. Each of these rankings could be criticized for various methodological and conceptual reasons, but our point is not whether they are accurate; it is that they have become an important set of counters in inter-urban competition. To what extent do cities make decisions in order to improve their positioning in some of the more influential rankings?

Certainly Calgary does need to restructure itself in various ways to make a better city. The pursuit of economic and demographic growth in the absence of adequate infrastructure has resulted in intense growth pains and costs imposed on everyone (Miller and Smart 2011). Calgary's experience highlights the management challenges for a booming city in a world of emerging talent shortages and the global flow of real estate investment. High real estate prices tend to attract outside investors. In Hong Kong, London, and New York, the cost of housing has relatively little connection to local wage rates, resulting in huge problems for not just the poor, but also the middle class. If options become available for good jobs in other cities, where lower salaries are compensated for by lower costs of living, labour shortages may become intensified. When, like Calgary, these cities do not have the same cultural attractions, the problem of retaining sought-after workers can become even greater. Higher wages might even make the situation worse; if economic migrants have a target they are working and saving for, paying them more may mean that they can leave sooner. As a result of these tensions, conventional global city measurements often compete with alternative rankings focused on quality of life.

Table 5.1 List of Calgary's recent rankings

Calgary's Ranking	Measure
1 (in the world)	Quality of Living Eco-City Ranking: Mercer – 2010
1	Canada's Best Places to Live, Work
1	Canada's Most Wired City (spending on internet services): *Maclean's*/Canadian Council on Learning – 2010
1	World Capitals of the Future (Emerging World Cities): *Forbes*
28 (against 221 cities)	Quality of Living: Mercer – 2010
3	Canada's Smartest City: *Maclean's*/Canadian Council on Learning – 2010
4	Canada's Most Cultured City: *Maclean's*/Canadian Council on Learning – 2010
6	Canada's Most Socially Engaged City: *Maclean's*/Canadian Council on Learning – 2010
6	Canada's Most Active Cities: *Maclean's*/Canadian Council on Learning – 2010
26 (out of 154 Canadian cities)	Canadian Business/*MoneySense* – 2010

Source: Calgary Economic Development.

Increasing traffic congestion and commute times feed widespread perceptions that Calgary's quality of life has deteriorated as the city has grown. Some studies lend credence to this perception. A study in the 1990s placed Calgary as having the highest quality of life among thirteen Canadian cities (Giannias 1998), while a more recent international survey of fifty cities ranked Calgary twenty-fourth for quality of living, the lowest among the five Canadian cities included (Mercer Human Resource Consulting 2007). Growth has generated pressures on every element of infrastructure, so much so that in the last five years, almost every poll asking Calgarians about the main issues facing the city has had infrastructure as the top answer (White 2007). Interestingly, these challenges of growth have been reframed with the use of global indices to benefit Calgary's image. Increasingly, policy development and public discourse about Calgary's economic development and quality of life draw on global cities discourse. City of Calgary publications examining quality-of-life matters, including diversity, public safety, arts and culture, recreation, and, of course, economic prosperity, look to a range of scores to measure Calgary's standing. Calgary Economic Development, charged with developing the municipality's long-range economic strategy, points out to potential employees looking to relocate that the city ranks among the top five places to live in the world, listing this as the number one reason to move. Though the brochure fails to identify the index that placed Calgary on top, it further points to the city as being the safest place to live, and as being in the top five Canadian cities for performance arts (Calgary Economic Development 2011). In a full book developed to attract highly skilled workers to the city, CED highlights Calgary as the world's healthiest city in which to live (2009, 49). Clearly, these rankings do not mention the critical need for affordable housing and infrastructure in the city, instead glossing it with indices comparing Calgary to places such as Hong Kong and New York.

Even concerns over housing affordability, which have consistently plagued the city's image as unkind to the poor and homeless, have been reinterpreted in a positive light. Calgary has a contested image in national media highlighting the wealth and deprivation co-existing in the city. Increasingly, Calgary has been portrayed as a heartless city, beset by homelessness and inequality. Such imagery can discourage the movement of the workers that Calgary's economy needs. The Royal Bank Housing Affordability Index measures a house price in relation to the total payments required for a mortgage, utilities, and property tax. The higher the measure, the more difficult it is to afford a house. The Index has been used by social agencies, such as the United Way of Calgary Poverty Reduction Coalition, to make a case for increased funding for affordable housing during the 2005 boom. However, using the same index, CED argues that in 2010, Calgary offered "more affordable housing than Vancouver, Edmonton, Toronto, Montreal, Ottawa and the National average for a standard two-storey house."[1] In this case, the relative ranking of Calgary against other cities with respect to housing affordability was reframed as a positive indicator and an enticement for relocation. Of course, this discounts some of the arguments calling for concerted action to address this social issue.

The main theme in promotional materials remains Calgary's entrepreneurialism and rapid economic growth, "with no signs of slowing down" (CED 2009, 42). CED's claims are backed up by the Conference Board's 2007 City Magnets report, where Calgary's robust economic performance lifted it to the top of all twenty-seven Canadian cities. In CED's 2009 Global Scorecard on Prosperity report, the agency developed a measurement to gauge Calgary's status on the international stage. Compared to twenty-two other cities around the world, Calgary was ranked number one for overall economic prosperity. The report aims to provide policy-makers and business leaders with intelligence to guide decisions about the future of the city. The report, however, cautions that "Calgary's perch at the top of our league of 23 global metropolises ... Calgary's continued domination is currently under threat, as weaker energy prices and tighter credit conditions have slowed oil and gas activity in the province of Alberta" (CED 2009, 15). With this "threat" to the city's rankings top of mind, the report calls for concerted action from city leaders to ensure Calgary "stays on top." The rankings against other cities are seen as a "pulse" that informs strategy development for economic growth. In this sense, the indicators used to build rankings, such as quality of life, safety, diversity, and infrastructure, are interpreted in light of the need for labour and infrastructure to maintain the city's competitiveness in the attraction of investment.

Recent attention to the attraction of big business to Calgary has focused on the concentration of head offices in the city. CED points out that "with the highest concentration of corporate head offices, Calgary is well-known as a centre of regional, national, and international corporate activity" (CED 2009, 42). A later report on Calgary's attractiveness to company headquarters was developed by CED "in order to better understand the importance of this sector of the economy and the impact head offices have on Calgary's community" (2010, 10). The report notes that by 2009, Calgary reached a concentration of 9.3 head offices per 100,000 population – double Toronto's rate of 4.7. In fact, as the "major centres of Toronto, Montreal and Ottawa suffered losses in head office concentration over the last 10 years, Calgary's rate rose by 13.4 percent during this same period." Once again, the city's relative ranking in relation to other Canadian centres becomes an impetus for policy development. The report concludes that "it is important to implement policies that create a business environment that allows for local companies across all sectors to innovate, grow and prosper on the global stage" (14). Despite also aiming to analyze the impact of headquarters on the locality, the report's main thrust is to identify strategic directions that create a climate that continues to "attract and maintain head offices" – retaining the city's tax advantage, promoting a high quality of life to attract skilled workers, and developing infrastructure to sustain economic development.

City rankings play an unquestionable role in decision-making about the economy, public safety, the arts, social issues, and so forth. Election platforms for mayoral candidates in the October 2010 campaign echoed CED's platforms on a vibrant economy, public safety, and infrastructure, particularly roads. Ric McIver, the frontrunner and past alderman, noted that his "vision for our city is to make Calgary the economic heart of Canada – a beacon of opportunity and affordability for all."[2] Like his top two competitors, Barb Higgins,[3] a local TV anchorwoman, and Naheed Nenshi,[4] a college professor, McIver's campaign focused on improving Calgarians' quality of life by building infrastructure, promoting vibrant and safe communities, and maintaining the city's economic advantage. A major plank in all candidates' platforms was municipal government cost efficiency and accountability – which is not surprising, given government concern with recessionary impacts on budgets. Higgins and Nenshi promoted Calgary's cultural vibrancy and the arts as part of their platforms, echoing CED identification of these areas for development to attract the creative class, and to cement a place for Calgary on the global stage. Nenshi and McIver also emphasized the lack of affordable housing in their platforms, with diverse policy initiatives including secondary suite legalization (Nenshi) and attainable homeownership development (McIver) (Tanasescu, Chui, and Smart 2010).

These discourses on rankings have real effects on policy decisions and governmental strategies. To take a recent example, the issue of safety and Calgary's ranking relative to other Canadian cities has had considerable impact on public expenditures on law enforcement and police practice. The questioning of policing costs by mayoral candidate (and eventual winner) Naheed Nenshi was used by Police Chief Rick Hanson to criticize Nenshi's election platform. Arguing against Nenshi's analysis, Hanson pointed out that "Calgarians can be assured that they not only enjoy arguably one of the safest cities in this country, but it is done so in a very cost-effective and efficient manner."[5]

This line of argument was also used by the Calgary Police Service to effectively oppose a proposed five percent cut to their budget in 2010. Further, support for the CPS proposal was raised from the business sector represented by the Downtown Association.[6] To protect the budget, the Calgary Chamber of Commerce, Calgary Crime Stoppers, the Calgary Downtown Association, the National Energy Security Professionals, and Penn West Energy bought a full-page newspaper ad, urging Calgary's city council to protect the police from cuts, reading: "Police budget cuts would result in a significant setback to the public safety of all Calgarians."[7] The CPS reports that the city centre is safer and that crime is decreasing: in 2009, city-centre person crimes, property crimes, and disorder incidents reached five-year lows. Success is attributed to "Clean to the Core," a collaborative effort including more police officers patrolling on foot, and more bylaw and transit officers. According to a 2009 City of Calgary survey, a majority of Calgarians say the city's core is safer and cleaner than a year prior (Calgary Police Service 2010). According to the Calgary Police Commission Citizen Survey, there was a significant increase in 2009 in the number of citizens who agree that Calgary is a safe city in which to live, rising to 86 percent from 79 percent in 2008 (Environics 2009). Of course, all players in this case have particular motivations to oppose a cut to police services: for business owners in the downtown core, increasing police service is believed to increase the perception of public safety among shoppers and office workers; police service staff clearly have a material interest in maintaining, if not growing, their staff base; mayoral candidates are focused on appealing to the voting public's concern with public safety, particularly in inner-city areas perceived to be plagued by crime.

The "Clean to the Core" campaign has also been accused of targeting the homeless in attempts to make downtown more appealing to mainstream citizens. Past Executive Director of the Calgary Drop-In Centre Dermot Baldwin "says he's noticed an increase in harassment of the homeless and says it started when the city began work on revitalizing the East Village" (CTV 2009). The East Village redevelopment proposal, where the Drop-In (Canada's largest shelter, housing over one thousand homeless nightly) is located, has been fraught with controversy, mostly with respect to the City of Calgary's intentions vis-à-vis the homeless. In 2009, the Calgary Municipal Land Corporation (CMLC) – the independent development company the city created to help revitalize the East Village – unveiled a master plan for the area. It called for a mixed-use community with arts and cultural venues, and a vibrant waterfront in the fifty-hectare area east of downtown. The CMLC notes that the "master plan will transform East Village into a vibrant urban village and one of the most dynamic areas within the downtown core. The neighbourhood will offer some of the hippest shopping, dining, recreational and residential opportunities."[8] Following this aim to develop East Village into a premier downtown neighbourhood, City Council approved the addition by

CPS of fifty officers dedicated to patrolling downtown streets, including the Village. They also approved a public behaviour bylaw passed in 2007 with harsher penalties for loitering, public intoxication, and panhandling. According to the CPS, these efforts resulted in one-third fewer robberies downtown in 2010 (CBC 2010a). The Drop-In Centre questioned the motives of the City, CPS, and CMLC for increasing patrolling of the area, given private interest in developing real estate in the area. However, other social advocates are less critical, as we describe below.

Calgary has long been a conservative city in a province that has been conservative since the 1930s. Calgary's conservative politics, and strong influence from corporate business, has meant that NGOS attempting to influence urban policy have to adapt their tactics (Miller and Smart 2011). Effective social advocacy in Calgary requires making a case that action is in the interests of business or the city as a whole, rather than "merely" a matter of social justice. Corporations became quite supportive of the Calgary Homeless Foundation after research revealed that a very high percentage of the homeless population works full-time, and that it would be less expensive for taxpayers to solve the homelessness problem than to continue the status quo. In general, for a social policy initiative to have a chance of success, a business case must demonstrate the initiative's potential return on investment. Many NGOS feel that without corporate support for their initiatives, it is difficult to get support from government to move forward.

A recent response to the appetite for city rankings by the Calgary Foundation resulted in the yearly report card called "Vital Signs," which showcases diverse areas including safety, diversity, housing, and economic prosperity. The exercise aims to provide a critical alternative to mainstream focus on economic competitiveness, and to ensure the needs of marginalized populations are on the political agenda. Interestingly, the 2010 report card shines a positive light on homelessness and public safety; shelter use is decreasing, and crime in the city centre is decreasing, as is Calgarians' perception of it (Calgary Foundation 2007). This reframing of the negative side of Calgary's boom and bust cycles is encouraging shifts in political positions. The Calgary Chamber of Commerce, for example, has been advocating measures to address the growing problem of homelessness and affordable housing, and supporting the expansion of public transit and mixed-use, high-density neighbourhoods organized around transit hubs (Calgary Chamber of Commerce 2007). NGOS highlighting the social impacts of growth are using the same methods and even the same indicators as groups representing business interests and government agencies. Unfortunately, the race for indicators threatens to blur the dire demand for affordable housing and the high rate of homelessness in Calgary.

CONCLUSION

Our Calgary case study demonstrates the dynamic and important role global cities discourse plays in city-region development in a global era. By exploring the interplay between diverse government, NGO, and private sector actors in employing selective indicators of infrastructure, safety, economic prosperity, and vibrancy, we highlighted how indices impact urban governance, particularly for those aspiring to be "global."

Calgary aims to develop economic strategies to increase its standing on global cities ranking lists, and to attract TNC headquarters and the "creative class." Such economic strategies shape local governance through policy responses to "indicators" seen as important on global city indices, particularly the numbers of headquarters, crime rate, and cultural vibrancy. The need for infrastructure to support skilled workers and employers drives an agenda focused on economic competitiveness, even when couched in quality-of-life terms. The latter ultimately relate to the city's attractiveness to business, rather than its liveability for all residents. It is therefore not surprising to find global city discourse surfacing in promotional materials to attract workers and businesses to Calgary, but also in election campaign materials, as candidates presented their vision for Calgary in October 2010.

The aim to appear more global according to these indices also leads to direct increases in enforcement practices. We highlighted the interconnected way in which public safety measures, perceived by residents and reported by police, surface in connection to Calgary's attractiveness to investment and economic position in relation to other cities. The politicization of police budgets in the mayoral campaign – and the engagement of major business players to defend police spending – demonstrates the real effects of studying, indexing, classifying, and counting on particular subjects: in this case, the "criminal" and the "homeless." The case of East Village showcases how interwoven redevelopment, urban governance, and economic competitiveness have become, in large part through the use of global city rankings to justify governance actions. The minimal dissent against further marginalization of homeless populations is softened by NGO reports indicating improvement in safety and housing issues. The Calgary case study clearly shows how knowledge about cities can be used to gain consent for certain actions and foreclose others.

This chapter has problematized prevailing discourses on global cities as a "regime of truth." By continuing in this vein, we are producing and reproducing fields of knowledge with considerable impacts on social structures and subjects. While the focus on dissecting, classifying, and ranking diverse city characteristics has, in a sense, made the study of the global processes more real, in doing so, we have already assumed the city itself to be "real," something that is easier to do for politically unified Calgary than for more fragmented city-regions. It is therefore critical that we complement our understanding of globalized cities with a deconstruction of broader discourses on cities as well. Michel Foucault's deconstruction of the subject as an effect of discourse is particularly relevant to the critical analysis of the knowledge on cities. Given the plurality of discourses on cities, we can benefit from further examination of their rise in particular historical moments in relation to competing regimes of truth (Easthope and McGowan 2002, 69).

By problematizing the city, we can further explore the discursive strategies that give rise to the social construction of the urban. The uncritical acceptance of the veracity of the city as an ontological, material, and "real" object should be questioned; by examining the "idea of the city" as an ideological project, we can probe if and how the concept works to legitimize domination and obscure the institutionalization of political power. The city can be conceived as the result or "effect of everyday practices, representational discourses, and multiple modalities of power" (Sharma and Gupta 2008, 165). In Calgary's case, global cities discourse is playing a key role in the way it has come to be perceived as autonomous and cohesive. As a "wannabe" global city, Calgary's everyday practices highlighted above are particularly instructive, as they delineate the boundaries between what is considered global and non-global, and how these are culturally and historically constructed, reproduced, and challenged. Future examination of everyday practices of representation can further highlight the historically and culturally specific constructions of cities.

Calgary's focus on becoming more global also highlights the parallel Akhil Gupta observes between "development discourse" and global cities discourse: "development discourse makes people subjects in both senses that Foucault emphasizes: subjected to someone else by a relationship of control and dependence, and tied to one's own identity through self-knowledge" (1998, 39). One's position in the category of "global cities" is made possible through the measurement of the city on one of the relevant indices, or the construction of a rival index that measures features more relevant to what that city sees as its globally central feature. Jennifer Robinson sees urban development strategies that aspire to global-ness, creativity, or global competitiveness as involving mimicry in the same sense as development discourse: "to learn, follow, replicate, repeat, improve – these are the incitements of development discourse" (2006, 40). We can see the governments of wannabe cities, like the nation-states in Robinson's critique of development discourse, as "the subject that does all this learning and following." Ranking places cities in hierarchical relations, and reaffirms some cities as exemplars and others as imitators. In policy-related versions of these accounts, cities either absent from the world-cities map or in lower locations on the constructed hierarchy have an implicit injunction to become more like those at the top of the hierarchy of cities. If they do not want to lose out, they need to climb the hierarchy to get a piece of the (global) action. Being among the top-ranked global cities can be equally burdensome. Attaining and maintaining one's status encourages policy emphases "on only small, successful and globalizing segments of the economy and neglecting the diversity of urban life and urban economies in these places" (94). As Robinson further states, "world cities approaches ... operate to limit imaginations of possible urban futures, especially in relation to poorer cities, and the situation of poor and marginalized people in cities around the world. A post-colonial urban studies needs to move beyond categories and hierarchies and to abandon claims to represent some cities as exemplars for others" (94).

We have highlighted in this chapter the need to maintain a critical and reflexive approach to the ways in which the study of cities and their rescaling projects itself impacts the development of urban governance and the life ways of residents. Clearly, academic writing on global cities – even unquestionably critical perspectives on globalized urban development and policy approaches – has been interpreted to justify these directions. Future research must not only document the impact of such developments on the marginalized, but also consider its potential implications for urban futures. Gone are the days when academic researchers could lament the limited impact their work had on public policy and the lives of the marginalized; it is essential that we consider the possibility and responsibility that our work may have tremendous impacts, and that we should be careful what we wish for.

NOTES

1. http://www.calgaryeconomicdevelopment.com/liveWorkPlay/Live/quality OfLife.cfm.
2. http://www.ricmciver.ca/ric-releases-his-vision-for-calgary/.
3. http://barbhiggins.ca/assets/files/higgins_platformframe_latest.pdf.
4. http://www.nenshi.ca/new/policy.
5. http://www.calgaryherald.com/news/Mayoral+hopeful+Nenshi+Police+ Chief+Hanson+spar+over+election+claims/3572436/story.html#ixzz119 EhWRwd.
6. http://www.cbc.ca/canada/calgary/story/2010/07/14/calgary-police-budget-ad-cuts-letter-herald-penn-west.html.
7. http://www.cbc.ca/canada/calgary/story/2010/07/14/calgary-police-budget-ad-cuts-letter-herald-penn-west.html#ixzz119GGGhxn.
8. http://www.calgarymlc.ca/rivers_projects/east_village/about_east_village/.

REFERENCES

Amin, A. 2002. "Spatialities of Globalisation." *Environment and Planning* 34 (3): 385–99.

Barnard, A. 2000. *History and Theory in Anthropology*. Cambridge: Cambridge University Press.

Brenner, N., and N. Theodore. 2002. "Cities and the Geographies of 'Actually Existing Neoliberalism.'" *Antipode* 34 (3): 349–79.

Calgary Chamber of Commerce. 2007. *Renaissance Calgary: Blueprint for a 21st Century World-Leading Capital*. Calgary, AB: Calgary Chamber of Commerce.

Calgary Economic Development (CED). 2007. *Head Offices*. Calgary, AB: Calgary Economic Development.

– 2009. *Calgary: A Global Scorecard on Prosperity*. Calgary, AB: Calgary Economic Development. http://www.calgaryeconomicdevelopment.com/sites/default/files/globalScorecardProsperity.pdf. Accessed 7 July 2011.

– 2010. *Home Base: What Drives Head Office Locations and Calgary's Place as a Global Business Hub*. Calgary, AB: Calgary Economic Development.

– 2011. *Calgary E-Brochure*. Calgary, AB: Calgary Economic Development. http://www.calgaryebrochure.com/genpdf.php. Accessed 5 July 2011.

Calgary Herald. 2008. "In an Ideas Economy, Cities Must Attract 'Creative Class.'" 13 May.

– 2010. "Mayoral Hopeful Nenshi, Police Chief Hanson Spar over Elections Claims." 24 September.

Calgary Municipal Land Corporation. 2011. *Explore Projects – The Rivers District*. http://www.calgarymlc.ca/exploreprojects/rivers-district. Accessed 5 July 2011.

Calgary Police Service. 2010. *Annual Statistical Report 2005–2009*. Calgary, AB: Calgary Police Service.

Castells, Manuel. 1998. *End of Millenium: The Information Age Volume 3*. Oxford, UK: Blackwell Publishers.

CBC. 2010a. "East Village Safer as Crime Drops: Residents." 15 July. http://www.cbc.ca/canada/calgary/story/2010/07/14/calgary-east-villagesafer-crime.html.

– 2010b. "Police Cuts Won't Hurt City, Say Calgary Groups." 14 July. http://www.cbc.ca/canada/calgary/story/2010/07/14/calgary-police-budget-ad-cuts-letter-herald-penn-west.html.

Clarke, J., J. Newman, N. Smith, E. Vidler, and L. Westmarland. 2007. *Creating Citizen-Consumers: Changing Publics and Changing Public Services*. London: Sage Publications.

CTV. 2009. "Calgary Police Criticized." 15 August. http://calgary.ctv.ca/servlet/an/local/CTVNews/20090814/CGY_Homeless_Police_09084/20090814/?hub=CalgaryHome.

Douglass, M. 2001. "Intercity Competition and the Question of Economic Resilience: Globalization and Crisis in Asia." In *Regions: Trends, Theory, Policy*, edited by A. Scott, 236–62. New York and Oxford, UK: Oxford University Press.

Easthope, A., and K. McGowan. 2002. "Subjectivity." In *A Critical and Cultural Theory Reader*, edited by A. Easthope and K. McGowan, 67–71. Toronto: University of Toronto Press.

Environics Research Group. 2009. *Calgary Police Commission 2009 Citizen Survey*. Calgary, AB: Calgary Police Commission.

Florida, Richard. 2002. *The Rise of the Creative Class*. New York: Basic Books.

Flusty, S. 2006. "Culturing the World City: An Exhibition of the Global Present." In *The Global Cities Reader*, edited by N. Brenner and R. Keil, 346–52. London and New York: Routledge.

Foran, Max. 2009. *Expansive Discourses: The City of Calgary, the Land Developers and Residential Urban Sprawl, 1945–1978*. Edmonton: Athabasca University Press.

Foucault, M. 1980. "Power and Strategies." In *Power/Knowledge: Selected Interviews and Other Writings, 1972–1977 by Michel Foucault*, edited by C. Gordon, 134–46. New York and Toronto: Random House.

– 1991. "Governmentality." In *The Anthropology of the State: A Reader*, edited by A. Sharma and A. Gupta, 131–43. Malden, MA, Oxford, UK, and Carlton, VIC: Blackwell Publishing.

Friedmann, J. 2002. *The Prospect of Cities*. Minneapolis: University of Minnesota Press.

– 1986. "The World City Hypothesis." *Development and Change* 17 (1): 69–83.

Friedmann, J., and G. Wolff. 1982. "World City Formation: An Agenda for Research and Action." *International Housing of Urban and Regional Research* 6 (3): 309–44.

Ghitter, G., and A. Smart. 2009. "Mad Cows, Regional Governance and Urban Sprawl: Path Dependence and Unintended Consequences in the Calgary Region." *Urban Affairs Review* 44 (5): 617–44.

Giannias, D.A. 1998. "A Quality of Life Based Ranking of Canadian Cities." *Urban Studies* 35 (12): 2241–51.

Hall, S. 2002. "The Spectacle of the Other." In *Representation: Cultural Representations and Signifying Practices*, edited by S. Hall, 223–90. London: Sage Publications Ltd.

Harvey, D. 2005. *The New Imperialism*. Oxford, UK: Oxford University Press.

Herod, A., and M. Wright. 2002. "Placing Scale: An Introduction." In *Geographies of Power: Placing Scale*, edited by A. Herod and M.W. Wright, 1–13. Oxford, UK: Blackwell.

Jonas, A., and D. Wilson. 1999. "The City as a Growth Machine: Critical Perspectives Two Decades Later." In *The Urban Growth Machine: Critical Perspectives Two Decades Later*, edited by A. Jonas and D. Wilson, 3–20. New York: State University of New York Press.

Keil, R., and K. Ronneberger. 2000. "The Globalization of Frankfurt am Main: Core, Periphery and Social Conflict." In *Globalizing Cities: A New Spatial Order*, edited by P. Marcuse and R. van Kemplen, 228–48. Malden, MA, and Oxford, UK: Blackwell.

King, A. 2006. "World Cities: Global? Postcolonial? Postimperial? Or Just the Result of Happenstance?" In *The Global Cities Reader*, edited by N. Brenner and R. Keil, 319–24. London and New York: Routledge.

Leitner, H., C. Pavlik, E. Sheppard, A. Herod, and M. Wright. 2002. "Networks, Governance and the Politics of Scale: Inter-Urban Networks and the European Union." In *Geographies of Power: Placing Scale*, edited by A. Herod and M.W. Wright, 274–302. Oxford, UK: Blackwell.

Lui, T.-L. 2008. "City Branding Without Content: Hong Kong's Aborted West Kowloon Mega-Project 1998–2006." *International Development Planning Review* 30 (3): 215–26.

Magnusson, W., and A. Sancton. 1983. *City Politics in Canada*. Toronto: University of Toronto Press.

Mercer Human Resource Consulting. 2007. *2007 Quality of Living Survey*. New York: Mercer Human Resource Consulting.

Miller, B. 1997. "Political Action and the Geography of Defense Investment: Geographical Scale and the Representation of the Massachusetts Miracle." *Political Geography* 16 (2): 171–85.

Miller, B., and A. Smart. 2011. "'Heart of the New West'? Oil and Gas, Rapid Growth, and Consequences in Calgary." In *Canadian Urban Regions: Trajectories of Growth and Change*, edited by L.S. Bourne, T. Hutton, R.G. Shearmur, and J. Simmons, 269–90. Oxford, UK: Oxford University Press.

Miller, B., and A. Smart. 2012. "Ascending the Main Stage? Calgary in the Multilevel Governance Drama." In *Sites of Governance: Multilevel Governance and Policy Making in Canada's Big Cities*, edited by M. Horak and R. Young, 26–52. Montreal: McGill-Queen's University Press.

Mitchell, T. 1999. "Society, Economy, and the State Effect." In *The Anthropology of the State: A Reader*, edited by A. Sharma and A. Gupta, 169–86. Malden, MA, Oxford, UK, and Carlton, VIC: Blackwell Publishing.

Ni, P., and P.K. Kresl. 2010. *The Global Urban Competitiveness Report 2010*. Cheltenham, UK: Edward Elgar.

Olds, K., and H.W.C. Yeung. 1999. "Reshaping 'Chinese' Business Networks in a Globalising Era." *Environment and Planning D: Society and Space* 17 (5): 535–55.

Peck, J. 2005. "Struggling with the Creative Class." *International Journal of Urban and Regional Research* 29 (4): 740–70.

Richards, J., and L. Pratt. 1979. *Prairie Capitalism: Power and Influence in the New West*. Toronto: McLellan and Stewart.

Robinson, J. 2006. *Ordinary Cities: Between Modernity and Development*. New York: Routledge.

Rose, N. 1991. "Governing 'Advanced Liberal Democracies.'" In *The Anthropology of the State: A Reader*, edited by A. Sharma and A. Gupta, 144–62. Malden, MA, Oxford, UK, and Carlton, VIC: Blackwell Publishing.

Rutheiser, C. 1996. *Imagineering Atlanta: The Politics of Place in the City of Dreams*. London: Verso.

Sassen, S. 2002. *The Global City: New York, London, Tokyo*, 2nd ed. Princeton, NJ: Princeton University Press.

Sharma, A., and A. Gupta, eds. 2008. *The Anthropology of the State: A Reader*. Malden, MA, Oxford, UK, and Carlton, VIC: Blackwell Publishing.

Smart, A. 2001. "Restructuring in a North American City: Labour Markets and Political Economy in Calgary." In *Plural Globalities in Multiple Localities: New World Borders*, edited by M. Rees and J. Smart, 167–93. Lanham, MD: University Press of America.

Smart, A., and G.C.S. Lin. 2007. "Local Capitalisms, Local Citizenship and Translocality: Rescaling from Below in the Pearl River Delta Region, China." *International Journal of Urban and Regional Research* 31 (2): 280–302.

Smith, N. 1996. *The New Urban Frontier: Gentrification and the Revanchist City*. New York: Routledge.

Tanasescu, A., E. Chui, and A. Smart. 2010. "Tops and Bottoms: State Tolerance of Illegal Housing in Hong Kong and Calgary." *Habitat International* 34 (4): 478–84.

TD Economics. 2007. "The Tiger that Roared Across Alberta." Toronto: TD Bank. Accessed 7 July 2011. http://centralalberta.ab.ca/assets/documents/TD%20Economics%20Update%202007.pdf.

Tyner, J.A. 2000. "Global Cities and Circuits of Global Labor: The Case of Manila, Philippines." *Professional Geographer* 52 (1): 61–74.

White, R. 2007. "Shared Vision Needed for Calgary." *Calgary Herald*, 23 October.

Wilson, D., and R. Keil. 2008. "The Real Creative Class." *Social & Cultural Geography* 9 (8): 841–7.

6

"Localism" in an Age of Austerity: Inequalities and Governance Dilemmas in the Sheffield City-Region

DAVID ETHERINGTON

INTRODUCTION

Recent years have witnessed a burgeoning literature on the "new regionalism" in the social and political sciences (see Boudreau 2003; Brenner et al. 2003; Keating 1998; 2001; Keating et al. 2003; Rossi 2004). Protagonists have argued on the existence of regions, and city-regions more recently, as successful models of economic and social development. There is recognition that city-regions can comprise local strategic capacities – locally based government agencies, civic associations, private-public partnerships, or a host of other possible institutional arrangements, considered appropriate for mobilizing "windows of locational opportunity" for capturing and developing an increasingly specialized reordering and rescaling of economic activity.

However, the actual benefits, distributional consequences, or pivotal inter-linkages of city-regional growth strategies are never specified, and, as shall be argued in this chapter, this "new urban renaissance" (HM Treasury et al. 2006, i), and now currently the new "localism," has the potential to cause adverse and damaging impacts in terms of social and labour market inequalities (4). The purpose of this chapter is to explore, by focusing on the Sheffield City-Region (SCR) as a case study, how the emergence of city-region governance and regulation can reinforce rather than resolve the problems of spatial and social inequalities and uneven development.

The SCR represents a particularly interesting example of dominant actors struggling with the policy discourses of competitiveness. Its employment and occupational structure has been transformed over the past twenty years from a highly paid employment economy with a plentiful supply of skilled jobs in the coal, steel, and engineering industries, to a de-industrialized economy where many of the new jobs created in the service sector tend to be low-paying, and where significant segments of the working-age population are economically inactive.

The remainder of this chapter is structured as follows. The next section situates our arguments within current New Regionalist academic discussion. This is followed by an analysis of the development of the SCR and its strategies, and we outline how Sheffield's labour market is represented within policy documents. We then attempt to empirically draw out the nature of labour inequalities within the SCR, and in this context, the chapter explores the actual and potential impacts of the new Coalition Government policies with respect to its welfare reforms and "localism" strategy. The chapter concludes with an appraisal of the findings for academic and policy debates. The research draws on, and updates, earlier research by Etherington and Jones (2009) and Jones and Etherington (2009), with a follow-up study undertaken in 2010 involving document collation and with interviews undertaken with a number of "stakeholders" in employment policy. These included officials from local authorities, Health Authorities, Employment Services, NGOs involved with delivering welfare-to-work programs, welfare rights organizations, trade unions, and policy think-tanks.

THEORETICAL PERSPECTIVES
ON CITY-REGIONALISM AND INEQUALITY

Intensified Competition in the Face of a Global Recession

Critics of the new regionalism point to the continued significance of national state power in underpinning regional and city-regional competitiveness strategies, their dynamics, and future trajectories (Hudson 1999; Lovering 1999; Musson et al. 2005). In turn, heightened attention has now been paid to the links between the state and the political economy of scale, and the ways in which regions are embedded in a politics of territory (see Mackinnon 2011 for an insightful survey of the debates). Important here is research that highlights the underlying problems of neoliberal city-region strategies, and conflicts between securing economic competitiveness for city-regions and managing the everyday politics of collective consumption and social reproduction in these spaces in particular (for examples, see Ward and Jonas 2004; Jonas 2012).

According to these perspectives, new regionalist literatures are myopic because they focus heavily on supply-side aspects of global-regional economic development, and city-regional capacities are accordingly treated as functional to the needs of this model of neoliberal growth and change. This significantly dodges issues of redistribution, conflict, counterstrategies, and politics more broadly. They shift our attention away from the spectacle of globalization and its reordering of political-economic space towards more micro- and urban-scaled social geographies.

This approach is useful in that it acknowledges the links between city-regions and the politics of uneven development (Cox 2004; Gonzalez 2011). City-regions as new "state spaces" embody alliances and social forces rooted in strategy formation responding to processes of economic restructuring and social inequalities, as well as promoting competitive advantage. However, as Brenner observes, there are limitations and contradictory outcomes to this:

> For in their current, market-led forms, metropolitan institutions likewise tend to intensify intra-national sociospatial inequality, uneven development and interspatial competition, and thus to undermine the territorial conditions for sustainable economic development. Moreover, despite their explicit attention to problems of interscalar coordination and meta-governance, metropolitan political institutions cannot, in themselves, resolve the pervasive governance failures, regulatory deficits and legitimation problems that ensue as public funds are spread out ever more thinly among a wide number of subnational entrepreneurial initiatives. (Brenner 2003, 317)

In the face of a global recession, as economic competition intensifies, so do the tensions in terms of resolving the problems and potential conflicts that arise from this. Of critical importance within this analysis as outlined by Brenner is that neoliberalism involves fiscal redistribution away from working-class and disadvantaged communities, as well as overall reduction in public investment as a strategy to restructure the market economy (Gough and Eisenchitz 2006).

Government and Governance Failure

The above analysis – and in particular Brenner's observations – provides some insight into what lies behind the causes and sources of city-region governance failure. The shift towards regionalization and localization represents "variegated" attempts to improve the effectiveness of policy and governance arrangements in the area of employment, because institutions and actors are mobilized to intervene and plan at the spatial scale of local labour markets and economies (see Jones 1999; OECD 2008; Sunley et al. 2006). Yet the process of devolution leads to developments that pose challenges to policy formation and delivery at the sub-national level. First is the apparent tension between devolving responsibilities in relation to policy formation and implementation, and the tendency towards centralization in decision-making whereby local actors are charged with implementing nationally determined targets and programs. The challenge here is the adaptation of national programs to local conditions. Second is the increasing tendency towards institutional and policy fragmentation at the sub-regional level, with issues of accountability being raised (see North et al. 2009). As Jessop (2002) states, governance becomes a new site for conflicts and political mobilization arising from the involvement of more and more "actors" and "stakeholders" involved in the design and delivery of labour market programs.

Outcomes at one scale may depend upon performance at another scale of governance, so coordination dilemmas occur. Furthermore, these coordination mechanisms may have different "temporal horizons," and there may be continuous tensions between short-term and long-term planning goals in policy planning. Third, and related, is the failure of current policies to address deep-rooted problems of labour market inequalities compounded by shortfalls in funding (see Keep et al. 2006; Etherington and Jones 2009). Under capitalism, the state can only modify the contradictions endemic in the commodification of labour power, and under neoliberalism, the emphasis is upon the state and governance providing the conditions for the market to resolve these problems – social inequalities, de-skilling, marginalization, discrimination, and poverty. These contradictions are heightened under neoliberal modes of governance and policy interventions, of which market failure in employment and skills is a clear expression (Keep et al. 2006).

Underpinning entrepreneurialism are supply-side policies in the form of welfare-to-work and employability programs. This dominance of workfare – where benefits are conditional on unemployed people participating in employment/training schemes – tends to be locked into managing decline and substantial swathes of surplus populations, rather than preparing labour for new and sustainable employment opportunities (see Cochrane and Etherington 2007; Jones and Etherington 2009). The effect of these policies, as highlighted in the research of Martin et al. (2001), is to make labour markets more competitive and reinforce their contingent nature. Workfare, because of its compulsory nature, removes any (supposed) barriers to employers obtaining a ready supply of labour. Groups who enter welfare-to-work and training programs tend to be vulnerable and disadvantaged. The "work first" principle tends to give prominence to the first job offer and to the assumptions that work will be sustained and that there will be some sort of upward mobility. Additionally, workfare increases competition or "workfare churning" as a result of substitution, as subsidized employment is used to replace "real" jobs. The direction of the unemployed to low-paid work creates a "crowding" effect on the labour market, which puts even more downward pressures on wages in certain sectors (Peck and Theodore 2000; 2010).

City-regional strategies tend to pay scant attention to the distributional consequences of competitive policies, and there is little, if any, focus on the nature and extent of poverty and social inequality, the need to establish poverty reduction targets, or any assessment of how policies are likely to reduce poverty rates. The discourses and representation by "hegemonic interests" of state spaces in relation to how problems are analyzed and policy solutions offered are of crucial importance to shaping policy agendas.

THE MAKING OF SHEFFIELD'S CITY-REGIONAL GOVERNANCE

The Sheffield City-Region is formed around the economic base of the former South Yorkshire and North East Derbyshire coal field, along with "traditional" industries such as steel and engineering.

The SCR is made up of the local authority districts of Sheffield, Barnsley, Doncaster, and Rotherham (as part of the South Yorkshire conurbation), as well as Chesterfield, North East Derbyshire, Bolsover, and Derbyshire Dales in the North East Derbyshire area.

The city of Sheffield, the largest local authority district in the city-region (and the fourth largest in England), is the area's main economic driver. However, the process of de-industrialization, a prevalent feature of the English economy, severely impacted Sheffield, and it has seen a decline in the steel, coal, and heavy engineering industries since the 1960s, which has forced the sector to rationalize its employment base. The pit closure program implemented by the Thatcher-led Conservative government involved the loss of thousands of jobs in the South Yorkshire Coalfield, impacting the mining communities of Barnsley, Doncaster, and North East Derbyshire.

> The collapse of the Sheffield steel industry and the restructuring that followed led to massive redundancies and unemployment reached record levels in the 1980s with an estimated two thirds of the local registered unemployed in Sheffield coming from the loss of jobs in the steelworks ... Another critical juncture in the city's political and economical history was the British Coal pit closure program which had devastating consequences for the regional economy leading to the loss of 10,311 jobs. (Thomas et al. 2009, 8)

The Sheffield region was characterized by a strong trade union and labour movement, with the (former) Communist Party heavily influencing the Trade Union Congress (TUC), and the Labour Party holding overall control of the local authorities. Redundancies and closures of the traditional industries weakened labour's organizing capacity because of the loss of unionized jobs; employment restructuring has basically been premised on the creation of jobs that have tended to be part-time and low-paid in non-unionized workplaces in the service sector. The retention of a trade union presence has been within the public sector (local authority and health services), where union densities have been traditionally high.

City-Region Economic Governance under New Labour

State rescaling under New Labour involved devolution of governance and policy interventions that included the establishment of the

Regional Development Agencies (RDAs) and investment in economic and social programs through the sub-regional strategies within South Yorkshire. The latter was financed by European Regional Development Funds, an economic development initiative to counteract the severest impacts of previous closures and job losses in steel and coal mining. At the end of the program in the early 2000s, the city-region became established as the South Yorkshire Partnership – initially covering the South Yorkshire local authorities, and then eventually, in 2008, incorporating the local authorities in North East Derbyshire. This was a growth strategy with the RDA given the powers and responsibilities to promote and lever in private sector investment in the regions. It represented a shift from an interventionist redistribution strategy that characterized regional policy in the 1960s, to a reliance on market forces to resolve the problems of inequality. The problems of regional and city-regional differences, according to the government, can be addressed by enhancing competitiveness through the mobilizing of resources within city-regional spaces by local actors who would bring about a renewal of private sector–led investment. In effect, the resources allocated to the RDAs and other programs were small in relation to the massive structural problems that characterize the economies (North et al. 2007).

An upbeat tone was evident in statements about how the Sheffield City-Region and its knowledge-based economy should be seen and narrated, which reinforced the strategies of the RDA. Repeated statements and discourses on the economy develop an almost scientific truth status with respect to the benefits of market-based growth-oriented strategies, which are in turn used to justify local state intervention (Fairclough 2001; Etherington and Jones 2009).

Similarly, the earlier *Sheffield City Strategy 2002–2005*, produced by the Sheffield First Partnership (a city-wide partnership bringing together public, private, voluntary, community, and faith sectors to coordinate regeneration activity), asserted:

> As late as 1999 it was legitimate to pose the question – 'can Sheffield re-discover the inventiveness which previously made it a world wide brand, or is the City locked in a downward spiral in which talented people and organizations will progressively migrate elsewhere?' *By 2002 there was convincing evidence that such questions are now irrelevant – the City has turned the decisive corner and is now 'on the up.'* (Sheffield First 2003, 10, emphasis added)

In many respects, the Sheffield First Partnership (Local Strategic Partnership) and other partnerships within the city-region were responding to increasing economic and development activity by over-hyping progress being made and presenting an "image" to attract inward investment.

The previous government's agenda in relation to signing up partners with respect to welfare-to-work programs set in motion an attempt to galvanize partnership working at the city-region level through the submission of a successful City Strategy Pathfinder (CSP) in 2006 on behalf of the South Yorkshire local authorities. This brought about a closer working relationship between the Employment Services (Job Centre Plus) and other partners in the face of increasing economic inactivity and worklessness in the sub-region. In 2007, the South Yorkshire Partnership was dissolved as the Sub Regional Partnership, to be replaced by the City Region Forum, whose executive director was appointed in 2008. A Work and Skills Board was established within the Sheffield First Strategic Partnership with the remit of bringing together the demand and supply sides of the local labour market in efforts to raise employability and skills levels; to put employer needs at the heart of employability and skills programs; and to ensure funding agencies align resources in support of employability and skills objectives (Sheffield Work and Skills Board 2007, 1).

The Coalition Government: New "Localism" and Policy Discourses

Perhaps the most significant element of the Coalition Government's strategy with respect to the regions and city-regions was to "hollow out" the state even further in the regions and cities by dismantling the RDAs and other sub-national governance and partnership structures. Within the "localism" agenda, there is a greater reliance on local actors supporting the development of the market to resolve the differences between cities and regions. Local Enterprise Partnerships (LEPs), which are created to replace other sub-national governance structures, tend to comprise coalitions of local authorities, with many LEPs comprising existing city-region partnerships – including the SCR (see Figure 2.2). The LEPs are required to encourage that a greater role is played by the private sector in the leadership of the board. The SCR proposal (SCR 2010) for the LEP is, in some ways, a condensed version of its previous strategies, although with a much greater emphasis upon the role of the private sector. A Regional Growth Fund (RGF) was established to lever in private investment that LEPs bid for on a competitive basis. The RGF resources are small-scale, compared even to the relatively modest budgets of the former RDA, and reflect the thinking that tackling the deficit with reduced public investment and increasing the role of the market are two sides of the same coin.

In parallel with the localism agenda, the Coalition Government has introduced significant changes to welfare-to-work programs (McNeil 2010; Newman 2011). The first aspect of the policy change is that the devolution of powers in terms of delivery of employment programs, which were carried out through the city strategies, has been scrapped, and the LEPs have been identified as bodies who could link in with the welfare agenda. In terms of programs for long-term unemployed on sickness benefits, the Coalition Government has established the Single Work Programme, whose main purpose is to simplify the benefits system, with the key focus on work capability assessments (WCA) as a means of moving people from the (more expensive) Employment Support Allowance (ESA) to the (less generous) Job Seekers Allowance insurance-based benefits. The program also involves a number of employability support measures that help to signpost people to the labour market. The other key element to the SWP is that it is administered by the Job Centre Plus (Employment Services) at the regional level, constituting contract package areas for competitive tendering for SWP providers.

DIMENSIONS OF GOVERNANCE AND POLICY FAILURE IN THE CITY-REGION

This section draws together assembled data derived from secondary data and commissioned research as well as key informant/stakeholder interviews.

Failure to Address and Policies Reinforcing Underlying Inequalities

Narrowing the gap between the regions was at the forefront of the thinking of New Labour's regional agenda around the establishment of the Regional Development Agencies. Research on the devolution

Table 6.1 Growth differences between the Sheffield City-Region and South of England

Area	Population (000s)	Workforce	GVA (£)*	GVA per head
Leeds	2,804	1,197	45,490	16,220
Manchester	3,199	1,361	50,941	15,920
Sheffield	1,653	658	24,230	14,660
LMS	7,452	3,216	120,661	15,760
London	7,452		211,512	28,040
South East	8,173		167,239	20,460

Source: Sheffield City Council 2010.

* GVA – Gross value added is a measure of an area's output and indicates the economic performance of an area, so a high GVA will reflect a comparatively stronger economy.

of economic governance (North et al. 2009) raised various questions about whether this was possible, given that government policy for all regions, including the most successful, is to grow and become more competitive. The devolution process also placed a greater emphasis upon the role of city-regions in terms of economic development, and to some extent, this has been latched onto in the localism discourse of the new Coalition Government in the development of LEPS by promoting the collaboration of local authorities. It is possible, therefore, to identify continuities in the politics of inequality shaped by neoliberal notions of entrepreneurialism and competition. Social inclusion and equality remain of little, if any, prominence in policy agendas.

This persistent – and even widening – regional inequality is a source of tension in central and local relations, as political and economic elites look towards London and South East, and within them, the more prosperous city-regions around Greater London, which display consistently higher growth rates and are seemingly far more immune to the impact of the government's austerity measures. Table 6.1 shows the unequal growth rates and sources of labour demand between the SCR and other northern city-regions and London/South East.

Just to underline this point, the Sheffield City-Region Development Plan has produced some frank messages about the state of the economy – indeed a point of departure from the optimistic messages in the early 2000s, as mentioned above. Some of the key issues identified by the SCRDP, which are also highlighted in Table 6.1, are that Gross Value Added (GVA measures the contribution to the economy of each individual producer, industry, or sector) is significantly below the national average. High numbers of people classified as workless and reliant upon welfare benefits (see below), combined with relatively large numbers of people in low-paid jobs, contribute to the lower levels of GVA. Local policy-makers recognize that creating significant numbers of new jobs will address regional income inequalities – it is estimated that 27,000 new jobs need to be created so that GVA will approach the national average.

A key feature of neoliberal political strategies is a greater reliance upon the market and reductions in social and welfare expenditures. Assessments have been undertaken on the impact of the Coalition Government's cuts in expenditure and the recession on Northern England's economies. One local trade union official has commented that the traditional industrial regions bear the brunt of the cuts because they tend to rely heavily on public sector employment and welfare services to support the impact of unemployment and low incomes (Interview). This view is supported by other research. For example, the Institute of Public Policy Research (IPPR) found that "[a] large proportion of this year's cuts are coming from the Area Based Grant, which represents a significant source of funds for Northern Councils and props up a wide range of services, not least to the most deprived neighbourhoods" (IPPR 2010, 10).

Similarly, the Centre for Local Economic Strategies (CLES) conducted their own assessment of the impact of the cuts:

> Fairness as an outcome is best pursued by calibrating cuts according to vulnerability and sensitivity to wider criteria and not applying a 2 percent locality ceiling. Regions provide a useful lens for analysis of this kind and regional sensitivity to cuts demonstrate unfairness of outcome and exacerbate spatial uneven development. Cuts have disproportionate effect on areas with weakest private sector, most workless and highest reliance on public sector employment. (CLES 2010)

The SCR Economic Assessment states that the SCR's capacity to adapt to and recover from the recession is also limited, and the SCR comes ninth out of sixteen city-regions on the basis of resilience indicators:

> The most serious consequence of the recession is however on employment ... in the long term the SCR is predicted to have a much slower job recovery period than the UK. The UK is not

expected to reach 2008 levels of employment again until 2016,
or eight years after the recession began. However the SCR is not
expected to reach its 2008 levels until 2023, 15 years later ...
The long term effects of the recession will be borne by our communities and should be reflected in high levels of unemployment
for some years to come. (2010, 131)

Between 1981 and the mid-1990s, thousands of jobs were lost in the
SCR economy. Those in employment declined by a staggering 12.4
percent between 1981 and 1991, and a further 5.4 percent between
1991 and 1996 for the Sheffield local authority area alone (Dabinett
2004). Furthermore, during this period, employment replacement
occurred but tended to be based in retail, hotels, and construction. In
stark contrast to the high-Fordist era of steel and manufacturing with
highly paid, highly skilled "jobs-for-life," new labour market opportunities were invariably precarious and based on part-time, low-paying,
insecure contracts. And during the past twenty years, employment
growth has not necessarily been accompanied by relative prosperity.

As Table 6.2 shows, there are significant numbers of people claiming sickness benefits in the SCR, and this is a major and persistent
social and economic problem. The reasons for an increase in incapacity benefit claims relate to the nature of the labour market.
During the 1970s, when skilled men were out of work, a lower proportion withdrew from the labour force. When the labour market
became more competitive, with rising unemployment and fewer
unskilled jobs being created that men could access, this group found
that they could get higher benefits by claiming invalidity benefits
(IB). Transfer to IB was officially sanctioned by the Employment
Service at that time as a strategy for reducing the claimant count.
Today, inactivity is four times higher than in the 1970s, and reflects
quite dramatic changes in the nature of demand for certain types of
skills and the type of jobs being created (see Beatty et al. 2010). The
authors argue that hidden unemployment characterizes the older
industrial regions such as the SCR because of the move from insur-
ance to IB, and that people who experience health conditions nevertheless may be able to still access some form of employment in
conditions of high demand (see also Beatty at al. 2011).

This vulnerability to the recession, and the extent and conditions
of labour demand, are illustrated by the nature and trends in registered unemployment in the SCR. The overall trend (Table 6.3)

Table 6.2 Worklessness and benefit claimants in the Sheffield City-Region

Local authority	Worklessness as % of working-age persons	Out of work benefits (%)	Incapacity benefit and employment support allowance (%)
Derby Dales	17.4	5.6	4.5
Chesterfield	23.6	9.1	9.7
N.E. Derbyshire	24.7	9.7	7.3
Bassetlaw	25.2	11.1	8.9
Bolsover	25.9	11.2	10.7
SCR	28.3	12.0	8.7
Doncaster	29.2	12.2	9.4
Sheffield	29.6	12.3	7.1
Rotherham	29.6	13.1	9.2
Barnsley	31.7	14.4	11.5
England	25.8	9.2	6.6

Source: Adapted from tables in Sheffield City-Region Executive 2010.

Table 6.3 Unemployment in the Sheffield City-Region

Long-term unemployment	2007	2010	Claimant unemployment
England	15.2	18.3	4.2
Barnsley	8.8	20.0	5.5
Doncaster	19.0	23.5	6.1
Rotherham	12.7	20.9	5.7
Sheffield	12.3	20.4	4.8
Bassetlaw	10.9	14.3	3.6
Bolsover	12.9	21.4	4.6
Chesterfield	12.4	20.6	4.7
Derby Dales	16.2	20.5	1.9
N.E. Derbyshire	14.3	21.8	3.7
Sheffield City Region	13.3	20.9	5.0

Source: Sheffield City Region Executive Team 2010.

nationally is towards a marked increase: 79.8 percent for England, compared with 99.7 percent for the SCR. Long-term unemployment (over twelve months) has increased "dramatically" over the period, and in Barnsley, it is five times the pre-recession level. Youth unemployment (under twenty-five years), which has been seen as a key issue at the national level, is 4.3 percent higher in the SCR (Sheffield City Region 2010a; Table 6.3).

Associated with the employment crisis is a skills crisis as identified by "educational underperformance." And the message in the SCRDP is particularly frank:

> The City Region's skills challenge is particularly acute. It can be characterized by a legacy of educational underperformance, a glut of skills (if not qualifications) associated with declining sectors and skills gaps and shortages in knowledge based sectors which must grow to achieve economic transformation ...
> Therefore unless the SCR is able to raise its game in this respect, it faces the prospect of a low skills equilibrium where the low expectations and commitment of both employers and employees, in terms of training and upskilling, will suppress productivity and income levels, inhibit the survival and growth of indigenous businesses and discourage inward investment. (SCRDP 2010, 14–15)

Some key aspects of this skills shortfall include the facts that almost a third of working-age populations have no qualifications; that where two thirds of employers recognize the value of workforce training, only half engage in it; and that there are insufficient opportunities to persuade those leaving to stay (Sheffield City Council 2010, 53).

Whilst there seems to be some consensus that worklessness and "dependency" upon long-term benefits is a cause of poverty, there are fewer acceptances from official government channels about the connection between level of benefits (what people actually receive in cash) and poverty.

"Workless" refers to all people of working age who are not in employment – these include those claiming benefits and those who are not in work but are not entitled to benefits (economically inactive). Out-of-work benefits are those work-related benefits that people receive when not in paid employment. They comprise Job Seekers Allowance (as the main unemployment benefit) and Incapacity Benefit/Employment Support Allowance (IB / ESA), and other income-related benefits. The people claiming IB / ESA are those who are deemed too sick to work, and the majority of these suffer mental health and behavioural disorders (Table 6.2).

As the Child Poverty Action Group (CPAG) – an advocacy organization around poverty – states:

Despite the Government's concern about the generosity of benefits acting as a deterrent to work, high levels of poverty among disabled people indicate that they do not provide an adequate financial safety net. It is hardly surprising that IB (currently a meagre £78.50 a week) is failing to safeguard disabled people from living in poverty. Although it is an 'earnings' replacement benefit, rates are between 16 per cent and 30 per cent of average earnings. While the long term rate of IB is more generous than JSA (Job Seekers Allowance), this is an indication of the inadequacies of JSA, not the generosity of IB. (Preston 2006, 101)

Partnerships have recognized that the low level of benefits in the UK[1] causes financial difficulties, poverty, and debt. According to the Derbyshire Unemployed Workers Centre (DUWC), which proveides benefit and welfare rights advice, the Job Seekers Allowance (JSA), an insurance-based benefit, is worth £64.50 per week compared with the average weekly earnings of £576.80 (figures for 2008). In other words, the level of benefits has been kept well below average earnings. They state: "Thousands of people in Derbyshire are having to make decisions on prioritizing eating or heating, getting into debt with all the well known consequent impacts on health both physical and mental" (DUWC 2010, 6).

Low pay and poor work are closely connected; people in low-paid employment (particularly in part-time work) tend not to have access to training and other "benefits," such as trade union representation, pension schemes, and sick pay – and the reality is that there are limited opportunities of upskilling and career/employment progression as routes out of low pay. Low pay has been defined as a wage comprising sixty percent of full-time median earnings (Cooke and Lawton 2008). The largest single sector where low-paid jobs exist is the retail and wholesale sector (although there are significant numbers in the public sector). In terms of the proportion of jobs in low-paid employment, the hospitality industry (hotels and restaurants) has half of its employees in low-paid employment.

Given the imminent (at the time of writing) threat of job losses in the public sector and the cuts in social and health provision that have been underway since 2009, it is likely that women will be adversely affected. Earlier studies (Yeandle et al. 2004; Etherington and Jones 2009) have highlighted the barriers faced by women and black and minority ethnic groups in the region in terms of accessing sustainable employment.

Challenges with Coordinating City-Region Partnerships and Policy Interventions

As scalar shifts require an enhanced role for the national state to manage rescaling processes, a tendency towards two often contradictory tendencies occurs: centralization of state power, and devolution and decentralization, which gives rise to tensions around policy and institutional coordination at vertical (between central and local) and horizontal levels (across institutions and partnerships within a defined locality) (Brenner 2003). These tendencies are discernable in the Sheffield City-Region. The (former) City Strategy Pathfinder (CSP) – an initiative designed to devolve some decision-making and improve coordination of welfare-to-work programs – involved a more centrally controlled model of decision-making through the commissioning process of contracts that were steered closely from the centre. At the same time, problems also arose as partnerships attempted to align performance targets and objectives. Evaluation of the City Strategy reveals that this initiative involved "centralized localism" whereby the outsourcing of welfare-to-work programs by the DWP was organized at the central level, commissioning providers to operate within the Strategy areas but not obliging them to work with local partners, and in particular, the newly created employer-led Employment and Skills Boards (Green and Orton 2010).

In fact, outsourcing and privatization, which became increasingly central features of New Labour's labour market policy, cause increasing tensions and conflicts within partnerships. The other underlying problem of the governance architecture around employment and skills was their legitimation, as a consequence of the lack of inclusion of a voice for, or representation of, those organizations who represent disadvantaged groups in the labour market (Interview with local trade union official). As the Coalition Government rolls out an increasingly market- and workfare-orientated welfare-to-work strategy, the links between local actors, partnerships, and providers seem to be weakened further due to the increasing emphasis placed on the private sector to deliver labour market programs. The main challenge is for local partners to grasp some form of control over the government's welfare-to-work program, as more and more strategic policy and program implementation is being driven by the prime contractors.

The implementation of the Coalition Government's Work Programme is creating tensions within the strategic partnerships because of the fear that welfare-to-work contractors will override employment strategies produced by local partnerships, as occurred in certain instances under the CSP. As one stakeholder commented, "there is little incentive for the contractors to engage with the partnerships" (local authority official). The rolling out of the Work Programme creates considerable challenges of accountability of contractors to partnerships, and the Sheffield local authority has attempted to negotiate with one of the prime contractors ways in which their activities could be monitored and evaluated. As one interviewee observed, "contractors are advised to link with local partnerships and it is not mandatory. Nor is there likely to be any sanctions if they don't" (Interview with local authority partnership manager).

A number of Sheffield local authority partnership stakeholders questioned how the prime contractors will engage with the various partnerships, and whether there will be any adoption or borrowing from good practice that has been developed within Sheffield and other localities. As prime contractors are operating at the South Yorkshire spatial scale, the degree to which they will become embedded in the local partnerships is open to question. "Prime contractors are likely to be of national standing and probably have weak local connections. There is a risk that they will not be connected to the city's strategies and services, market intelligence and the economic development from which job opportunities could flow" (Sheffield City Council 2011, 9). A key element of the previous City Strategy for improving coordination was to bring in employers within the current partnerships, which the new privatized approach is likely to undermine: "Depending on which prime contractors are successful, links to local employment opportunities may not be strong and lead to a loss of confidence in relationships built with employers within the city to date. Prime contractors have raised a concern around where jobs will come from, given the current climate, and may look to the city to galvanize local employers" (Sheffield City Council 2011, 9).

A struggle is being waged to bring the contractors to account, improve coordination, and avoid marginalization from policy- and strategy-making processes (Interview with Senior NGO Officer). The Sheffield City Council is reviewing and reconfiguring partnership structures and composition, including the role of the Local Strategic

Partnership Executive Board; the creation of a South Yorkshire Work Programme Group; and proposals to replace the Multi Agency Employment Group (which deals primarily with health and employment) with a partnership covering a broader remit to embrace employment and skills (Interview with a Health Services Mental Health Worker; see Table 6.2). The scepticism about the contracting model seemed to be prevalent amongst stakeholders, and the evidence suggests that attempts to develop contracting have already been under critical scrutiny (Finn 2009; 2011; NAO 2010).

Government austerity measures and fiscal reductions are a cause of barriers to, and tensions around, coordinating and sustaining partnerships. The reduction of resources to those projects and services that facilitate labour market entry – such as social, health, and child care support provided by local government, the health services, and voluntary sectors (or "wrap around services") – is potentially undermining the objectives of the Work Programme. These cuts will therefore have impacts on the capacity of partnerships to transform labour markets, and there is already evidence of tensions within the partnerships over the distribution and allocation of increasingly scarce resources. For example, in Sheffield, budget cuts have been implemented to services to young people, including career guidance[2] (and also significant cuts to the voluntary sector, which provides social and employability services to disadvantaged groups within the labour market). In Rotherham, £2 billion regeneration programs are under threat; these are usually supported by the Regional Development Agency, which has since been abolished and was due to close in 2012. The scope for the private sector to absorb the increasing numbers of unemployed is limited. Doncaster Chamber of Commerce, an employer organization in the Doncaster local authority area, stated: "However, the real term cuts for department budgets of a record 25 percent across the board are troubling. 59 percent of Doncaster businesses are deeply concerned by the impact this is likely to have on their efforts to grow in the coming year. A sizeable proportion of private sector turnover in Doncaster is, at present, still reliant on the public sector" (Doncaster Chamber of Commerce 2010, 14).

As the expenditure cuts bite deep, this will bring about increasing tensions amongst the SCR partners as local authorities are coming to terms with making significant redundancies and as certain sections of the business community will feel the consequences of a reduction in incomes in the local economies.

CONCLUSIONS: ASSESSING NEOLIBERAL LOCALISM AS A POLITICS INEQUALITY

Neoliberalism as a strategy that gives priority to market forces comprises two elements with respect to the role of the state (Newman 2011, 93). One is the "rolling back" (or hollowing out, in Jessop's terms) of the state, which involves the dismantling of institutions (e.g. Regional Development Agencies), privatization, cuts in social expenditure, deregulation, and the contracting-out of services. The other element is "rolling out," which involves a proactive form of intervention that seeks to embed neoliberalism via state spatial strategies in the form of workfare and active labour market policies (such as through the Work Programme), as well as promoting local private investment (such as the Local Enterprise Partnership–sponsored Regional Growth Fund).

The Coalition Government has sought to rely more heavily on the market (rolling back) to develop the city-regional economy, and the new discourse is about "rebalancing the economy," whilst at the same time the spending review will involve a rationalization of the public sector through reductions in resources and via outsourcing of activities and functions. Within the employment and skills aspect of the LEP strategy, the focus is on "private sector led local solutions ... the key principles underlying our approach will be that it is private sector led, responsive and aligned to the local economy" (Sheffield City Region 2010b, 15–16).

Neoliberalism is an inherently unstable strategy because of the way it underpins and reinforces uneven development and inequality. The Coalition Government's austerity measures are already having severe consequences, exacerbating the deep and longstanding inequalities in the labour market. Since 2011, there have been numerous instances of large-scale protests against the cuts around the spending reductions and redundancies in social and care sector within the individual districts making up the city-region. Furthermore, the SCR authorities experiencing higher unemployment rates and worklessness are likely, as a response to political and social pressures within their constituencies, to shape policies and strategies that mitigate the adverse impacts of the recession and austerity measures. The prospects for the economy of Sheffield have been given a sober assessment in the *Economic Masterplan*: "If we can raise the prosperity of Sheffield to the national average it will represent the most dramatic turnaround of any UK city in living memory" (Sheffield City Council 2010, 5).

The second tension relates to the way the cuts will potentially destabilize the partnerships, as those areas of local authority functions that will be responsible for carrying out LEP activities (for example, planning, economic development, and regeneration) will not be immune to redundancies and outsourcing. The other possible challenge to the stability of the partnership is the continued commitment of the private sector to the LEP governance, and their continued commitment and participation on the Board and within the networks that are being established. The partnership can also experience problems in terms of coordinating those strands of policies that create new jobs, and those that attempt to signpost unemployed people into employment. This coordination problem is already prevalent as the Work Programme is rolled out because of the different scales of intervention in terms of the City-Region and Job Centre Plus administrative region.

The rebalancing of the local economy and reducing of "welfare dependency" is dependent upon the new jobs growth and the effectiveness of the Work Programme. In addition to the issue of coordination highlighted above, the other challenge to the WP relates to its design, with providers of welfare-to-work programs operating on a performance and results basis. This is likely to exacerbate the "creaming" and "parking" of unemployed – i.e. those who are job-ready are the most likely to access new jobs. The possible impact will be persistent long-term unemployed and a resultant increase in poverty (see Newman 2011).

NOTES

1 See Newman (2011, 102); according to the Joseph Rowntree Foundation, Job Seekers Allowance and Income Support (now being phased out) are worth what they were in 1997 accounting for inflation, and are equivalent to 41 percent of the Minimum Income Standard, i.e. the amount required to purchase clothes, food, and shelter, and the opportunities to participate in society. The more "generous" Employment Support Allowance (ESA) is around 60 percent of the MIS. However, this analysis does not take account of the income reductions that benefit "migration" will result in, nor, of

course, the cuts in certain benefits and the linking of benefits to the Consumer Price Index as opposed to the Retail Price Index (Kenway et al. 2010).

2 http://www.unitetheunion.org/news_events/latest_news/sheffield_council_cuts_hit_the.aspx.

REFERENCES

Beatty, C., S. Fothergill, D. Houston, R. Powell, and P. Sissions. 2010. *Women on Incapacity Benefits*. Sheffield, UK: Centre for Regional Economic and Social Research.

Beatty, C., S. Fothergill, T. Gore, and R. Powell. 2011. *Tackling Worklessness in Britain's Weaker Local Economies*. Sheffield, UK: Sheffield Hallam University.

Boudreau, J. 2003. "Politics of Territorialization: Regionalism, Localism and Other Isms … The Case of Montreal." *Journal of Urban Affairs* 25 (2): 179–99.

Brenner, N. 2003. "Metropolitan Institutional Reform and the Rescaling of State Space in Contemporary Western Europe." *European Urban and Regional Studies* 10 (4): 297–324.

Brenner, N., B. Jessop, M. Jones, and G. MacLeod. 2003. "Introduction: State Space in Question." In *State/Space: A Reader*, edited by N. Brenner, B. Jessop, M. Jones, and G. MacLeod, 1–26. Oxford, UK: Blackwell.

Bristow, G. 2005. "Everyone's a Winner: Problematizing the Discourse of Regional Competitiveness." *Journal of Economic Geography* 5 (3): 285–304.

Centre for Economic and Social Inclusion. 2005. *More Jobs, More Skills – The Future for Sheffield's Labour Market*. London: Centre for Economic and Social Inclusion.

Centre for Local Economic Strategies. 2010. *Public Sector and Local Government Cuts*, Bulletin No. 75. Manchester, UK: Centre for Local Economic Strategies.

Christopherson, S. 2003. "The Limits to 'New Regionalism': (Re)learning from the Media Industries." *Geoforum* 34 (4): 413–15.

Cochrane, A., and D. Etherington. 2007. "Managing Local Labour Markets and Making up New Spaces of Welfare." *Environment and Planning A* 39 (12): 2958–74.

Cox, E., and K. Schumueker. 2010. *Well North of Fair: The Implications of the Spending Review for the North of England*. London: IPPR.

Cox, K. 2004. "The Politics of Local and Regional Development, the Difference the State Makes and the US/British Contrast." In *Governing Local and Regional Economics Institutions Politics and Economic Development*, edited by A. Wood and D. Valler, 247–76. Aldershot, UK: Ashgate.

Dabinett, G. 2004. *Uneven Spatial Development and Regeneration Outcomes in the UK: Reversing Decline in the Northern City of Sheffield?* Sheffield, UK: Sheffield University (mimeograph).

Derbyshire Unemployed Workers Centre. 2010. *Annual Report.* Chesterfield, UK: Derbyshire Unemployed Workers Centre.

Doncaster Chamber of Commerce. 2010. *Economic Review 4 Quarter.* http://www.doncaster-chamber.co.uk/content/pages/doncaster-economic-review-q4-2010.php. Accessed 17 February 2012.

Etherington, D., and M. Jones. 2009. "City Regions and New Geographies of Uneven Development and Inequality." *Regional Studies* 43 (2): 247–65.

Fairclough, N. 2001. *New Labour, New Language?* London: Routledge.

Finn, D. 2009. "The 'Welfare Market' and the Flexible New Deal: Lessons from Other Countries." *Local Economy* 24 (1): 38–45.

– 2011. *The Design of the Work Programme in International Context, Report for the National Audit Office.* Portsmouth, UK: University of Portsmouth, Centre for Economic and Social Inclusion.

Gonzalez, S. 2011. "The North/South Divide in Italy and England: Discursive Construction of Regional Inequality." *European Urban and Regional Studies* 18 (1): 62–76.

Gough, J., and A. Eisenschitz with A. McCulloch. 2006. *Spaces of Social Exclusion.* London: Routledge.

Green, A., and M. Orton. 2009. "The Integration of Activation Policy at the Sub National Scale: A Case Study of the City Strategy Initiative in an English Region." *International Journal of Sociology and Social Policy* 29 (11/12): 612–23.

Hudson, R. 1999. "The Learning Economy, the Learning Firm and the Learning Region: A Sympathetic Critique." *European Urban and Regional Studies* 6 (1): 59–72.

HM Treasury, DTI, and ODPM. 2006. *Devolving Decision Making: 3 – Meeting the Regional Economic Challenge: The Importance of Cities to Regional Growth.* London: Stationery Office.

Jessop, B. 2000. "Governance Failure." In *The New Politics of British Local Governance*, edited by G. Stoker, 11–32. London: Macmillan.

– 2002. *The Future of the Capitalist State.* Cambridge: Polity Press.

Jonas, A.E.G. 2012. "City-Regionalism: Questions of Distribution and Politics." *Progress in Human Geography* 36 (6): 822–9.

Jones, M. 1999. *New Institutional Spaces: TECS and the Remaking of Economic Governance.* London: Routledge.

Jones, M., and D. Etherington. 2009. "Governing the Skills Agenda: Insights from the Sheffield City Region." *Local Economy* 24 (1): 68–79.

Jones, M., and G. MacLeod. 2004. "Regional Spaces, Spaces of Regionalism: Territory, Insurgent Politics and the English Question." *Transactions of the Institute of British Geographers* 29 (4): 433–52.

Keating, M. 1998. *The New Regionalism in Western Europe: Territorial Restructuring and Political Change.* Cheltenham, UK: Edward Elgar.

– 2001. *Nations Against the State: The New Politics of Nationalism in Quebec, Catalonia and Scotland.* London: Palgrave.

Keating, M., J. Loughlin, and K. Descouwer. 2003. *Culture, Institutions and Economic Development.* Cheltenham, UK: Edward Elgar.

Keep, E., K. Mayhew, and J. Payne. 2006. "From Skills Revolution to Productivity Miracle – Not as Easy as It Sounds." *Oxford Review of Economic Policy* 22 (4): 539–59.

Lovering, J. 1999. "Theory Led by Policy: The Inadequacies of the 'New Regionalism' (Illustrated from the Case of Wales)." *International Journal of Urban and Regional Research* 23 (2): 379–95.

Mackinnon, D. 2011. "Reconstructing Scale: Towards a New Scalar Politics." *Progress in Human Geography* 35: 21–36.

McNeil, C., ed. 2010. *Now It's Personal: The New Landscape of Welfare-to-Work.* London: Institute of Public Policy Research.

Musson, S., A. Tickell, and P. John. 2005. "A Decade of Decentralization? Assessing the Role of Government Offices for the English Regions." *Environment and Planning A* 37 (8): 1395–1412.

National Audit Office. 2010. *Support to Incapacity Benefit Claimants through Pathways to Work.* DWP available on http://www.nao.org.uk/publications/1011/pathways_to_work.aspx. Accessed 17 February 2012.

Newman, I. 2011. "Work as a Route out of Poverty: A Critical Evaluation of the UK Welfare to Work Policy." *Policy Studies* 32 (2): 91–108.

North, D., D. Syrett, and D. Etherington. 2009. "Tackling Concentrated Worklessness: Integrating Governance and Policy across and within Spatial Scales." *Environment and Planning C: Government and Policy* 27 (6): 1022–39.

Organization for Economic Co-operation and Development (OECD). 2008. *Making Local Strategies Work: Building the Evidence Base.* Paris: OECD.

Peck, J., and N. Theodore. 2000. "Work First: Welfare-to-Work and the Regulation of Contingent Labour Markets." *Cambridge Journal of Economics* 24 (1): 119–38.

– 2010. "Labor Markets from the Bottom Up." In *Handbook of Employment and Society: Working Space*, edited by S. McGrath-Champ, A. Herod, and A. Rainnie, 87–105. Cheltenham, UK: Edward Elgar.

Rossi, U. 2004. "New Regionalism Contested: Some Remarks in Light of the Case of the Mezzogiorno in Italy." *International Journal of Urban and Regional Research* 28 (2): 466–76.

Sheffield City Council. 2010. *Sheffield Economic Masterplan*. Sheffield, UK: Sheffield City Council.

– 2011. *Unemployment and Worklessness in Sheffield*. Sheffield, UK: Children and Young People's Services Lifelong Learning and Skills.

Sheffield City Region. 2010a. *Strategic Economic Assessment*. http://www. sheffieldcityregion.org.uk/economic-assessment. Accessed 17 February 2012.

– 2010b. *Proposal for a Sheffield City Region Local Enterprise Partnership*. Sheffield, UK: Sheffield City Region.

Sheffield First. 2003. *Sheffield City Strategy 2002–2005*. Sheffield, UK: Sheffield First Partnership.

Sheffield Work and Skills Board. 2007. *Draft Terms of Reference*. Sheffield, UK: Sheffield Work and Skills Board.

South Yorkshire Partnership. 2005. *South Yorkshire Investment Plan*. Barnsley, UK: South Yorkshire Partnership.

Sunley, P., R. Martin, and C. Nativel. 2006. *Putting Workfare in Place: Local Labour Markets and the New Deal*. Oxford, UK: Blackwell.

Thomas, B., J. Pritchard, D. Ballas, D. Vickers, and D. Dorling. 2009. *A Tale of Two Cities: The Sheffield Project*. Sheffield, UK: Sheffield University Department of Geography.

Ward, K., and A. Jonas. 2004. "Competitive City-Regionalism as a Politics of Space: A Critical Reinterpretation of the New Regionalism." *Environment and Planning A* 36 (12): 2119–39.

7

Ottawa: Would "Telling Its Story" Be the Way to Go?

CAROLINE ANDREW

INTRODUCTION

This chapter presents a "what if" argument around the post-amalgamation development in Ottawa, Canada's capital city. It develops an alternative vision for the development of the new city-region, based on arguments about the strength of storytelling as a method of planning and place-making. It contrasts this trajectory for developing city-regions with the path actually followed by Ottawa, and speculates on the relative strengths of the two strategies for identity-building and the capacity for collective action. It builds on the very rich literature on storytelling, but particularly focuses on its relation to planning and to place-making. Given the relatively slow and rather conflictual nature of the post-amalgamation development in Ottawa, it seems worthwhile to imagine the possibilities of a storytelling process of city-region identity-building. And, in doing so, this chapter explores the development of alternate regional narratives, and engaging a more diverse range of communities in these stories as they are being crafted, told, and enacted.

THEORETICAL FRAMES: STORYTELLING IN PLANNING

Within the very broad literature on storytelling and planning, there are a number of important points that have helped to construct this chapter. Eckstein and Throgmorton's introduction to *Story and Sustainability* sets the stage:

[W]e encourage you to keep four aspects of story and storytelling in mind. First, storytellers have the power to imagine communities ... Second, story and imagined communities always have a spatial dimension and make a geographic claim ... Third, storytelling is a constitutive part of democratic practice, and democratic practice is constitutive of sustainability. To serve both sustainability and democracy, stories need to be understood as multiple and listened to with an ear for surprise. And last, the ability to listen with an ear tuned to surprise takes education – formal and informal – in how stories work. (2003, 6)

Mandelbaum (2003) adds some significant aspects of storytelling in his description of narrative as being one of four equal and interrelated tools for planning. After describing the other three (theory, model, and information system), he underlines the importance of stories focusing on the foreground, and of clearly distinguishing foreground and background. In addition, Mandelbaum insists on the importance of narratives having a beginning and an end. And finally, narratives need to give recognizable identities to the individual and social entities that exist within them. The emphasis on the foreground is important for our description of Ottawa; the stories need to highlight the construction of an identity within a specific space, and need to have a beginning and an end rooted in the creation of a city-region in Ottawa.

The importance of a beginning and an end to stories introduces the issue of the multiplicity and diversity of stories, and how storytelling can deal with multiple voices – and therefore with the possibilities of conflicting and contradictory accounts, including conflicting beginnings and ends. In an earlier article, Mandelbaum (1991, 212) describes the great difficulty planners have in dealing with "narrative conflicts," and advocates a strategy appropriate to open moral communities that "embraces controversy rather than seeking either to resolve or to ignore it." This is certainly the position we adopt in this chapter, recognizing, of course, that it is much easier to embrace controversy in a book chapter than in a plan destined to be implemented by a municipal government. The question of diversity within stories is, in fact, central to our intent.

We have adopted the same choice of multiple genres of stories as does Finnegan (1998) in her analysis of the stories of Milton Keynes in the United Kingdom – itself the product of radical planning narratives in the 1960s. In her account, Finnegan brings together descriptions by urban theorists, planners' accounts, and residents' recollections, telling stories of urban life and highlighting the role of reflective and creative individuals in constituting urban communities: "I decided to pursue the rather different endeavor of bringing together a series of stories of the city that are more often kept separate and analyzing them within the same narrative framework. Their interaction and overlaps can tell us something about the actualization of our mythologies of urban life" (ix).

Finnegan's pursuit engaged multiple genres, but also multiple perspectives. So, not only do we want to bring together official documents, personal stories, and academic literature, but we want to ensure that these different kinds of material tell many versions of the story. And here there are different views about the potential of storytelling. Soja (2003) argues that storytelling often underplays the spatial element, and certainly space must be central to our story of Ottawa. Other authors are more sanguine about the capabilities of storytelling to encompass multiplicity and diversity; Little and Froggett (2010, 459) describe storytelling as a prime means of "allowing a complex and ambivalent view of aspirations, actions and motivations." Sandercock (2003, 153) writes of the search for diversity, community, and sustainability, and therefore of the need for "organizing hope, negotiating fears, mediating memories, and facilitating community soul searching and transformation." For Sandercock, this "acknowledges that the work of planners involves both the creation and the use of stories and storytelling" (163).

Beauregard (2003) adds to the discussion of storytelling and diversity by linking public storytelling, public spaces, and the potential for a robust discursive democracy. He argues for a wide variety of public spaces – from formal to informal – where strangers can meet and debate common concerns. As does Finnegan, Beauregard describes these deliberations as being of multiple genres: "the instrumental and linear presentations of policy analysts and planners, the strategic calculations of elected officials, the commentary of public intellectuals, and the personal stories of common citizens" (2003, 68). This also is inspiration for our attempt to re-imagine a process of building a democratic city-region in Ottawa.

Storytelling is also place-making. Schneekloth and Shibley describe it in the following way:

Place making as an alternative professional practice seeks to create relationships between people and places, and relationships

among people and places. Making relationships and communities
is the goal, and making places is the vehicle for this practice ...
The first task of place making is to open a space for a conversation about place: a dialogic space. This is the most important
task, as it is within this open space that we share goals, concerns,
hopes and desires for places and it is also within this space that
we trust each other enough to argue and disagree. (2008, 207–8)

The authors go on to describe the democratic nature of this process,
building on inclusive processes of melding a variety of forums of
knowledge, and putting together their professional expertise with
the lived experience and tacit knowledge of the residents. They
describe the project as "intensely pragmatic and deeply imaginal"
(205); it is about building globally competitive city-regions, and also
about "who we are and where we are." It was a project built on storytelling that reinforced the sense of place:

Our place making work in the Niagaras has attempted, through
an open dialogic space, to bring stories into the conversation and
to join them in an inclusive and relational manner. Rather than
work with a single theme, we are weaving a complex fabric, finding places for individual perspectives within a framework that
structures and contains them. The new cloth must make the individual threads legible and accurately reflect who we are, in a way
that is saleable as deep structural representations of the region's
history and cultural landscape. (215)

A reference that combines the focus on storytelling within the context of organizations (such as the City of Ottawa), and that builds
on multiple dimensions of complexity with a recognition of numerous actors with individual stories in interaction, is David Boje's work
on *Storytelling and the Future of Organizations* (2011). Boje builds
on the idea of agency, and combines this with what he calls the "collective dynamics of storytelling complexity and chaos" (4). Boje continues by defining storytelling as a discourse that combines three
genres – narrative, living story, and antenarrative – to create a combination defined as Collective Storytelling Dynamics:

Collective Storytelling Dynamics (CSD) is the interplay of antenarratives, linear narratives, and living story networking. CSD

applies this complexity to three interdependent storytelling genres: narrative retrospective sense-making, living story networks unfolding in the present and antenarrative prospective sense making into the future. CSD is all about patterns of complexity of storytelling sense making. (12)

Antenarratives are defined as bets on the future pattern, and therefore open up possibilities for agency on the part of actors to do other than continue past patterns. But defined as a bet, this does not ensure change; it merely conceives of the possibility. Narrative is described as the dominant force in storytelling and as being a story with a beginning, middle, and end. On the other hand, living stories are in the here and now, are nonlinear, and it is the antenarratives that bridge the spaces of narratives and the spaces of living stories.

Boje's frame, similar to that of Schneekloth and Shibley for place-making, is both "intensely pragmatic and deeply imaginal" (2008, 205). In fact, it suggests some very concrete guidelines for composing regional stories: the importance of having past, present, and future in constant interaction; the possibility of putting different and even competing stories, different voices, and different narratives together as parts of a larger whole; the importance of taking real account of agency; and, finally, the possibility that the regional story is not necessarily linear, but can take a variety of shapes, including cycles and spirals. The idea of cycles in the regional story is relatively simple; electoral systems are cyclical, and so too is the socio-economic pattern of development. Spirals are more complex, with unexpected movements and the non-assumption of linearity. Spiral development relates to the idea of antenarrative, and the potential for shifts in direction.

This introduction has served to outline the possibilities of storytelling on a regional level. Before attempting to apply this perspective to the example of Ottawa post-amalgamation, it is important to understand the actual amalgamation process as it took place in Ottawa, and to fully comprehend how dramatically different the process was from the democratic and inclusive spaces of dialogue just described.

OTTAWA'S AMALGAMATION PROCESS

The city of Ottawa, Canada's capital, has its history in the lumber trade and in its position on the banks of the Ottawa River as a strategic military and trading site. From these early origins, the city has grown to be the fourth largest urban area in Canada, and a centre for government, education, and high technology industries. Culturally, the city has been influenced by its location on the border between English and French Canada, although more recently the cultural importance of the indigenous First Nations people is beginning to be acknowledged. Each of these characteristics tells us something about the stories that might be told about the city of Ottawa. However, these narratives have struggled against recent amalgamation strategies, and provided limited scope in the emergence of community histories.

First, and most importantly, amalgamation was imposed on Ottawa. There had been an initial, more participatory process, in which a committee of three (chosen by the Regional Government of Ottawa-Carleton and the City of Ottawa) chose a Citizen's Forum of twelve members who were charged with making recommendations about the future form of the region. However, once the Ontario government proceeded with the amalgamation of Toronto – despite massive citizen mobilization against it – citizen action in Ottawa fell apart. The Citizen's Forum disbanded, arguing that the local governments were not willing to listen to them. There had been some local efforts to propose appropriate structures in addition to the early work of the Citizen's Forum, such as the Centre on Governance's report on the idea of borough governments to give some measure of local control within a regional structure. Citizen participation was even further discouraged when Claude Bennett, a former Ottawa alderman and close political ally of the Ontario premier, Mike Harris, became the Transition Board Chair. He took on the role with the declared intention to reduce the size and scope of the local government. The Transition Board was given a mandate of one year to recommend a structure for the new City of Ottawa. Its first effort was to suggest the possibility of part-time councillors (the City of Ottawa had a tradition since the 1960s of full-time councillors, remunerated in consequence), as a way of encouraging candidates from the business community to run for office. This was rejected by all the existing elected representatives, and by a large coalition of civil society groups. The idea was dropped by the Transition Board. Towards the end of the transition year, some civil society mobilization took place around the representation of ethno-cultural diversity and youth, but essentially the Transition Board ran out of time to radically restructure the City of Ottawa.

The amalgamation created a new City of Ottawa comprising all the urban area of the Ontario side of the Ottawa River, all the suburban areas, and a large section of rural territory. If this territory could be seen as making sense in terms of planning (as most of the rural area could be seen as urbanizing), it certainly made for a challenge in terms of the creation of a regional identity. The territory of the new city covered the quasi-totality of the Census Metropolitan Region on the Ontario side of the Ottawa River.

Other institutional features also added to the challenge of creating a regional identity. For instance, the region is bisected by the Ottawa River, with Ottawa situated in Ontario, and the City of Gatineau located in Quebec. These trans-border relations, and the cultural, political, and territorial divisions between them, create challenges, as well as opportunities (as we argue below), to creating a cohesive regional identity. Similarly, the federal-local relationship over the past century created a very particular dynamic in which the City of Ottawa saw itself as a provider of basic services, leaving to the federal government questions of vision, identity, and the more high-end services (Andrew and Chiasson 2012). Even though the self-image that municipal Ottawa has had of itself may be in the process of changing, it influenced the post-amalgamation in terms of the actions of the city and its "love-hate" relationship with the federal government.

The new City of Ottawa did try to set a new direction for itself by organizing an Ottawa Summit in the summer of 2001, a few months after the official creation of the new city. The Summit tried to build on the highly participative planning process that had existed immediately prior to amalgamation, Ottawa 2020, which had generated a vision of a more compact, environmentally friendly, and socially mixed City of Ottawa. The summit was a largely top-down process in that it was organized by the city in a rather short timeframe, but it did generate a progressive urban vision as a future direction for the city.

However, the following period was dominated by a risk-averse municipal government and a very divided electorate. Half the voters had believed the declarations emanating from the Conservative premier of Ontario, Mike Harris – that amalgamation would reduce taxes – and the other half had feared that any reduction in taxes would be because of cuts to services. The polarization of the electorate, coupled with a timid and risk-averse municipal leadership, led to municipal politics dominated by individual councillors thinking almost exclusively of their ward interests and nothing larger. Ward interests tended to mean handling individual complaints, as this was seen as the path to successful re-election.

The lack of municipal direction continued after the 2006 election. The election had seen the victory of a largely unknown mayoral candidate, Larry O'Brien, promising no tax increase for the four years of his mandate. O'Brien was unable to deliver on his promise, in part because the entire former municipal council had been re-elected having made no such promise; in part because of the weak mayoral system; and in part because O'Brien did not have a sus-tained interest in building a majority among the councillors. The dissatisfaction of citizens grew throughout the 2006–10 period, and debates were launched around issues such as limiting councillors' terms, introducing political parties, encouraging new candidates, enhancing the mayor's powers, and transforming ward boundaries. That the debates were largely around institutional issues is indica-tive of the way the region thought of reform. The number of sepa-rate institutional issues debated indicated general dissatisfaction with the functioning of the municipal government, but no agreement on the definition of the problem, nor, therefore, the solution. This directionless dissatisfaction was demonstrated by the results of the 2010 election: a large number of new councillors representing a wide variety of political positions, and the defeat of O'Brien by a new mayor, Jim Watson, a former provincial cabinet minister and former mayor of the City of Ottawa. The new mayor certainly understands the municipal system better than his predecessor, but he is risk-averse and committed to minimal tax increases. One could argue a strong path dependency of the basic services orientation of the City of Ottawa, as described earlier.

This introduces the complexity of the trans-border regional com-ponent of the Ottawa-Gatineau Census Metropolitan Area. This single economic region is defined largely by federal government employment, but also by employment in the high technology sector (Andrew, Ray, and Chiasson 2011). Clearly, from an environmental point of view, Ottawa-Gatineau is a single region dominated by the Ottawa River, being joined by the Rideau River and Canal on the Ontario side, and the Gatineau River on the Quebec side. Although there are relatively limited contacts between the Ottawa and the Gatineau municipal councils, there is one planning exercise that involves Ottawa, Gatineau, and the National Capital Commission (NCC), and that has a hundred-year horizon for planning. Despite some citizen participation, this exercise, Choosing Our Future, has been a relatively technical, top-down process.

Working in collaboration between Ottawa and Gatineau is not easy as few of the Ottawa planners are bilingual, creating a situation of inequality where the Gatineau planners are at a disadvantage. As this reproduces the more global power relations between Ottawa and Gatineau (based on population and wealth distribution), it does not create easy working relations.

The role of the NCC also adds rigidity. As we have described earlier, the City of Ottawa sees the federal government as, to some extent, imposing its views on the municipal government. However, the role of the NCC has diminished substantially over the past twenty years in terms of its planning activities. Although it is still an important regional agency, it has become more an organizer and promoter of events and festivals, and much less a planning body. The report on the NCC drafted for the federal government in 2006 by economist and former President of the Royal Society of Canada Gilles Paquet did outline a scenario to restructure the agency so as to give it an important voice in national debate (and indeed, as a storyteller); however, the government has not followed the direction suggested by the report.

In conclusion, the amalgamation of Ottawa was imposed by the provincial government, and the municipal structure has done little to take control of the direction of the region. A combination of risk-averse or inconsistent leadership, extremely local ward politics, and a discontented and divided electorate have contributed to an ongoing pattern of lackluster municipal politics. This whole evolution is dramatically different from the potential for place-making through storytelling that we outlined above. We will turn now to the efforts made in Ottawa to tell a story or to brand the region, before concluding with how Ottawa might tell its story.

THE STORIES THE REGION HAS TRIED TO TELL

There have been a variety of attempts to tell a story about the region. The Greber Plan, completed in the immediate post-war period under the political leadership of Prime Minister Mackenzie King and the planning vision of French landscape architect Jacques Gréber, was based on a Le Corbusier–type vision of urban design. It was based on a planning vision that placed imposing buildings in beautiful natural settings. The demarcation of a large, crescent-shaped greenbelt bounding the city against the Ottawa River, and the conservation of 361 square kilometres of forest and lakes – Gatineau Park – were seen as allowing the juxtaposition of city and nature. In reality, urban development simply jumped across the greenbelt. The NCC over time built on the image of the green capital before deciding that it needed to develop a more urban image. The decision to place federal buildings in Gatineau was based partly on politics, and partly on an urban vision of re-centring federal government buildings close to the Parliament buildings (Andrew, Ray, and Chiasson 2011, 228–9). The NCC also reflected on the representation of the units of the federation in the capital, in part based on similar Australian thinking. The Australian plan had included both the political units of the federation and the economic components of the federation, but the only concrete result in Ottawa of this thinking is a totally uninspiring and almost invisible "Garden of the Provinces" across the street from the National Archives.

More specific urban visions exist. One can be seen in Prime Minister Pierre Elliott Trudeau's decision in the early 1980s to build two "world-class" buildings: the National Gallery, designed by Moshe Safdie on the Ottawa side of the river, and the Museum of Civilization, designed by First Nations architect Douglas Cardinal. This can be seen as a story of Ottawa as the capital of a modern "world-class" urban nation, and also as recognition of the importance of the Aboriginal presence in the capital. However, as the federal government has since refused to allow Victoria Island to become an Aboriginal presence in the centre of the capital, the symbolism of the recognition of Aboriginal culture in Ottawa has been seriously undermined.

Comparisons of tourism branding in Ottawa and Gatineau illustrate its disparate elements: important federal cultural buildings and a somewhat urban story on the Ottawa side, and regional and nature-focused images on the Gatineau side (Chiasson and Andrew 2009) – certainly not one story, but rather two somewhat fuzzy efforts at branding. Still another story can be told of the War Museum, first thought of as part of a revisionist reading of Canadian history that attempted to re-establish the triumph of the military and male leaders at war as more central to nation-building than social history, feminist history, and labour history. However, the building was finally designed by a Japanese architect with personal connections to the internment of the Japanese population in British Columbia during the war. As a result of these mixed messages, the museum, in trying to be representative of both the triumph and the tragedy of war, is neither (Andrew 2007).

The most explicit attempt to brand the region was the effort by The Ottawa Partnership (TOP). TOP had been created to develop an economic development strategy for the region by bringing together leaders from the high-tech sector, the post-secondary sector, and the City of Ottawa around a cluster strategy for the region. The process started during the period of high-tech development, and the City of Ottawa strongly supported the idea of an economic development plan based on the private sector rather than on the federal government. The cluster process was led by a group of American consultants, and, as part of the overall exercise, they designed a branding strategy for the City of Ottawa. The brand was launched with great fanfare at a large breakfast meeting, bringing together private sector representatives, government, and civil society organizations, and the brand chosen was "Technically Beautiful." Undoubtedly this was an effort to amalgamate the green capital image with the high-tech economic boom; however, it failed miserably, and the audience was bewildered or sarcastically amused. The post-high-tech downturn, which in Ottawa involved the bankruptcy and sale of the telecom giant Nortel, certainly forced the Ottawa Centre for Regional Innovation (OCRI) to rethink its messages. The OCRI had been created in 1983 as a partnership between the high-tech sector, the regional government, and the post-secondary institutions of the region to focus on the economic development of the region, and certainly in its early years, the OCRI was seen as a great success. A recent promotional presentation by the OCRI is entitled "Ottawa: Canada's Creative Economic Capital," and focuses on the new economy as driven by knowledge and innovation. It quotes Richard Florida's high ranking of Ottawa as having a high percentage of creative class workers (Darch 2008; see also Smart and Tanasescu, this volume). The OCRI has recently been replaced by Invest Ottawa, which has rebranded itself as being downtown, young, and hip rather than suburban and bringing together large firms. Another new discourse for Invest Ottawa is giving more priority to recent immigrants, and arguing that they are by nature risk-takers, and therefore entrepreneurial.

One can see that all these attempts fail in terms of some of the lessons outlined in the above discussion of the literature. Almost none include past, present, and future in interaction; they tend to be a "present" orientation, or a single-minded re-reading of the past. Most are composed of one or two elements, and tend to homogenize the elements rather than leave them in creative tension. They are mostly linear, with little appreciation of the impact of the cycles of political and economic activity. And finally, they have almost all been top-down and only timidly participatory; citizen participation has tended to be in terms of choosing between alternative models presented by official planning bodies. Could another process, more in line with place-making through storytelling, be possible for Ottawa?

COLLECTIVE STORYTELLING DYNAMICS OF OTTAWA

This section attempts to build a story for Ottawa by building on past and present initiatives, and by imagining ways of developing emergent community narratives for the future.[1] It starts with the need to build back into the roots of Ottawa's working-class history: the lumber industry, and even more, the tensions and meeting places of the Irish and the French – the Shiners' War, but also the taverns and physical prowess of the workers in the lumber trade. There is a monument, again almost invisible, along the side of the Rideau Locks that bears witness to the heroism of those early workers. Roots need to be built back into that recognition of the tension-filled but significant meeting of the "other": in this case, the Irish and the French.

Roots also have to be established to a bottom-up history of the Francophone presence in early Ottawa. Their institutional role has been touched upon – establishing the General Hospital, the Cathedral, and the University of Ottawa – but the more collective creation of the stories of Francophone neighbourhoods, parishes, and institutions is in its initial stages. The CRCCF (Centre de recherche en civilisation canadienne française) at the University of Ottawa has worked on this, and is now starting an enlarged project of the history of Francophone Ottawa. This project needs to be seen as an integral, and independent, element of the history of Ottawa, and as an experiment in creating space for dialogue and debate within the story of Ottawa. The meeting with the "other" – Francophone and Anglophone – has played a significant role in the Ottawa story, and the roots to the Francophone building of community need to be part of the story.

The Francophone-Anglophone story can also include relations between the two sides of the river, and understanding this interaction not so much as a Canadian story, but as the story of the region. There are multiple levels of Anglophone-Francophone meetings, such as the Anglophone Pontiac in dialogue in the Outaouais, and the changing patterns of Francophone-Anglophone settlement on the Ontario side, with the now new Francophone population in the western communities of Ottawa.

The growing diversification of the Ottawa population has brought a variety of stories and a variety of storytelling methods of the different ethno-cultural communities. For example, there is a video of the development of the Ottawa Chinese community.

The Ottawa Local Immigration Partnership (OLIP; for information on the Local Immigration Partnerships in general, see Bradford and Andrew 2011) has also brought a rich understanding of the meeting of recent immigrants and the host society. Building a story of the economic advantages to Ottawa to better foster the integration of recent immigrants – and indeed, beyond that, the story of the successful economic competition by Calgary and Edmonton because of their better strategies of integrating recent immigrants – is a major part of the broader story of the OLIP. Making better use of the talents, entrepreneurial spirit, and global connections of recent immigrants is crucial, and this requires not only economic actions but also social, cultural, and educational strategies to successfully grow the diversity of Ottawa.

Immigration also builds on the story of the meeting of Francophones and Anglophones, as recent immigrants belong to both the Francophone and Anglophone communities. The OLIP's story is one of a partnership with the Support Network to Francophone Immigration of Eastern Ontario (le Réseau de soutien à l'immigration francophone de l'Est de l'Ontario) that builds on the historical and complex relationships of Francophones and Anglophones in Ottawa. The OLIP is itself a partnership of the settlement sector, the City of Ottawa, the educational sector, the social service, and the health sector, along with many others. It is an effort to build a welcoming community in which recent immigrants and long-time residents learn to better understand and value each other. The OLIP planning process involved experiments in dialogue, storytelling, and democratic practice, and continues to build on a history of social innovation in Ottawa's social sector. The website builds on this story of continuity between past, present, and future, and therefore the innovation created in the past is living in the present and will thrive in the future. Among the examples of innovation are the creation of LASI (Local Agencies Serving Immigrants), a coalition of the major settlement sector agencies; LASI World Skills, an employment-oriented agency co-created by the LASI members; the now Canada-wide SWIS program (Settlement Workers in Schools), which originated as Ottawa settlement agency OCISO; and the Coalition of Community Resource and Health Centres across Ottawa.

Ottawa also has a small but quickly growing Aboriginal population, and there is an Aboriginal Working Group, co-chaired by an Aboriginal leader (in this case, the president of an Aboriginal housing corporation) and the City. This recognition needs to be part of the Ottawa story, on the one hand going back to the three rivers as the transportation corridors for the Aboriginal populations, and on the other, building on the past, present, and future understanding of the central importance of the meetings and recognition of Aboriginal and non-Aboriginal populations in Ottawa.

There are perhaps two processes that most clearly exemplify a collective storytelling of Ottawa: the creation of the Equity and Inclusion Lens of the City of Ottawa, and the startup of Citizens Academy. The Equity and Inclusion Lens was created by the City for All Women Initiative (Initiative: une ville pour toutes les femmes – CAWI–IVTF; see also Klodawsky, Siltanen, and Andrew 2013) for the City of Ottawa when the city decided it would be preferable to create a single tool for city employees to help them be more inclusive of the full diversity of Ottawa in all phases of municipal policymaking. The creating of the Lens was complex, an initial group of eleven people who represented the eleven groups seen to be marginalized in the City of Ottawa – the five groups covered by the Equity and Diversity Policy of the City (Aboriginal peoples, persons with disabilities, visible minorities, women, and the GLBTQ community) plus six others: immigrants, youth, the elderly, people living in poverty, Francophones, and people living in the rural sector. The eleven members were chosen as people able to speak for one of these groups, but speaking as individuals rather than as representatives of organizations. The working group also included some city staff working in areas relating to one of these groups, and each of the City's Advisory Committees that related to one of the groups named a member as a liaison to be consulted on elements relating to that group. There were deep, and often conflictual, discussions, but there developed a considerable level of trust. The resulting document goes through the different phases of policy-making, raising questions about inclusionary practices. The Lens was accompanied by eleven profiles, one for each of the groups, which described the group's history in Ottawa, their common elements and the common barriers they face, the policies that affect them at the municipal, provincial, and federal levels, and specifically, the diversity of each group. The message of the Lens is intersectionality; Aboriginals are women and men, they are young and old, some belong to the GBLTQ community, some have disabilities. Similarly for the elderly: some are Francophone, some Anglophone, some are recent immigrants, some live in the rural area, some belong to the GBLTQ community, and some live in poverty. This message of identity, intersectionality, and complexity created the trust that created the Lens, but it was trust that came through debate, through disagreement, through negotiated words and sentences, and through the push and pull of city and community.

The Equity and Inclusion Lens integrates past, present, and future; it captures separate stories within a larger story. The eleven profiles create a sense of story about each of the communities that help to make up the diversity of Ottawa. It can be seen as spiral or cyclical, as inclusions within a group become exclusions to other groups before coming back to the possibility of inclusion. It is not linear, as even the phases of policy-making play out as a continuing cycle. It is about intersectionality and the possibility of multiple and complex identities. It has roots in a variety of histories, both in Ottawa and across the world. It is about democratic practice. However, it does not include an environmental dimension; the economic dimension is more about employment and revenue than about economic development; the cultural dimension is relatively limited; and it is, to a degree, homogenized within a document of the City of Ottawa. The slowness of the Lens's implementation across the city relates to the lack of resources, both human and financial, but it also relates to the functioning of the city as controlling the process of implementation. If the city could open itself to the process of sense-making through storytelling, it might see the potential in a complex story of the overlays of meetings with "others," and see itself as having been enriched by these meetings – Aboriginals and non-Aboriginals, Francophones and Anglophones, immigrants and non-immigrants, the GBLTQ community and the heterosexual community, the able-bodied community meeting with those with disabilities, women and men meetings as equals, young and old engaging in intergenerational dialogue, and rural, urban, and suburban meetings, all understanding their interrelationships and separate identities.

The most recent initiative to plan for Ottawa through storytelling is Citizens Academy. The description on the website indicates that "Citizens Academy is designed to break down these barriers by inviting people representing the full diversity of the city to experience a democratic dialogue. In that dialogue, they will learn together what are the big challenges to our future, how the City works, how decisions are made, and how the community can be part of the solution." So far three pilot sessions have been held, and the group is working to ensure that a full program will be in place for the fall of 2013. And within this overall project of dialogue and storytelling across the full diversity of the population is the intent of building the leadership of the Ottawa of tomorrow – a leadership capable of planning for a more complex and more diverse urban region. One very concrete tool of storytelling that is in the process of being produced is a series of capsules about the important decisions that have created the Ottawa of today. If Citizens Academy is to create the leadership of tomorrow, it is important that there be a way of coming together around some common understanding of the past, and given the increasing diversity, this needs to be created through the tool of the decision capsules. Storytelling is to create a place for discussion and dialogue on the ways in which the past has shaped the present, thus allowing a choice of directions for the future.

CONCLUSION

All these meetings with "others" are what Sandercock describes as the urban condition: the excitement of cities and the story of the urban. As we have shown, though, in general the City of Ottawa has not embraced place-making by storytelling, and rather has simply continued with "business as usual" in terms of the imposed definition of the city-region. However, as we have described, there are a variety of examples, some failures and some partial successes, that could be used to build a robust, democratic, and highly participatory collective storytelling dynamic. This is not the route Ottawa has chosen post-amalgamation.

The major conclusion to the Ottawa post-amalgamation account is the dramatic contradiction between the spatial and social potentialities of the city-region idea and the humdrum reality of the institution that was imposed on the local population. Ottawa did not have the chance to think about being a city-region or to think about whether it could be, or wanted to be, a city-region. The global-local interconnecting of city-regions could have built on Ottawa's role as the capital, and created a strong sense of being able to connect the world to Ottawa and Ottawa to the world. However, the imposition of a city institution by the provincial government – and this without agreement or even discussion – certainly made it clear to the citizens of Ottawa that they were not to be given an enhanced role of intermediate between the local and the global.

The imposition of a conventional municipal structure certainly did not help to liberate Ottawans' imaginations around place-making, as the "place" had been made, and not by them. But at the same time, we should not suggest that the lack of storytelling only stems from the imposed municipal amalgamation. It also emerges from the fairly self-satisfied image of itself that Ottawa has tried to maintain. After all, it can be seen as a story of victory, of going from a small, dirty, and somewhat dangerous lumbering community to the fourth largest city in Canada, with most signs of the lumbering past being well-hidden. However, it is perhaps this self-satisfaction that is beginning to change as signs of slower economic growth and/or stagnation begin to be felt. This is why we have highlighted, as exceptional, the two current processes that seem to have most incorporated the values of storytelling for successful planning and place-making.

REFERENCES

Andrew, C. 2007. "Trying to Be World-Class: Ottawa and the Presentation of Self." In *Urban Communication*, edited by T. Gibson and M. Lowes, 127–40. Lanham, MD: Rowman and Littlefield.

Andrew, C., B. Ray, and G. Chiasson. 2011. "Ottawa-Gatineau: Capital Formation." In *Canadian Urban Regions*, edited by L. Bourne et al., 202–35. Toronto: Oxford University Press.

Andrew, C., and G. Chiasson. 2012. "The City of Ottawa: Symbolic Representation and Public Image." In *Cities and Languages: Governance and Policy*, edited by R. Clement and C. Andrew, 41–8. Ottawa: Invenire Books.

Beauregard, R.A. 2003. "Democracy, Storytelling, and the Sustainable City." In *Story and Sustainability*, edited by B. Eckstein and J.A. Throgmorton, 65–77. Cambridge, MA: MIT Press.

Boje, D.M. 2011. "Introduction to Agential Alternatives that Shape the Future of Organizations." In *Storytelling and the Future of Organizations: An Antenarrative Handbook*, edited by D.M. Boje, 1–19. New York: Routledge.

Bradford, N., and C. Andrew. 2011. *LIPs Gathering Momentum: Early Successes, Emergent Challenges, and Recommendations for the Future*. Ottawa: Report prepared for Ontario Region, Citizenship and Immigration Canada.

Chiasson, G., and C. Andrew. 2009. "Modern Tourist Development and the Complexities of Cross-Border Identities within a Planned Capital Region." In *City Tourism: National Capital Perspectives*, edited by R. Maitland and B. Ritchie, 253–6. Wallingford, UK: CABI.

Darch, M. 2008. "Ottawa: Canada's Creative Economy Capital." Powerpoint Presentation. Ottawa: OCRI.

Eckstein, B., and J.A. Throgmorton, eds. 2003. *Story and Sustainability*. Cambridge, MA: MIT Press.

Finnegan, R. 1998. *Tales of the City*. Cambridge: Cambridge University Press.

Klodawsky, F., J. Siltanen, and C. Andrew. 2013. "Urban Contestation in a Feminist Register." *Urban Geography* 34 (4): 541–59.

Little, R.M., and L. Froggett. 2010. "Making Meaning in Muddy Waters: Representing Complexity through Community Based Storytelling." *Community Development Journal* 45 (4): 458–73.

Mandelbaum, S.J. 1991. "Telling Stories." *Journal of Planning Education and Research* 10 (3): 209–14.

– 2003. "Narrative and Other Tools." In *Story and Sustainability*, edited by B. Eckstein and J.A. Throgmorton, 185–94. Cambridge, MA: MIT Press.

Sandercock, L. 2003. "Dreaming the Sustainable City: Organizing Hope, Negotiating Fear, Mediating Memory." In *Story and Sustainability*, edited by B. Eckstein and J.A. Throgmorton, 143–66. Cambridge, MA: MIT Press.

Schneekloth, L.H., and R.G. Shipley. 2008. "The Public Realm: Weaving a Regional Civic Life." *Landscape Journal* 27 (2): 205–18.

Soja, E.W. 2003. "Tales of a Geographer-Planner." In *Story and Sustainability*, edited by B. Eckstein and J.A. Throgmorton, 207–26. Cambridge, MA: MIT Press.

8

Calibrating the Regional Map to Enhance City-Region Competitiveness

MICHAEL R. GLASS

DEVELOPING BOUNDARY REFORM SOLUTIONS FOR UNITED STATES CITY-REGION COMPETITIVENESS

The dynamic nature of urban places is a familiar subject for policy research and debate. Intra- and inter-urban shifts in employment and population patterns, economic activity, and relative competitiveness, as well as shifting patterns of investment, disinvestment, and reinvestment, converge to challenge the capacity of planners and politicians to influence city-region competitiveness in a proactive manner. Such challenges are exacerbated because urban political boundaries cannot be adjusted at the same pace at which global economic change creates new demands; indeed, political boundaries are often highly static, with many American city-regions governed using the same borders and boundaries designed for the nineteenth-century city.[1]

Local decision-makers faced with the challenge of boosting their region's economic performance have often selected between two broad options for city-region governance reform. On the one hand, functional reforms reorganize the responsibilities for urban management, ignoring the thorny issue of political boundary reform and further complicating regional governance with additional political spaces. On the other hand, structural political reforms intend a fundamental reorganization of a city-region's political geography:

erasing parochial municipalities to create new scales for urban governance. Regional reform advocates consider structural reforms a precondition for growth, especially when perceived competitors are engaged in similar reform efforts.

However, whereas boundary changes might seem appropriate in light of seemingly standard policy "best-practice" models observed in other regions, this chapter argues that following the template established by other regions is problematic because the local sociopolitical and geographic context of a city-region matters for how a reform plan will be received. The outcomes are uncertain, even when a particular model is copied perfectly. Difficulties in transferring standard strategies for city-region governance reform indicate that indigenously developed reform plans are occasionally preferable to the familiar and popularized models of city-county consolidation or special district formation.

The tension between these policy prescriptions is evident in cities across the United States, including in Pittsburgh, Pennsylvania – a post-industrial city that has experienced significant population and economic shifts over the past thirty years. Pittsburgh's reputation for being politically fragmented led to several failed attempts at city-county consolidation.

The persistent claims by local advocates that Pittsburgh and the surrounding Allegheny County required greater cooperation led to new initiatives which sought a different path toward enhancing city-region collaboration. Pittsburgh's new Congress of Neighboring Communities (CONNECT) seeks common cause between the city and its thirty-five contiguous municipalities, pursuing a third way between structural and functional reforms that sets aside structural boundary reform for a form of ad-hoc regionalism, creating a potentially significant lobbying bloc.

This chapter evaluates the evolving debates over city-region governance in Pittsburgh, which culminated in two recent attempts at regional governance: the Citizens Advisory Group (CAG) report on regional governance, and the CONNECT initiative. These efforts to enact greater city-region cohesion in governance will be framed by a discussion about the standard pathways toward city-region competitiveness – structural and functional governance reforms. The chapter concludes by questioning whether the CONNECT initiative reflects a shift away from "one size fits all" models of regional reform, and toward more endogenously based models that could provide more significant results for particular city-regions.

PITTSBURGH'S REGIONAL REFORM HISTORY

Introduction

The City of Pittsburgh and Allegheny County have had many proposals for realignment of their political boundaries (Glass 2007). During the twentieth century, periods of urban growth, decline, and resurgence caused the region's political boundaries to be reassessed, since replication of services by small municipalities seemed to create a drag on the overall competitiveness and efficiency of the county.

1920–50s: Early Regionalism and Managing Growth

The county's first significant effort at boundary reform occurred during the 1920s, when local civic reformers sought to join a (still thriving) City of Pittsburgh to the broader region, creating a Greater Pittsburgh. There were two key reasons for this early attempt at structural governance reform. First, the City of Pittsburgh was losing population to the surrounding municipalities. This concerned local boosters, as the population loss would lower Pittsburgh's comparative population ranking among cities in the 1930 Census. Second, metropolitan reform plans were popular nationally during the Progressive era. Civic reformers advocated structural reforms, arguing that fragmentation reflected outdated needs which did not match twentieth-century urbanism (Fishman 1992).

Pittsburgh's political, civic, and business leaders heeded calls for merging city and county services, yet the compromises of the political process only added confusion to the municipal structure of the county (Glass 2011). Allegheny County next attempted structural reforms in the 1950s. By this stage, suburbanization had further weakened the City of Pittsburgh.[2] Local and national reformers again called for a new metropolitan government to enhance good regional governance by bolstering the role performed by Allegheny County's government. These plans were again stymied, as municipal leaders feared regionalism as a socialistic plot against local control and freedom (Jensen 2004, 87–90).

1970–90s: De-industrialization and Managing Stagnation

Until the late 1970s and 1980s, the question of regional reform for Pittsburgh was posed in terms of how to manage economic decline.

The closure of steel mills greatly affected the communities of Allegheny County, which were faced with significant legacy costs in the form of pension obligations and civic infrastructure, while tax revenues collapsed with the loss of businesses and residents. This created a challenging environment for regional politicians, who, for the first time, had to consider urban governance in the face of economic stagnation and decline.[3]

By the 1980s, the Pittsburgh region's governance framework still reflected its early-twentieth-century roots, in spite of several attempts to modernize government through a home rule charter (Lonich 1991). While local communities continued to resist functional reforms of the region's governance, Councils of Government (COGs) provided a framework for localized cooperation.[4] Eight COGs operated in Allegheny County, enabling contiguous municipalities to share services and work toward common goals, such as responding to the challenges of de-industrialization. As this system developed, the City of Pittsburgh was facing significant population decline – Pittsburgh's population had fallen from 671,659 in 1940 to 423,959 in 1980 (Table 8.1). The "hollowing out" of the city-region's core would continue to prompt several calls for boundary reform between 1980 and 2000.

Attempts at structural consolidation were floated periodically, as the situation was considered untenable – a common complaint levied was that, with 130 minor civil divisions, 8 Councils of Government, and numerous school districts and other administrative units, the county was a national "poster child for fragmentation," and that something needed to be done for the reputation and competitiveness of the Pittsburgh city-region. Consequently, by the early 2000s, new studies were commissioned to reconsider the century-old notion of city-county merger.

2000s: Determining a New Path for Post-Industrial Pittsburgh

By the mid-2000s, elected officials were again interested in exploring the prospects for enhancing city-county consolidation. New Pittsburgh Mayor Luke Ravenstahl and Allegheny County Executive Dan Onorato empanelled the Citizens Advisory Committee on the Efficiency and Effectiveness of City-County Government (CAG) in October 2006. The CAG was tasked with refreshing the debate on city-county governance by constructing a profile on the history of regional reform attempts, and considering the county's options in

Table 8.1 Allegheny County population statistics, 1910–60

	1910	1920	1930	1940	1950	1960	Cumulative change (%)
PITTSBURGH	533,905	588,343	669,817	671,659	676,806	604,332	
Decadal change (%)		10	14	0	1	-11	
Pittsburgh as % of county	52	50	49	48	45	37	13
BALANCE OF COUNTY	484,558	597,465	704,593	739,880	838,431	1,024,255	
Decadal change (%)		23	18	5	13	22	
Balance as % of county	48	50	51	52	55	63	111
COUNTY	1,018,463	1,185,808	1,374,410	1,411,539	1,515,237	1,628,587	
Decadal change (%)		16	16	3	7	7	60

Source: US Census.

the wake of prominent examples of successful reform, with the Louisville–Jefferson County case cited as a best-practice model. Chaired by University of Pittsburgh Chancellor Mark Nordenberg, the CAG's name shows the dual emphasis for their work – the evaluation of regional government efficacy and efficiency. The project findings (released in April 2008) defined these terms by focusing on economic imperatives for the city-region in the context of increasing global inter-urban competition.

The CAG report focused solely upon the city and county; none of the other 129 local governmental units, or any of the special districts (specifically, schools), were to be considered as part of the committee's work. The final report took a favourable perspective toward consolidation for the benefits it could provide for economic development goals – benefits such as unity of leadership, increased planning capabilities, and a reduction of intergovernmental competition (Citizens Advisory Committee 2008, 9–11). The CAG was also dubious that such reforms could be enacted in the city-region, given the numerous historical failures of reform efforts.

Drawing upon the rhetoric of economic competitiveness and the logic of governmental efficiency, the findings of the CAG report echo the suggestions of successive generations of municipal scholars. The CAG report therefore represents the next iteration in a long series of reports that considered structural city-region consolidation to be the next phase for regional governance. Such an emphasis on structural consolidation for city-regions is not particular to Pittsburgh. In the next section, the two broad strategies of political reform used by regional reformers are outlined: structural and functional reforms. Each reform model has specific limitations, which Pittsburgh's recent CONNECT plan is attempting to circumvent.

GOVERNANCE REFORM PATHWAYS TO CITY-REGION COMPETITIVENESS

Boundary Reform Initiatives

Reform advocates argue that the comparatively static nature of political boundaries creates costs for city-region competitiveness; it is akin to playing sports with outmoded equipment, or fighting a battle with the maps and logistics of an earlier age. Patterns of employment, financial distress, and urban development change rapidly and leap across jurisdictional lines, frustrating the policies of urban politicians who seek to control such processes. Consequently, political boundary adjustment is one potential solution within the broader set of regional policy choices available to metropolitan planners seeking to address waning regional fortunes. Two general consolidation strategies – structural and functional – are used to correct urban political geographies that are considered outmoded. However, despite the prevalence of such strategies in policy debates over reshaping regional futures, four significant qualifications exist to boundary reform attempts.

First, although city-regions can try to alter boundaries to improve metropolitan competitiveness, boundary adjustment takes longer to implement than social or economic changes take to occur. For instance, the city of Louisville, Kentucky, began discussing a merger with the surrounding Jefferson County in 1982, with plans enacted in 2000, before consolidation was finally achieved in 2003. Meanwhile, the regional population continued to shift, with Louisville having lost 42,000 residents during the 1980–2000 period[5] (Table 8.2). This situation is not isolated to Louisville, and the lengthy legislative and consultative processes needed to achieve boundary adjustment will usually mean that boundary reform supporters are always going to engage in a process of catch-up with forces reshaping urban regions.

Second, despite their prominence and importance to national economies, city-regions are still constrained as "creatures of the state," a term coined by the nineteenth-century Justice Dillon of Iowa: minor civil divisions that are incapable of enacting structural reforms without the support of the state or states of which they are part. Under the so-called "Dillon's Rule," minor civil divisions have only those powers expressly granted to them under their state constitutions. Likewise, Dillon provided states with expansive rights to construct or destroy minor civil divisions within their borders as they saw fit. Such latitude for state control of their minor divisions has subsided with the rise of home rule charters and other mechanisms to protect existing municipalities, but the situation remains that any municipality wishing to alter its dimensions will need to receive the blessing of the state.

Third, boundary reform initiatives are subject to resistance by local constituencies who fear that changes to the political status quo would negatively impact their resources or quality of life. Boundary

Table 8.2 Jefferson County & Louisville population statistics, 1960–2000

	Jefferson County population	Percent change	Louisville population	Percent change
1960	610,947		390,000	
1980	685,004	+12.12	298,694	–23.41
2000	693,604	+1.26	256,000	–14.29

Source: US Census; Kentucky State Data Center.

reforms are reactions by specific constituencies to perceived inefficiencies or inadequacies. However, such perceptions are not necessarily universally shared; what is to one planner an anachronistic municipality deserving of dissolution may be to another planner – let alone a neighbourhood resident – a significant historic district worthy of protection. Such conflicts may be political, social, or economic in nature, with concerns over loss of representation, identity, or opportunity. The bottom line is that boundary reform initiatives require an often lengthy consultative process to receive support from local and regional stakeholders who could otherwise extend or scuttle the process.

Finally, metropolitan regions are highly sensitive to exogenous processes and events, such as global market shifts. The location decisions of transnational corporations, funding allocations from state and federal sources, and market shifts in housing desirability are just a few of the factors beyond the control of any city-region. Since these shifts cannot be directly controlled by metropolitan areas, the best-laid plans for metropolitan regions can be derailed, including plans for structural or functional boundary reform.

Despite these significant limitations on city-region action, boundary reform conversations persist, often for the stated purpose of enhancing economic competitiveness. The solution that many city-regions have implemented to address the issue of seemingly outdated political boundaries is to reform their boundaries, bringing them – at least temporarily – into alignment with the social and economic patterns that are influencing their area. Reform projects fall under two broad rubrics: structural reforms, whereby the political jurisdictions of a metropolitan region are redrawn; and functional reforms, which accommodate and circumvent the inherited political maps of a region by reorganizing the responsibilities and relationships of regional actors. The next section outlines each of these pathways to city-region competitiveness, before I note some problems for policy-makers who seek to adopt these familiar strategies within their own regions.

Functional Reform

Functional reform refers here to governance reforms that reorganize the responsibilities for local or regional authorities in charge of assets such as infrastructure, emergency services, and transportation. Special districts for the management of assets such as water services, policing, or other activities may be created at either local or regional scales. Such districts are defined as "independent, limited-purpose local governments that exist as separate legal entities with substantial administrative and fiscal independence from general-purpose government" (Marlow 1995, 569), and can be considered a type of functional consolidation intended to construct efficiencies through economies of scale and to reduce redundancies created by service replication in adjacent municipalities. Such reforms may be conducted on a service-specific basis, and do not directly affect the political geographies of city-regions, although the "layering" of several special districts for specific services onto the base political map of a region can serve to create its own set of complexities, as the number of districts multiplies, and the number of stakeholders invested in the new districts increases.

The use of functional reforms and special districts has complicated the political map of the United States. In 2007, there were 36,011 general-purpose sub-county administrative units, consisting of municipalities, towns, and townships. By comparison, the United States had 37,381 special districts (special-purpose administrative units, not including school districts) in the same year, representing an increase of 5,826 (or nearly 18.5 percent) since the 1992 Census of Governments (US Census 1997; US Census 2007). Therefore, there are more than double the total number of sub-county administrative units, and special districts account for 90 percent of the growth in local governments within the United States during the second half of the twentieth century (Miller 2002, 43). This situation implies both that metropolitan regions are likely to be characterized by a complex political mosaic, and that local communities are finding at least some utility in using special districts to enhance municipal management.

Councils of Government (COGs) and Metropolitan Planning Organizations (MPOs) are two types of regional special districts that

have sought to reform city-region governance through federal mandate. COGs developed out of post-1945 federal planning initiatives,
and were by the mid-1970s run by locally elected officials and
administered with HUD 701 funding (Conant and Myers 2006,
252–3). COGs had limited authority to pursue city-region planning
initiatives, depending (as is often the case) on the priorities and abilities of the local officials serving on a given COG. MPOs are another
form of regional special district arising from federal legislation –
namely the Intermodal Surface Transportation Efficiency Act (1991).
This legislation was intended to enhance regional planning in
America's city-regions by requiring that each metropolitan area in
the United States designate an MPO to act as a clearinghouse for
federal transportation funding. The MPOs have amassed a mixed
record: while they have provided a conduit for some regional planning, recent studies have found that their capacity to enhance
regional cooperation is limited (Vogel and Nezelkiewicz 2002), and
that MPO boards have not been representative of their local communities, with central cities and minorities frequently marginalized
from representative participation when compared to the suburban
and rural communities of the region (Sanchez 2006).

City-regions may choose to develop special districts for very specific purposes, such as the pooling of assets to support and sustain
facilities that are considered regionally significant. Such districts can
be considered metropolitan-scale examples of similar mechanisms
that function at neighbourhood scales, such as Business Improvement
Districts. In the regional case, asset management districts are used to
support regional development and communal assets through the levy
of some tax vehicle assessed across the entire district. For example, in
1994, Allegheny County and the City of Pittsburgh (along with associated public and private partners) passed legislation enacting the
Allegheny County Regional Asset District, which created a new one-
percent sales tax to support regional assets (Turner 1995). Another
example of a regional asset district is the Twin Cities Metropolitan
Area Fiscal Disparities Program, centered on the cities of Minneapolis–
St Paul (Hinze and Baker 2005). This program, enacted in 1975,
shares forty percent of the growth in commercial-industrial property
tax between the seven counties surrounding the Twin Cities in order
to reduce regional development inequalities, which can occur through
business development (such as stadiums, freeway interchanges, or
shopping complexes) potentially located in a particular area of the

city-region. Goetz and Kayser (1993) evaluated the proposition that this asset-sharing district could act as a disincentive for competition between municipalities within the region, but found that this cooperative asset plan had not depressed competition between municipalities within the district – thus suggesting that this form of functional reform could enhance regional cooperation without negatively affecting regional economic development.

Structural Reform

Structural reforms differ from functional reforms by involving the direct redrawing of regional political boundaries. These reforms attempt to reflect contemporary or anticipated socio-economic patterns for a given metropolitan area, and are usually the consequence of sustained deliberative action by local and regional actors who seek boundary changes. Structural reforms are frequently (and historically) presented using the rhetoric of economic competitiveness, with a particular regional configuration depicted as inefficient or ineffective in that regard. For instance, the city-county consolidation recommended for Pittsburgh in 1929 was one example of structural reforms recommended by Progressive-era reform institutions such as the National Municipal League, who published reports promoting the perspective that consolidated city-regions could provide services with greater efficiency, while fragmented regions were not practical for meeting the needs of modern American cities (Studenski 1931). While the economic efficiency claims of structural reformers are contested by public choice proponents – such as in the classic defense by Tiebout (1956) – city-region consolidation reforms remain a popular policy goal for regional advocates. Proponents such as David Rusk (1995) argue in favour of metropolitan government to combat comparative regional decline or intra-regional population shifts, expanding city boundaries to counteract the "hollowing out" of central cities. Structural boundary reform may also be recommended to counteract urban sprawl (Carruthers and Gudmundur 2002), with other supporters arguing that consolidated city-region governments provide more effective land use planning tools to promote "smart growth"–type anti-sprawl policies (Griffith 2001).

The process of structural boundary reform is prone to regional variation. As with functional boundary reforms, the legislation governing minor civil division changes varies between states. Additionally, the presence of unincorporated land in states such as Texas, Arizona,

and Florida provides a lower barrier to annexations along city boundaries. David Rusk (1995) argues that states with unincorporated territory provide a "dowry" to cities wishing to expand their total land
area, making structural boundary reform a likelier course of action
under these conditions. In contrast, states such as Pennsylvania and
Ohio lack any unincorporated land, with every square acre of those
states "belonging" to a given minor civil division. In areas such as
these, compromise between competing local governments is required
to facilitate any such structural changes, making the process more
complicated, and less likely to occur.

A prominent example of structural political consolidation in the
United States occurred in 2003, with the merger of the city of
Louisville, Kentucky, with Jefferson County. Louisville's political
experience during the mid-to-late twentieth century is similar to that
of many other mid-sized American cities, with population loss to the
surrounding suburbs, industrial transformation, and legacy costs
related to infrastructure and pension funds. Table 8.2 shows that the
relative shifts in population for Louisville and Jefferson County
were significant – while the central city lost 134,000 residents from
1960 to 2000, Jefferson County gained over 82,000 residents during
the same period (US Census figures accessed through Kentucky State
Data Center). While these figures do not reflect a direct population
shift, they are indicative of the centrifugal forces experienced by
urban core areas during the past half-century. Such forces, when
added to somewhat antagonistic relationships between the city and
county, and the loss of employment away from the "core" of the city-
region, provoked Louisville's business and political leaders to call for
consolidation with Jefferson County, which would again elevate
Louisville's population, improve its tax base, and, most importantly,
enhance its economic competitiveness.

Economic imperatives performed a central role in advocacy for
structural boundary reform between Louisville and the surrounding
Jefferson County. Beginning in the early 1980s and continuing for
the next twenty years, business leaders in the City of Louisville continued to emphasize the city's economic health and declining competitiveness in the advocacy for merger plans with the county. The
economic justification behind structural boundary reform is based
in two arguments. First, that a consolidated city-region can speak
"with one voice" on matters of economic development policy, hence
providing greater leverage to attract or retain firms. Such leverage
has historically been tied to the increased population of the

combined region, providing a tool for city boosters who can argue that their city is the *n*th largest in the United States. Second, promoters of city-region consolidation argue that the economies of scale and reduction of duplicated services implied in boundary reform result in more efficient governance, which may reduce waste and taxes.

The city-county merger for Louisville and Jefferson County was a lengthy process, driven in part by the antagonistic relations between the city and county, and partly because of the complex nature of structural reforms. From the early 1980s, boosters for consolidation gradually converged on a plan to combine the city and unincorporated portions of the county to enable cost savings, greater capacity for economic coordination, and the perception of increased national stature through increasing the city's population (Savitch and Vogel 2004). By 2000, the plan was approved by Kentucky's state legislature; it was ratified by the region's population in 2001, and the newly merged city and county came into effect in 2003. Beyond the actual success of the merger, analysis is guarded as to what structural reform meant for the Louisville region. In an early evaluation of the consolidation, Savitch and Vogel argued that the merger reduced African-American political representation within the new city-region, and diluted advocacy for the central city. In a later evaluation of the merger's impact on the city-region, Savitch, Vogel, and Ye again found little real regional economic benefit arising from the new structure (Savitch, Vogel, and Ye 2009). Whereas it is true that less than a decade of evidence is insufficient to make claims about the long-term viability of the Louisville–Jefferson County merger, the early evaluations by Savitch and Vogel make clear that structural boundary reforms have uncertain consequences for city-regions. Nevertheless, structural reforms remain on the table for metropolitan areas with perceived failings in regional governance or economic competitiveness. The Louisville merger, as the most significant consolidation in the United States during the past thirty years, is now used as a potential model for structural reforms in other city-regions, including Pittsburgh (Citizens Advisory Committee 2008).

Transferring Best Practices Is Problematic

While boundary change may seem an appropriate strategy for regions facing socio-economic shifts or comparative decline, and "doing nothing" during periods of regional stress may not be palatable politics or policy, the functional and structural reform options outlined in this section do not necessarily provide pathways that other cities should emulate. Specific models of regional governance – such as the Louisville–Jefferson County merger, or the Twin Cities Metropolitan Area Fiscal Disparities Program – are considered "best practice" plans in settings beyond their source regions because they suggest a familiar, well-documented, "turn-key" solution that a city-region seeking a new approach might adopt with relative ease.

However, specific functional or structural reform plans are not necessarily suitable for adoption by other cities – in a large sense, place-based context matters. For instance, the presence or absence of unincorporated land, the strength and willingness of political stakeholders at the local, state, and federal scales to cooperate with intended governance reforms, the relative strength of the regional economy, the institutional history of the region, and the relationships between municipal units within a given city-region can all influence the ways in which reform plans are received and translated in different regions. Such difficulties in transmitting standard strategies for city-region governance reform suggest that indigenously developed reform plans are occasionally preferable to the familiar and popularized models of city-county consolidation or special district formation. The next section examines one such policy alternative.

PITTSBURGH'S CONNECT INITIATIVE

Introduction

After the long history of failed attempts at both structural and functional governance reforms, proponents for regional governance in the Pittsburgh city-region embarked upon a new path, which I argue provides a third way toward partnerships for economic competitiveness. Led by advocates familiar with the pitfalls inherent in both structural and functional reforms described above, the new CONNECT program is neither structural reform (as it does not alter the political geography of the Pittsburgh region), nor purely functional reform (as it operates on a case-by-case basis, and is hence more fluid than special districts). Rather, the CONNECT program provides flexibility for local communities to act communally when appropriate, and individually when desired.

Formation

CONNECT originated in the University of Pittsburgh's Innovation Clinic, led by Dr David Miller. The primary rationale supporting CONNECT's formation was the combined economic and political strength of Allegheny County's thirty-six "core communities" – Pittsburgh and the thirty-five contiguous municipalities. Taken as a set of political jurisdictions, the CONNECT constituency accounts for a significant amount of the Pittsburgh city-region's population, employment, and political representation. With seemingly no good short- to medium-term prospects for the structural reform of the Pittsburgh city-region's political spaces, the erection of a new form of inter-jurisdictional network gained interest, and a steering committee was empanelled in 2007 to identify the way forward to create new connections between the thirty-six targeted municipalities.

The steering committee argued that the proposed Congress of Neighboring Communities could leverage greater results for the members by acting in unison. By bringing together the City of Pittsburgh with the thirty-five municipalities that shared a common border, CONNECT assembled a diverse set of communities that held significant collective social, economic, and political power. As of 2009, the CONNECT communities accounted for 56 percent of Allegheny County's population, and 75 percent of the county's jobs. The CONNECT communities also accounted for a majority of the political representation for Allegheny County, with fourteen of fifteen County Council districts, seventeen of twenty-three Pennsylvania House districts, and all three federal House of Representatives districts that overlap the county also overlapping the core CONNECT region.

The early stages of organizing support for CONNECT involved negotiating with political leaders in the City of Pittsburgh and the surrounding municipalities. The City of Pittsburgh was presented as an equal partner to the thirty-five smaller municipalities present at the meeting, which marked a shift from the traditional hierarchal manner in which the city presented itself when dealing with its political neighbours.

Structure of the CONNECT Program

The planning for CONNECT was completed by 2009, with monthly planning meetings among a small group of CONNECT representatives (including the City of Pittsburgh, Allegheny County, and municipal officials). During these initial planning meetings, the decision was made to focus on public transportation and water/sewer issues, given their significant and explicit character as problems of inter-jurisdictional interest. The inaugural congress was held on 19 June, with thirty-four of the eligible communities choosing to actively participate. Economic development imperatives were explicit to the purpose of CONNECT from the outset, and were a key justification for the coordinating function of the new initiative. This goal was introduced at the initial congress, where the official mission statement of CONNECT was declared as follows:

> CONNECT coordinates the collective activities between the city of Pittsburgh and the 35 municipalities that share its border through: Advocating for and voicing the collective interests of the urban core and its 680,000 residents; developing and enhancing ways the 36 municipalities work together to deliver important public services; and maintaining a forum for the discussion, deliberation, and implementation of new ways to maximize economic prosperity for Western Pennsylvania. (Resolution 09-01, CONNECT 2009)

CONNECT sought to identify the formal and informal inter-governmental arrangements that currently operated amongst the core communities of the Pittsburgh city-region, in order to identify new opportunities to leverage existing regional arrangements. From a practical perspective, the organizational structure of CONNECT enabled all members to have a role in planning and coordinating the functions of the organization. Three standing committees – an executive committee, a policy committee, and an operational committee – were created to oversee the functions of CONNECT (Table 8.3).

Each municipality serves on the Executive Committee on an ongoing basis, while each community serves a two-year term on either the Policy or the Operational Committees (CONNECT 2010). The distribution of committee assignments follows an algorithm based in municipal population size rather than geographical location, since the communities of CONNECT vary greatly in population (from 427 to 311,218 in 2009; see Figure 8.1).

Table 8.3 CONNECT committee functions

Committee Name	Functions	Membership
EXECUTIVE	• Determines direction for CONNECT • Initially charged with writing by-laws • Empowered to act on behalf of CONNECT between sessions	• Representation from each CONNECT community
OPERATIONS	• Examines existing inter-governmental agreements • Identifies spaces for new intergovernmental arrangements • Recommends new service-sharing arrangements to Executive Committee	• Eighteen CONNECT communities • Two-year terms • Population-based membership algorithm
POLICY	• Provides arena for policy-level discussion • Identifies issues of common concern among CONNECT membership • Educates residents on relevant policy issues • Recommends issues to Executive Committee	• Eighteen CONNECT communities • Two-year terms • Population-based membership algorithm

Source: CONNECT Bylaws 2010.

Preliminary Successes and Challenges

Even as the CONNECT organization was launched, significant challenges awaited the successful implementation of its planned programs. One of the potential challenges facing the CONNECT organization is the lack of an official mandate to act on behalf of the region it purports to represent. Despite the ratification of CONNECT's mission of intergovernmental cooperation by its constituent members, there is no electoral mandate from the populations of CONNECT's community to act regionally on their behalf – in essence, CONNECT could be perceived as yet another special district in a region already crowded by such districts. In addition, other intergovernmental organizations (such as the COGS and county government) have more established and legitimate voices in urban

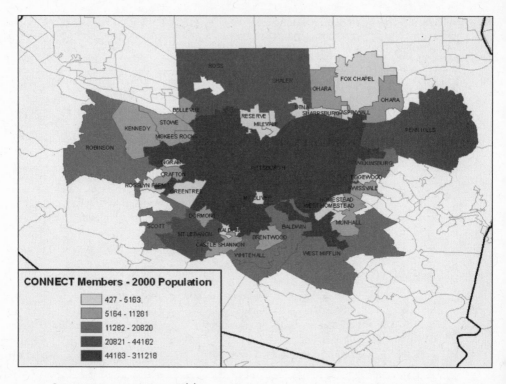

8.1 CONNECT communities

governance beyond the municipal system. In order to address this potential conflict, CONNECT argues that it supplements the role of Allegheny County's eight local COGs by focusing on the Pittsburgh city-region's "urban core," whereas the COGs focus on communities which radiate outwards from the core (CONNECT 2010).

Another problem that CONNECT could face is if the parochial interests or uneven power of specific communities interfere with the primary mission of the broader organization. From the outset of CONNECT's planning process, suggestions were raised that rather than a regional organization, a set of sub-regional groups be convened to address "local concerns." Also, the varying political and economic power of the municipalities might lead to a less-than-equitable division of resources and power, although the rotating committee structure of the organization is intended to prevent that from occurring. Despite the potential problems that are inevitable in start-up enterprises such as CONNECT, by mid-2010 the organization had achieved significant early successes. First, the organization had obtained initial funding from the regional foundation community, enabling the hiring of full-time staff to guide the organization and lobby for additional support from state and private sources. Second, a set of local intermediaries (termed "expeditors") were identified for each CONNECT municipality. These intermediaries provide first points of contact for liaisons between CONNECT and the municipalities, and enable a secondary system for discussing inter-municipal collaboration beyond the formal committee structure of CONNECT. Third, the organization began the process of identifying existing inter-municipal agreements, and facilitated the participation of four CONNECT communities in a reverse energy auction, providing total savings of $530,792 for the municipalities (CONNECT 2010, 10).

REFORM CHALLENGES FOR CITY-REGIONS – THE PITTSBURGH CASE

While the jury remains out on the long-term efficacy of CONNECT to provide a new pathway toward city-region cooperation for Pittsburgh's municipalities, we can conclude by considering two issues – CONNECT's role as a boundary reform platform, and the potential for boundary reform initiatives to provide solutions to the perceived problems facing other city-regions. With regard to CONNECT's role, I will return to the three preliminary questions for this chapter: whether CONNECT forms a middle path between traditional boundary reform pathways, how the participation of regional stakeholders influences the chances for boundary reform, and whether the Pittsburgh experience represents a shift away from a "one size fits all" model of regionalism. I then close with two key points – first, the significance of geographic context to boundary reform initiatives, and second, the ultimate vulnerability of city-regions to exogenous forces.

Evaluation of CONNECT as a Boundary Reform Platform

American city-regions seeking political boundary reform have usually chosen between two general and traditional policy choices – the structural reform of local political units, and the functional revision of regional responsibilities for governance. From the preliminary evidence regarding CONNECT, it seems that this boundary reform initiative is charting a "third way" between these two choices. The CONNECT program is not an example of structural reform, as it is not seeking to change the political boundaries of the Pittsburgh city-region; and yet the program is codifying new relationships among the thirty-six municipal members. At the same time, whereas there is a degree of functional boundary change occurring through the definition of the thirty-six communities as members of a shared congress, the partnerships that are emerging occur on a case-by-case basis, providing flexibility for local control and individual action when desired. The CONNECT program holds boundary reform conversations for the stated purpose of improving economic competitiveness, but with the flexibility to adjust as conditions warrant – hence, CONNECT seems to provide something between functional and structural boundary reform.

The next question is whether CONNECT represents a shift away from "one size fits all" models of regional boundary reform. For both structural and functional boundary reform, there are a limited number of cases considered to provide "best practice" models for other regions to follow. The Louisville–Jefferson County, Kentucky, merger is a prominent example of structural reform, cited in several Pittsburgh-based reports considering the idea of boundary change. Likewise, city-regions interested in pursuing functional reforms often study models of regional asset sharing (such as TCMA or ARAD). The problem with evaluating and adopting best practice models from other places is that the place-specific contexts of model source-regions will probably mean that attempts at replicating a particular best practice model in different areas will produce different results. Despite the uncertainty of policy outcomes, regional leaders need not be paralyzed when choosing between different reform plans – what is required is the capacity to first evaluate the conditions that made a specific plan work in a given geographic context, and then to consider whether those conditions are present in the target city-region.

This evaluative process was followed in the Pittsburgh case, where CONNECT is leveraging local knowledge about the (failed) history of boundary reform to create something novel to the Pittsburgh city-region. A beneficial feature of CONNECT is the voluntary nature of the regional associations that are being entered into by the thirty-six member municipalities. This is significant; voluntary mechanisms for regional governance give stakeholders incentive to participate more meaningfully, as there is little sense of coercion by other scales of government. John Debolske[6] summarized intergovernmental politics as a set of axioms shaped by the relative position of a government within the urban hierarchy, with politicians at a given scale acting according to the following rules: 1) the level of government I am with is good; 2) any level of government above me is putting it to me; and 3) any level of government below me cannot be trusted (Berman 2003, 1–18). Hence the type of horizontal collaboration embodied by CONNECT has the capacity to reduce suspicion regarding the motivations of other actors. Conversely, no electoral mandate accompanies CONNECT, and so there are likely to be limitations to the capacity for action as the program develops.

City-region consolidation is a long process in any context, as indicated by Pittsburgh's struggles with this issue (dating to the 1920s), or Louisville's twenty-year path to consolidation with Jefferson County. Regional leaders are best advised to understand that debates over regional futures take time, especially when a full array of stakeholders is involved, as is the case in the CONNECT example. While the jury, as stated, remains out on the long-term efficacy of CONNECT, the flexibility of the model means that it is easier to be "proactive" toward economic changes which might influence the Pittsburgh city-region in the future. Municipal boundaries remain intact within the framework of the organization, which leaves open the question of whether it is possible or necessary to circumvent "anachronistic" political boundaries under conditions of ad-hoc regionalism. For city-region reforms to be considered sustainable beyond the short term of electoral cycles, reform strategies should also be aligned to the broader economic and political processes that affect the city-region. For example, reforms to city-regions in the Southwest and Mountain West of the United States (e.g. Phoenix and Salt Lake City), which are characterized by rapid population growth and a larger geographic extent of minor civil divisions, require significantly different regional policy vehicles from those that would be appropriate in stagnating or declining city-regions.

Partnerships for Competitiveness: Links to Other City-Regions

This chapter has evaluated the prospect of political boundary reforms in American city-regions, with a particular emphasis on the Pittsburgh, Pennsylvania, case. After outlining Pittsburgh's history with urban political reform, I defined the two broad pathways to city-region competitiveness – namely, structural and functional boundary reforms. Regardless of which boundary reform is attempted, the rhetoric used to advocate for new plans is often similar – the attempt to circumvent anachronistic political divisions in order to enhance the economic performance of city-regions. While this argument for boundary reform is persuasive, the practice of boundary reform is more difficult, as re-spatializing a city-region takes a long time to complete, and is likely to lag behind socio-economic changes (see also Shields, this volume). The review of Pittsburgh's history with boundary reform exemplifies the problems with efforts to change the political map of a city-region. In Pittsburgh's case, unsuccessful reform efforts occurred from the 1920s until the 2000s – a testament to the reluctance of local citizens and stakeholders to amend the status quo, regardless of rapidly deteriorating economic conditions during the late twentieth century.

The resistance to structural and functional changes led to an attempted third way: the CONNECT program, housed at the University of Pittsburgh's Innovation Clinic. This program is defined as a form of ad-hoc regionalism, neither a structural nor a functional reform effort, whereby the City of Pittsburgh and the thirty-five contiguous communities come together to lobby for shared interests. While the program is still in its early stages of development, there are positive early signs about the efficacy of this approach to city-region partnerships.

Of course, when it comes to frameworks for intra-regional cooperation and boundary change initiatives, place matters – meaning that specific solutions used in particular locations might not travel well to different city-regions. The social, economic, political, and historical conditions of a given location all affect the type of policy solutions that can be used, and affect how policies imported from elsewhere will function. Despite the challenges of transferring governance models (or other policies) from place to place, policy transfer is increasingly prevalent, and is argued to signify the diffusion of particular ideologies of governance across space (Peck and Theodore 2010; Peck 2002). Bunnell and Das have termed the transfer of policies "serial seduction," as globally active consultancy firms and other proponents sell the promise of given policies from city to city, perhaps regardless of the "fit" that those models have for their intended recipient (Bunnell and Das 2010). At the same time as there are risks involved in adopting urban reform policies tailored for different contexts, there are two potential benefits to enhancing and accepting locally specific solutions, in the manner conducted by Pittsburgh's CONNECT program. First, there is a cost and time savings to consider, as a region need not spend time attempting to shoehorn a popular (yet inappropriate) model into its regional context. Second, there are competitive advantages to protecting local specificities, as that provides a point of difference from other city-regions. With that said, it remains important for city-regions to monitor strategies pursued by other areas – yet without rushing to emulate them. The examples of structural and functional reform as well as the "third way" approach of CONNECT therefore provide three questions for the leaders and policy-makers of city-regions to consider before pursuing reform:

1   Are the regional challenges we perceive significant enough to prevent them from being addressed by our current governance arrangements, and if so, do regional leaders have the time and resources to commit to finding a new model for city-region governance?
2   Does the reform model we are considering as a template for our own city-region have its roots in similar socio-economic circumstances, or is it being brought to us by consultants promoting a policy which does not fit our local context?
3   If we implement this new model of city-region governance, will we have sacrificed some part of our institutional character which differentiates ourselves from city-regions whom we consider to be competitors for investments, people, and/or prestige?

The structural and functional reform pathways discussed in this chapter offer city-regions the opportunity to consider and reshape their future trajectories. The emergence of "third way" solutions toward enhancing regional prosperity (such as the CONNECT program discussed here) indicate the continuing dynamism of contemporary city-regions. However, in closing, there must be a caveat. Cities remain vulnerable to exogenous forces, and to their position within broader national and regional political regimes. The position of Justice Dillon that minor civil divisions are "creatures of the state" remains true, and cities are only empowered to act to the degree allowed by state and national governments. At the same time, other shifts – such as economic crisis and opportunity – continue to shape the fortunes of city-regions in ways outpacing the capacity of cities to react. Finally, the inexorable dynamism of cities is what continues to draw people to live, work, and research in them. Just as cities changed from the form of the nineteenth century to the shape of the twentieth-century city, future regional shifts are inevitable, requiring that those interested in city-region governance must always be ready to adapt to changing conditions.

NOTES

1 Indeed, as Harrison points out in this volume, the city-region concept is used internationally as a means toward aligning urban-regional planning with state territorial strategies. As in his English and German examples, the US state orchestrates the strategies available to city-regions by regulating the capacity for structural or functional boundary reforms.
2 Between 1920 and 1960 the City of Pittsburgh's population increased from nearly 534,000 to 604,000 – a growth rate of 13 percent. However, in the same period, the rest of Allegheny County increased by 111 percent to slightly over one million residents, or nearly two thirds of the entire county population.
3 Pittsburgh's de-industrialization during the period is well recorded, and sits as part of the broader de-industrialization events that created America's "rustbelt" cities. Disinvestment, declining profits, economic globalization, and mismanagement are all cited as partial causes of the collapse of Pittsburgh's steel industry, but regardless of the culprit, the cumulative effect was severe for the city-region's economy and psyche.
4 These were enabled by Pennsylvania's Intergovernmental Cooperation Act (1972).
5 After the 2003 merger, the combined Louisville–Jefferson County area had a total population of 557,113.
6 John Debolske was affiliated with the League of Arizona Cities and Towns.

REFERENCES

Berman, D. 2003. *Local Government and the States*. New York: M.E. Sharpe.
Bunnell, T., and D. Das. 2010. "Urban Pulse – A Case of Serial Seduction: Urban Policy Transfer from Kuala Lumpur to Hyderabad." *Urban Geography* 31 (3): 277–84.
Carruthers, J.I., and F. Ularfsson Gudmundur. 2002. "Fragmentation and Sprawl: Evidence from Interregional Analysis." *Growth and Change* 33 (3): 312–40.

Chinitz, B. 1961. "Contrasts in Agglomeration: New York and Pittsburgh." *American Economic Review* 51 (2): 279–89.

Citizens Advisory Committee. 2008. *Government for Growth: Forging a Bright Future Built on Unity, Efficiency, Equity, and Equality.* Pittsburgh, PA: Citizens Advisory Committee on the Efficiency and Effectiveness of City-County Government.

Conant, R.W., and D. Myers. 2006. *Toward a More Perfect Union: The Governance of Metropolitan America.* Novato, CA: Chandler & Sharp.

CONNECT. 2009. *First Annual Congress of Neighboring Communities.* Pittsburgh, PA: Congress of Neighboring Communities.

– 2010. *Second Annual Congress of Neighboring Communities.* Pittsburgh, PA: Congress of Neighboring Communities.

Fishman, R. 1992. "The Regional Plan and the Transformation of the Industrial Metropolis." In *The Landscape of Modernity: Essays on New York City, 1900–1940,* edited by D. Ward and O. Zunz, 106–25. New York: Russell Sage.

Glass, M.R. 2007. *Changing Spaces – Communities, Governance, and the Politics of Growth.* State College, PA: Unpublished PhD dissertation, Pennsylvania State University.

– 2011. "Metropolitan Reform in Allegheny County: The Local Failure of National Reform Advocacy, 1920–1929." *Journal of Urban History* 37 (1): 90–116.

Goetz, E.G., and T. Kayser. 1993. "Competition and Cooperation in Economic Development: A Study of the Twin Cities Metropolitan Area." *Economic Development Quarterly* 7 (1): 63–78.

Griffith, J.C. 2001. "Smart Governance for Smart Growth: The Need for Regional Governments." *Georgia State University Law Review.* Paper 993.

Hinze, S., and K. Baker. 2005. *Minnesota's Fiscal Disparities Programs.* Legislative Research Report. St. Paul, MN: Minnesota State House Research Department.

Jensen, B.K. 2004. *Masters of Their Own Destiny: Allegheny County Government Reform Efforts, 1929–1998.* Pittsburgh, PA: Unpublished PhD dissertation, Carnegie Mellon University.

Lonich, D. 1991. *Metropolitics in Allegheny County.* Pittsburgh, PA: Unpublished PhD thesis, Carnegie Mellon University.

Lubove, R. 1969. *Twentieth Century Pittsburgh: Government, Business, and Environmental Change.* New York: John Wiley & Sons.

Marlow, M. 1995. "The Influence of Special District Governments on Public Spending and Debt." *Applied Economics* 27 (7): 569–84.

Miller, D.Y. 2002. *The Regional Governing of Metropolitan America.* Boulder, CO: Westview Press.

Peck, J. 2002. "Political Economies of Scale: Fast Policy, Interscalar Relations, and Neoliberal Workfare." *Economic Geography* 78 (3): 331–60.

Peck, J., and N. Theodore. 2010. "Recombinant Workfare, Across the Americas: Transnationalizing 'Fast' Social Policy." *Geoforum* 41 (2): 195–208.

Rusk, D. 1995. *Cities Without Suburbs*. Washington, DC: Woodrow Wilson Center Press.

Sanchez, T.W. 2006. *An Inherent Bias? Geographic and Racial-Ethnic Patterns of Metropolitan Planning Organization Boards*. Washington, DC: Brookings Institution.

Savitch, H.V., and R.K. Vogel. 2004. "Suburbs Without a City: Power and City-County Consolidation." *Urban Affairs Review* 39 (6): 758–90.

Savitch, H.V., R.K. Vogel, and L. Ye. 2009. "Beyond the Rhetoric: Lessons from Louisville's Consolidation." *The American Review of Public Administration* 40 (1): 3–28.

Studenski, P. 1931. *The Government of Metropolitan Areas*. New York: National Municipal League.

Tiebout, C. 1956. "A Pure Theory of Local Expenditures." *Journal of Political Economy* 64 (5): 416–24.

Turner, J.W. 1995. "The Allegheny County Regional Asset District: Communities Thinking and Acting Like a Region." *Government Finance Review* 11 (3): 19–22.

US Census. 1997. *Census of Governments*. Washington, DC: US Census.

– 2007. *Census of Governments*. Washington, DC: US Census.

Vogel, R.K., and N. Nezelkiewicz. 2002. "Metropolitan Planning Organizations and the New Regionalism: The Case of Louisville." *Publius* 32 (1): 107–29.

9

Resilience and Governance in City-Regions: Lessons from Waterloo, Ontario

DAVID A. WOLFE

INTRODUCTION

Efforts to sustain the economic performance of regions through periods of disruptive change, such as we have recently experienced, prompt the need for a radical rethinking of our analysis of the factors that contribute to economic development. One such approach that has gained growing appeal in this period adopts the concept of resilience to understand why some regions are better able to resist or recover from external economic shocks, which disrupt their past growth pattern, while others are less so. Resilient cities and regions are those best able to adapt to changing economic and competitive circumstances, and to deploy their economic and institutional resources to respond to external threats and take advantage of new opportunities. They are able to focus their investments in research and innovation in areas where those investments are likely to have the greatest impact. However, the resilience of a region does not depend on economic or market forces alone. Rather, it involves a complex mix of private, public, and civic institutions working together to chart a new growth path for the region. Regional resilience requires a new approach to the governance mechanisms for policy development that incorporate regional exercises to identify and cultivate their assets, undertake collaborative processes to plan and implement change, and encourage a regional mindset that fosters growth (Wolfe 2010).

Canada is a highly urban society, and becoming more so with each passing decade. Its city-regions are not just the dominant sites of economic activity, but they are also the leading edge of innovation that will generate the new ideas, new products, and new industries that will drive the economy in the future. The accelerating trend towards globalization and the evolution towards a more knowledge-based and creative economy pose a set of challenges and opportunities for city-regions. However, their ability to respond to these challenges, and take advantage of the opportunities, depends upon their capacity to weather external shocks and to adopt new development strategies – in other words, their resilience. In order to appreciate their capacity to respond to these changes, we need to analyze how the interplay between the private economic dimensions of city-regions and their underlying political and civic institutions affect their pattern of development and their potential for resilience.

This chapter explores the way in which the intersection between path-dependent trajectories of development and the strategic choices made by regions affects their capacity to deal with external shocks. Efforts to sustain the economic performance of regions through periods of disruptive change need to commence with the institutional capacity of those regions to manage their transition. The concept of "regional resilience" has been applied with increasing frequency across a wide number of cases to analyze and understand why different city-regions display a highly different capacity to respond to external shocks and chart new development trajectories for themselves. This chapter examines the different approaches to the concept that have been used in the literature. It then focuses on one of those concepts, which emerges out of an evolutionary approach to economic geography, and which builds on the path-dependent understanding of how regional economies change and develop over time. It explains why an evolutionary approach to resilience requires more than a narrowly economic view of the concept, and borrows from the literature on governance and civic engagement to explain why the underlying civic institutions of a city-region are crucial to its economic resilience. It then applies this understanding to a case study of the mid-sized Canadian city-region of Waterloo, Ontario, to demonstrate how a mix of private, public, and civic institutions have been crucial to the region's ability to adapt to changing economic circumstances and chart a new developmental path for itself.

REGIONAL RESILIENCE AND THE SUSTAINABILITY OF CITY-REGIONS

Recent theoretical and empirical research on economic development describes city-regions as key drivers of economic growth and prosperity, as well as the primary locus where social dynamics of innovation play out "on the ground." This literature underlines the importance of agglomeration economies and proximity as key factors that facilitate the transmission of knowledge among the leading-edge sectors that are increasingly concentrated in urban regions. The same evidence indicates, however, that the fruits of knowledge-intensive economic activity are distributed unequally between cities of different sizes, industrial specialization, and labour markets, as well as between people within those cities (Wolfe and Bramwell 2008). Efforts to improve the economic performance of city-regions, especially small and medium-sized ones (which are viewed as being relatively disadvantaged in the emerging global economy), need to address considerations of both industrial transformation and their mechanisms of local governance at the same time. Increasing analytical attention is focused on cities' capacities to formulate responses to their own particular set of challenges. In this sense, there is growing interest in the abilities of cities to alter their trajectory of economic development, and a belief that "communities can affect the tenor and trajectory of regional economies through a concerted, organized, *organizing* approach" (Safford 2004, 39).

One aspect of resilience that underlies its recent popularity is the openness of the term, and the ease with which it has been applied to the study of a number of different subjects. Like the earlier concept of "general systems theory," the term originates with certain biological theories in the field of environmental studies. In this context, it describes the parameters or characteristics of an ecological system that allow it to absorb a sustained disturbance or external shock through changes in its underlying structure or forms of adaptive behaviour. From the ecological perspective, most definitions of resilience focus on the ability of a system to recover from an external shock and return to its previous state or trajectory of development. According to Walker et al., one of the widely cited authorities on the ecological approach and its socio-economic implications, "[r]esilience is the capacity of a system to absorb disturbance and reorganize while undergoing change so as to still retain essentially the same function, structure, identity and feedbacks" (2004, 2). From this perspective, the idea of resilience is closely related to two others: adaptability, which involves the capacity of actors in a system to affect its resilience, and transformability, which signifies the ability to create a new system when the ecological, economic, or social conditions of the current system are no longer viable.

Another approach that offers a second perspective on resilience draws from the discipline of engineering. It focuses on the susceptibility of different places to external hazards and natural disasters, and the potential of such events to undermine the stability of the system, with negative social and economic consequences. The emphasis in this approach is on attempting to anticipate the vulnerability of physical, ecological, or social systems to these external hazards or potential disasters, and to analyze the factors that might contribute to the continued stability of the system in the face of the disaster, or help the system return to its equilibrium point after the disruptive event occurs. Both the ecological and engineering perspectives draw heavily upon aspects of systems theory, and, as a consequence, tend to emphasize the way in which the interaction among component elements of the system contributes to or weakens its resilient capabilities in light of these external shocks (Pike, Dawley, and Tomaney 2010).

Both perspectives also emphasize the ability to return to a previous or new equilibrium point after the perturbation has occurred. For this reason, these perspectives have resonated with an economic approach to regional resilience that focuses on the potential of the regional economy to return to an original or new point of equilibrium. In economic terms, this highlights the ability of the regional economy to maintain its pre-existing rate of growth or pattern of development – or how quickly it can return to its previous level of economic output and employment after a shock occurs. This approach views the external shocks largely in terms of economic changes that affect the region's underlying competitive position: "Regional economies can be thrown off their growth paths through (a) *structural change* resulting from global or domestic competition, from changes in the region's competitive advantages for various products, and/or from changes in consumer demand for products the region produces, or b) other external shocks (a natural disaster, closure of a military base, movement of an important firm out of the area, etc.)" (Hill, Wial, and Wolman 2008, 5).

From an equilibrium perspective, resilience involves the way in which market mechanisms determine the ability of regions to respond to these shocks. Regions that return quickly to their equilibrium growth path are called *economically resilient*; those that avoid being thrown off their growth path are *shock-resistant*; and those that are unable to return to their previous equilibrium point are *non-resistant* (Hill et al. 2008).

Équilibrium approaches can be distinguished from an alternative view which draws upon the evolutionary economics literature. The evolutionary approach differs in its view of the diversity of developmental paths which regions follow, and the resulting variety in both the industrial and economic structures of the region. A key difference between the two perspectives lies in the question of whether resilience merely involves the process of "bouncing back" and returning to the previous growth path, or whether it involves a process of adaptation and adjustment to a new growth path. Implicit in this latter perspective is the distinction between whether there is one equilibrium point or multiple ones that the region can reach through a process of industrial restructuring and the development of new industries (Christopherson, Michie, and Tyler 2010). The evolutionary approach also attaches greater importance to the institutional underpinnings of resilience, and the extent to which political and civic institutions may frame the responses taken by different regions to the natural, economic, and social disruptions they experience. Finally, it recognizes the extent to which regions are embedded in broader political geographies, and understands that these "nested scales" shape and constrain both their potential and actual responses to external shocks (Pike et al. 2010; Bunnell and Coe 2001).

The evolutionary approach to regional resilience draws upon the complementary concepts of path dependence, increasing returns, and lock-in to understand the historical paths taken by regions and their core cities. It argues that economic systems change over time, but in ways that are shaped and constrained by past decisions, random events, and accidents of history. When applied to regional and urban phenomena, these ideas suggest that the developmental path of a specific city or region is rooted in a series of economic, social, and cultural factors that lie in its past. The challenge is to reconcile the significance of random or chance events in endowing a region with its specific industrial structure and institutional capabilities, while allowing for the role of political leadership in fashioning subsequent changes to its broader institutional structures and development strategies. For example, during the early phase of technology development, many different cities have the potential to emerge as the location where a technology and its corresponding industry take root and develop. Once a city or region has established itself as an early success in a particular set of production activities – through a sequence of random occurrences and locational advantages – its opportunities for continued growth are strongly reinforced by the impact of increasing returns to the technological and institutional advantages it enjoys. By the same token, ailing places may face greater challenges in improving their fortunes when their principal industries and technologies in their region begin to decline. Once a path-dependent trajectory of decline sets in, the capacity of local firms to shift to a new or emerging set of production activities, and the degree to which the region's institutional structures support this shift, become crucial (Wolfe and Gertler 2006).

Drawing upon previous work on the institutional transformation of post-socialist societies, Pike et al. (2010) make an important distinction between the concepts of *adaptation* and *adaptability*. Adaptation is seen as a short-run phenomenon that involves the movement back towards the original path of development, based on strong linkages between different social agents and the institutional underpinnings of the regional economy. In contrast, adaptability involves the capacity to shift the growth path of a region towards multiple and alternative trajectories of development, based on the ability to forge new linkages between social agents and alternative or emerging institutional structures. Thus, there is a certain tension between adaptation and adaptability as alternative forms of resilience; at the heart of this tension is the question of whether resilience refers to a region's ability to retain its underlying economic and institutional structure in face of an external shock, or whether it requires the ability to respond to the shock by adjusting those underlying structures. Adaptation involves the region's ability to adjust to a new, competitive dynamic in the global economy in order to maintain a previously successful growth pattern, whereas "resilience through adaptability emerges through decisions to leave a path that may have proven successful in the past in favour of a new, related or alternative trajectory" (Pike et al. 2010, 62; Simmie and Martin 2010).

Adaptability is the key feature that distinguishes resilient regions (regions that exhibit a strong degree of economic success over long periods of time in the face of different shifts in production technology, the emergence of new markets, and changes in international competition) from those that are able to adapt to short-run changes in the above conditions. Adaptability over the long run involves the ability of a region to transform its industrial structure, labour market, productive technologies, and supporting institutions to respond to external pressures. Simmie and Martin view this capability as something akin to Schumpeter's "notion of industrial 'mutation' that takes place via a process of 'creative destruction'" (2010, 30). The broader and more diverse the regional economy is, the greater the potential for multiple equilibriums to exist. As older industrial sectors decline in the face of new or emerging production technologies and new production locales around the globe, larger metropolitan regions have a greater potential to reinvent their local economies by nurturing and supporting the emergence and growth of new economic sectors (Swanstrom 2008).

A key question then involves the underlying conditions that differentiate between a region's resilience in terms of its potential for adaptation versus adaptability. One important factor is the extent of economic diversity versus specialization that characterizes the regional economy. A diverse industrial structure provides greater resilience, in that different economic sectors face differing changes in underlying production technology and international competitive conditions. A more diverse regional economy thus has a better chance of withstanding disturbances to its growth path, particularly if not all of its sectors need to adapt at the same time. A diverse economy also offers the potential for sectoral variety, which, according to a long line of theorizing that draws its inspiration from Jane Jacobs, is more conducive to innovation because of the potential to generate new ideas that can lead to new technologies, new products, and new markets at the intersection of existing economic sectors.

In the same vein, Jacobs (1969) emphasizes the potential for innovation that arises when new forms of knowledge circulate among a wide range of sectors within a city – in other words, from the dynamics associated with greater diversity in the economic structure of a city-region. The most important knowledge transfers originate outside the firm's specific sector, and the diversity of geographically proximate industries, rather than specialization *per se*, promotes innovation and growth. In her view, ideas that are commonplace or widely accepted within one particular sector of the economy may have novel value in another. Knowledge flows between firms in different industries drive innovation and growth, as new ideas form by combining older ideas, or by applying knowledge that is routine in one sector to emerging problems in another. Large urban economies, with their mix of different industries and occupations, increase the potential for knowledge flows between industries, and therefore exhibit faster growth and higher levels of innovative dynamism. The possibility of cross-fertilization arising from an economic structure with greater variety enhances the potential for the generation of new ideas and innovation within the local economy. The question of whether small and medium-sized cities can display the same degree of innovativeness across a range of sectors is open to further investigation. Recent evidence gathered by a national study of city-regions in Canada suggests that despite the greater challenge, it is possible for small and medium-sized cities to alter their development trajectory to support more innovative firms and industries (Wolfe 2009).

Central to the changing role of the regional scale in facilitating adjustment to a changing economic environment is how institutional ensembles adapt to changes in the principal industries and technologies at the core of the region's industrial structure. The key issue concerns the ability of firms, industries, and institutions in a specific city or region to adapt their existing knowledge base and localized capabilities to the generation and exploitation of new commercially valuable sources of knowledge. Resilient regions tend to be those in which existing clusters of firms prove to be adept at making the transition out of declining industries, while simultaneously exploiting their local knowledge infrastructure to cultivate new potential growth fields. In both instances, the structure of local and regional institutions is critical for those capabilities (Wolfe 2010). The undeniable result has been a shift in the relative importance of institutional structures at the national and regional scale, and an increasing emphasis on the importance of understanding "how locally distinctive and evolving institutional architectures, interacting with national and provincial institutions, local political dynamics and the agency of individuals and organizations help create particular evolutionary trajectories over time" (Gertler 2010, 11).

As noted above, another factor that conditions the resilience of regions is their institutional underpinnings. The evolutionary perspective draws attention to the importance of the social dimension in charting the developmental paths of different regions, but what is often missing from these discussions is the recognition that political relations play an important role in determining the range of institutions that can shape a region's potential response to external shocks, and thus help determine its resilience. This represents a key distinction between the equilibrium approaches that view resilience largely in terms of purely economic or market-driven responses to external shocks, and more evolutionary and institutional perspectives. Todd

Swanstrom (2008) draws our attention to this dimension, and goes further in arguing that there are three different institutional spheres that contribute to regional resilience: the private (firms), public (governments), and civic (networks and associations) sectors.

Municipal and regional governments also play a central role in creating new development strategies for their local economy, but they rarely do so in a vacuum. As noted above, this involves the role of governments in multiple geographic scales, not just those operating at the local or metropolitan level (see Guay and Hamel, this volume). The ability of local and regional governments to draw upon the fiscal and policy resources available from more senior levels of government may be important in shaping their ability to frame appropriate policy responses to help their regional economies shift to new sectors of potential growth and move towards a new developmental pathway. But, in some respects, governments represent the slowest-moving parts of the local or regional ecosystem, and therefore may pose the greatest challenge in helping frame a resilient response to new obstacles. Their ability to help their regions adapt is often reinforced by the presence of vibrant local civic associations.

Regions with strong and dynamic leadership from the civic sector – what Doug Henton and his colleagues term "regional stewards" – may prove more successful in working with the public sector to develop new strategies (Henton, Melville, and Parr 2006). Resilient regions are thus ones in which private market forces, a strong and flexible or dynamic civic sector, and local governments are capable of adapting to changing economic and environmental circumstances in order to respond to emerging threats, and take advantage of emerging opportunities. Local civic associations also help develop new strategies to promote the growth of their local and regional economies, and thus contribute to their potential resilience. Regions with a diverse cross-section of civic stakeholders can develop a set of innovative strategies that promote the future economic interests of the region. However, at the same time, local civic networks that have become excessively ingrown or self-replicating can be the source of an excessive degree of social rigidity that limits the potential for innovative solutions to emerge (Swanstrom 2008; Safford 2009).

It is important to recognize that none of these sectors act independently of each other. Much work has been devoted to explaining the emergence and growth of dynamic regions based on new technologies, as well as the challenge for older, industrial regions to break free of their locked-in paths of development. However, less attention has focused on the co-evolution of a region's industrial structure and institutional underpinnings. Rather, the path-dependent nature of development in regional economies involves the process by which these interdependent sectors co-evolve, as well as the process by which new institutional ensembles (composed of all elements of the three sectors outlined above) emerge in response to changing economic and environmental conditions. The question of how adaptable these institutional ensembles are to changes in the principal industries and technologies of the region's industrial structure lies at the heart of the issue of regional resilience. Critical is the ability of firms, industries, and institutions in a specific city or region to adapt their existing knowledge base and localized capabilities to the generation and exploitation of new commercially valuable sources of knowledge: "New paths do not emerge in a vacuum, but always in the contexts of existing structures and paths of technology, industry and institutional arrangements" (Martin and Simmie 2008, 186).

The Role of Civic Capital in Regional Resilience

Underlying the civic sector in local and regional economies is the complex set of social relations which exist in any community. The nature of these relations varies considerably across communities and city-regions, and the nature of that variation is a key factor in explaining the relative degree of resilience among them. Part of the explanation of that variation lies in the social mechanisms which can foster more effective coordination among civic actors at the regional and local level. Due to the benefits of proximity, the region is often the site within which better coordination develops. Among the relevant factors often considered to contribute to more effective coordination is the character of the relationships between actors in a region – described as social capital. Social capital is defined as the "social relations among agents, resting upon social institutions that allow for cooperation and communication" (Lorenzen 2007, 801; Maskell 2000). Lorenzen draws an important distinction between the business realm and the civic realm of social relations. Business relations include technological learning within a firm, and inter-firm trade and knowledge exchanges. Civic relations include those that exist between people in a community who interact with each other through their involvement with schools, various cultural and leisure activities, and other civic associations. He argues that the civic dimension of social capital is particularly sensitive to geographic distance because many of the activities that enhance the strength of civic relations are based on the specific catchment area of a civic association or membership in a cultural organization. These relations frequently entail face-to-face meetings that are constrained by distance.

Building on this distinction between the business and civic dimensions of social capital, we have formulated the concept of civic capital to analyze the contribution that more cooperative forms of behaviour make to the success of local and regional economies (Wolfe and Nelles 2008). Civic capital is defined as a set of relations that emerge from interpersonal networks tied to a specific region or locality, and contribute to the development of a common sense of community based on a shared identity and set of goals and expectations. It comprises formal or informal networks among individual actors or associations at the community level and between members of the community and regional or local governments (Nelles 2009). The bases of civic capital are its regional orientation and the key role played by civic leaders in fostering regional networks. Civic leaders, or civic entrepreneurs, are critical in articulating a regional orientation and intensifying and formalizing collaborative networks within and between communities. Civic entrepreneurs are bridge-builders, and help to connect localized networks and different communities of actors with one another. These leaders understand the importance of collaboration, and through their leadership bring various groups of actors together to negotiate and agree on regional goals. In doing so, they build civic capital by creating the fora and the initiatives for different segments of the local community to collaborate in pursuing these agreed-upon goals (Henton, Melville, and Walesh 1997, 31).[1]

The concept of civic capital provides insight into the processes and dynamics that contribute to more successful regional governance, and ultimately to regional resilience. In regions characterized by higher degrees of civic capital, the coordination required to sustain regional cooperation tends to result in more effective governance. Collaborative institutions often embody values and attitudes that are intrinsic to the region and further build civic capital. Successful regional economies benefit from the presence of collaborative institutions, which help communicate the respective needs of different community actors to each other, establish local and regional priorities for economic development, and build effective bridges across different segments of the economic community that might not otherwise be linked. Above all, they contribute to the articulation of a shared vision for the economic community and the local economy, and build a consensus among key civic actors and associations around that vision (Porter et al. 2001, 75). The emphasis on the role of local leaders in building civic capital and creating collaborative institutions underlines the importance of agency in overcoming the problems of lock-in and charting new developmental pathways for resilient regions, but even dynamic regions with the highest levels of civic capital are constrained by their existing mix of industries and technological capabilities.

The most effective strategies for sustaining regional resilience rely on acquired levels of civic capital and the existing endowment of regional institutions to chart new paths forward, but they do not always do it in an equally effective manner. Among the factors that determine their effectiveness are the ability to build on specialized regional assets, including public and private research infrastructure, as well as unique concentrations of occupational and labour market skills; the presence or absence of "civic capital" at the regional and local level; and the ability of local firms and entrepreneurs to adjust their business strategies in response to changing economic circumstances. Path dependence plays a role in determining the outcomes, but that role is contingent; it is framed by the strategic choices of local actors and the degree to which local institutional structures constrain or support the realization of their goals. No region gets to wipe the slate clean and start afresh. Or, as Christopherson et al. (2010) comment, "regions make their own resilience, but they do not make it as they please; they do not make it under self-selected circumstances, but under circumstances existing already" (7).

CIVIC GOVERNANCE AND REGIONAL RESILIENCE IN WATERLOO, ONTARIO

The case of the dynamic regional economy in Waterloo, Ontario, provides strong evidence and confirmation of how these factors come together to create the conditions needed for regional resilience. The Kitchener-Waterloo-Cambridge region, located about one hundred kilometres west of Toronto, has received a great deal of attention from policy-makers because of its successes in maintaining high regional growth rates and modernizing its economic base. Geographically,

Canada's Technology Triangle (as the region is also known) encompasses the four municipalities of Waterloo, Cambridge, Kitchener, and Guelph. The region has benefited from the unique blend of its status as a traditional manufacturing centre with roots dating back to the mid-nineteenth century, and the size and international reach of its concentration of information technology firms, dating from the 1970s. The dominant industrial sectors in the Waterloo region are manufacturing, retail trade, education, and professional, scientific, and technical services. Kitchener-Waterloo has been the home to major national and international corporations for more than a century, from Dominion Electrohome Ltd. to present-day success Research in Motion (RIM) – the manufacturer of the Blackberry, and Canada's largest information technology firm. Although the total population of the region is only about half a million, its diversified industrial base, as well as the success of some of its leading industrial firms, such as Electrohome (now Christie Digital), in making the transition from older industrial technologies to newer digital ones, has been a continuing source of economic resilience. A hallmark of the innovation process within the region has been the application of digital technology to advanced manufacturing processes, evidence of a relatively uncommon, but critical, dimension of knowledge transfer across two of the core areas of specialization within the regional economy (Krashinsky 2011).

The emergence and dynamism of the high technology sector in the Waterloo region owes its success to critical decisions taken by industrial leaders in the local economy in the years following World War II, which led to the creation of the University of Waterloo. The high technology cluster in the Waterloo region grew out of its strong industrial base in advanced manufacturing, combined with the early focus of the new university on engineering, math, and computer science. The University of Waterloo continues to play three critical roles in the development of the region's innovative economy. As a major research university, it is at the forefront of knowledge creation in a variety of fields. It also generates a critical supply of talent that has contributed to the growth of a "thick" labour market in the local economy, particularly through its highly successful cooperative education program, the largest in North America. Finally, through the process of knowledge creation and its strong support for entrepreneurship, the university has spun off several prominent firms in the area. While all three roles have had important effects on the shape of

the regional economy, the one that attracts the most obvious attention is its role in spinning off high technology firms. Two of the early
technology firms, WATCOM and Dantec Electronic, were spun off
from the University in 1974. A subsequent generation of firms followed in the 1980s, including Dalsa (1980), Virtek Vision (1986),
and Open Text (1989). RIM, although not technically a spin-off
from university research, was founded by University of Waterloo
students in the early 1980s, and has since grown to become the leading high technology company not only in the region, but in the
national economy as well. Although the university remains central
to the continuing development of the regional economy, its primary
contribution is no longer through the process of new firm formation,
as relatively fewer firms have spun off directly since the late 1980s;
its role in feeding the growth of the local talent pool, however, has
become a mainstay in contributing to the adaptability of the regional
economy (Bramwell and Wolfe 2008; Kenney and Patton 2011).

The industrial cluster in the Waterloo region is one of the most
dynamic sources of high-tech activity in Canada. Overall, the region
boasts more than seven hundred companies involved in the high
technology sector. Regional organizations are also working with
more than two hundred early-stage start-ups, some of which are
housed in the Accelerator Centre at the University of Waterloo
Research Park, others in the new Communitech Hub in downtown
Kitchener, and still others off-site (Communitech and Waterloo
Region Record 2010). The companies are spread across four key
subsectors: information and communication technology, scientific
and engineering services, advanced manufacturing, and the life sciences biotech and environmental subsector. Of these, information
and communications technology accounts for 62 percent of the high
technology firms and 45 percent of the total employment in the high
technology sector (Communitech 2006). Unlike other concentrations of high technology activity in Canada, the economy of the
Waterloo region is not dominated by one particular subsector, such
as telecommunications or Internet-based firms. The Waterloo region
faced the same set of economic shocks as many other mid-sized
manufacturing regions in North America from the mid-1970s
onwards. However, the diverse industrial base of the regional economy, the underlying strength of its knowledge institutions, and the
ability to mobilize its local assets to maintain its existing strength
and take advantage of emerging opportunities have helped the

region to weather these economic shocks, such as the post-2000 dot-com meltdown that devastated employment in other leading technology regions across the country.

Institutional Foundations of Regional Resilience in Waterloo

While Waterloo has long been one of the most prosperous regions of its size in Canada, its growing reputation as a high technology centre has really taken off in the past two decades. While many traditional manufacturing centres in central Canada and the US Midwest struggled to cope with the economic restructuring and de-industrialization of the 1980s, the Waterloo region accelerated its transition into new and emerging economic sectors. By the early 1990s, local firms had begun to carve out a niche in high technology and advanced manufacturing, while its post-secondary institutions gained international recognition. Much of the success of the Waterloo region can be attributed to its unusually active civil society, and the proliferation of mechanisms of strategic coordination and collaborative governance. This section of the chapter situates the major players in the Waterloo region, discusses how regional collaboration has evolved over time, and examines how the growth of civic capital has been an important factor in laying the institutional foundations for regional resilience. As the regional economy has evolved, new civic institutions at the regional scale have proliferated and expanded in scope. However, close examination of these initiatives reveals a bias towards economic development goals, in part due to the dominance of economic actors.

One of the hallmarks of regional resilience in the Waterloo region from the 1960s to the present has been the ability on the part of local firms and key institutional players to identify changing technology and market trends, and adapt their respective competitive strategies at both the firm and the regional level to take advantage of them. From the founding of the University of Waterloo in the 1950s to the establishment of Canada's Technology Triangle (CTT) Inc. and Communitech, the private sector has played an instrumental role in the economic development of the region (Nelles, Bramwell, and Wolfe 2005). While the Kitchener-Waterloo region has traditionally enjoyed the same cross-section of civic organizations found in most other local regions of North America – including the local Chambers of Commerce and United Way – the key to its civic success over the past two decades has been the gradual development of a new set of more focused organizations dedicated to promoting the growth of the region's high-tech economy. As Feldman, Francis, and Berkowitz (2005) note, this process is not uncommon in regions where technology entrepreneurs have built on their individual successes to strengthen the underlying organizational base of the region as a whole. The intensification of civic organizations in Waterloo region occurred in three stages. The first two stages involved civic entrepreneurs formalizing bonding ties within the high technology community and between local governments with the creation of Communitech and CTT Inc. As the organizations matured, bridging ties began forming with other community actors. The third stage built bridges between associations, local and regional governments, and economic and social actors through multi-stakeholder associations such as the more recent Prosperity Forum.

The dawn of more collaborative forms of regional governance in the Waterloo region can be traced to the foundation of two associations in the mid-1980s and early 1990s. CTT Inc. and Communitech were established by different communities of actors independently of each other in order to support and grow the high technology economy. However, as the two associations have evolved, they have developed increasingly close ties and coordinated capacity. While the early years were marked by a certain degree of competition and conflicting mandates between the emerging civic institutions in the Waterloo region, most of these issues were gradually resolved. Today, CTT Inc. and Communitech have expanded their mandates significantly beyond their original designs, and function as the core associations in contributing to civic collaboration in the region (Roy 1998; Leibovitz 2003).

CTT Inc. is a regional marketing and economic development association. The association was founded in 1987 by economic development officials in the cities of Kitchener, Waterloo, and Cambridge[2] in order to coordinate regional marketing and business attraction efforts. CTT Inc. was originally constructed as a political partnership between the three local governments, but evolved into a public-private partnership in 1999. In adopting public-private models of control over direction and strategy, the association passed from public to largely private hands. Previously, CTT Inc. was primarily a marketing corporation; however, its scope of regional activity now includes broader areas of regional economic development, such as land use, infrastructure development, and immigrant integration. Representation on the board of directors and corporate partners reflects the economic development mission of the association. Despite this wide range of development roles, CTT Inc. is wary of stepping on local toes and acknowledges the role that local economic development officials and offices play. From a collaborative perspective, CTT Inc. views itself as a node through which the interests of other regional actors can be expressed.

Communitech was established in 1997, though its roots stretch back to the early 1990s to an informal group of twelve CEOs called the Atlas Group, whose goal was to facilitate the exchange of ideas, and improve networking relations, between high technology companies. This partnership originally formed as these CEOs discovered they faced similar challenges stemming from the weak state of the regional information communication technology infrastructure. Although these functions remain central to the association's mission, as it has evolved, Communitech has embraced a broader role in regional governance. Like CTT Inc., its leadership and board of advisors represent private sector and economic development interests. An oft-cited benefit of Communitech membership is access to a pool of shared experiences and support by providing a variety of services to its members. This has led to partnerships between technology companies, service firms, academic institutions, business support organizations, and government – and a role as one of the most visible organizations for regional economic development in Waterloo. The association currently supports the technology community with a number of services, such as the Executive in Residence program; Peer2Peer networking events developed to provide a forum to discuss best practices for industry leaders (CEOs, CIOs, and CTOs) and management and technical professionals; and the development of the new Communitech Hub in downtown Kitchener (Bramwell, Nelles, and Wolfe 2008).

Both CTT Inc. and Communitech are associations that have transcended their narrowly economic initial mandates to become leaders in regional governance. Both associations have been described as catalysts of regional initiatives with the critical mass and political weight to bring people to the table in a wide variety of areas beyond economic development. Over time, the scope of their activities shows an increasing commitment to diversity, cultural vibrancy, and regional health. In fact, there are few genuinely regional partnerships in the region that do not include representation of some sort from either organization. Despite this expansion of their mandates, at their core, they remain economic development associations, and their involvement in cultural and social spheres is consistently in the name of regional prosperity.

A key feature of Waterloo's adaptability and resilience has been the foresight of local firms to recognize emerging technology trends, and to mobilize key segments of the local business community, civic associations, and the post-secondary research infrastructure in support of new initiatives to capitalize on those trends. A key initiative that CTT played a central role in was the establishment and marketing of the Research and Technology Park in partnership with the University of Waterloo, the government of Canada, the province of Ontario, the region of Waterloo, the City of Waterloo, and Communitech. The Research Park is located on the northern boundary of the University of Waterloo, and is the site of several new buildings, one of which houses the Accelerator Centre, the local offices of the Industrial Research Assistance Program, legal offices, and other support functions directed towards the promotion of local firms in the cluster. Other buildings in the Research Park house some of the leading firms in the region or provide space for growing firms to expand into, as well as a number of amenities deemed to be attractive to employees in high technology firms. The cooperative role played by all major levels of government plus the key regional actors in designing, financing, and developing the new Research and Technology Park is a strong testament to the collaborative form of governance that has contributed to the resilience of the region.

The Kitchener-Waterloo region has historically been known for its manufacturing strengths, as well as a focused but dynamic financial services sector. However, as the competitive dynamics of the information technology industry have shifted in recent years with growing competition in the hardware products that Waterloo firms excel at, key civic and business leaders have recognized the growth potential of digital media, and have been quick to chart a new course for the region to expand in this direction. Somewhat ironically, the cultural centre of Stratford, Ontario, is located just half an hour west of Waterloo, but until recently has not been considered an integral part of the region. This gap between the cultural and scientific sectors of the regional economy has been narrowed with a move by the University of Waterloo to establish a satellite campus in Stratford, followed closely by the creation of a new centre in digital media, linking Stratford directly into the Waterloo economy. This new branch of the University of Waterloo – the Stratford Institute, with a strong focus on the creation of content for digital media – is the centre of a national network to promote the growth of digital media across the country.

The Corridor for Advancing Canadian Digital Media (CACDM) is a collaborative initiative on the part of partners across the region and southwestern Ontario to develop a Centre of Excellence in digital media. This project combines two initiatives that emerged in 2008–09 to develop the region's digital media capacity. The first, spearheaded by the City of Stratford, located just west of Waterloo, initiated a satellite campus of the University of Waterloo and a digital media convergence centre in Stratford. The second established the Communitech Hub as a digital media convergence centre in downtown Kitchener to combine the regional expertise in digital media and mobile technology. The two separate initiatives were united to establish the first Centre of Excellence in the region, and both aimed to build on existing strengths to open new possibilities for future growth. The CACDM is supported by the University of Waterloo, Conestoga College, and the C3 network of universities. Other stakeholders include the municipal governments of Kitchener and Stratford, as well as economic development associations from other centres in southwestern Ontario. Local firms such as Open Text and Christie Digital have provided key support, and CTT Inc. and Communitech are also very involved in the strategy and direction of the initiative.

The goal of the Centre of Excellence is to create Canada's largest concentration of digital media R&D and commercialization expertise, and to develop internationally competitive and sustainable capacity in digital innovation. The vision of the Centre of Excellence is that arts and cultural content creation expertise can be combined with digital media in order to produce innovative ways to present and manipulate data and visualize processes. What is most innovative about the initiative is the inspiration to combine the well-established capabilities of the Waterloo region in digital technologies with the cultural and creative capabilities that the city of Stratford has long been recognized for. It represents a significant effort to shift the regional economy onto the path of becoming a preeminent site in the emerging cognitive-cultural economy. The CACDM is also significant from a collaborative governance perspective, as it is one of the first times that the civic leadership in the Waterloo region has engaged with municipalities beyond its regional boundaries (such as Stratford), and reached out to assume national leadership of an innovative research network.

The success of the region's civic and business leadership in attracting federal funding to support the CACDM was followed quickly by its success in winning a grant from the provincial government to further support the establishment of the Hub. In November 2009, the Ontario government announced plans to invest up to $26.4 million (24 percent of the $107 million project) in Kitchener to create the Communitech Hub: Digital Media and Mobile Accelerator, bringing the combined federal and provincial total to $31.4 million. The Hub, which opened in October 2010, has a unique ability to support the growth and commercialization of Ontario's digital media industry. It provides an attractive location in the heart of the region for entrepreneurs, companies, and academic institutions to interact in a 30,000-square-foot state-of-the-art centre. The Hub immediately filled its available space, and further expansion is under way. Among the many features of the Hub are the immersive 3D H.I.V.E (Hub Interactive Virtual Reality Environment) provided by Christie Digital, one of the key private sector partners; 3D-capable event space; and virtual conferencing facilities. In addition to Christie, the Hub also has representatives from some of the larger firms in the region, including RIM, Open Text, and Agfa. Through a wide range of programs administered by Communitech, the Hub's mission is to build global digital media by mentoring tenant start-ups, creating linkages with more established companies in the region, and helping secure financing for digital media ideas. The facility has space to accommodate more than one hundred digital media start-ups and, as noted above, Communitech is already working with more than two hundred start-up firms in the region through its Executive in Residence program and mentoring activities. The Hub also has space for some of the legal and consulting companies that provide services to the high technology sector, and serves as the headquarters of the Canadian Digital Media Network (CDMN), and through that, is the sponsor of the highly successful Canada 3.0 conferences which have been held in Stratford for the past three years (Knowles 2011).

Even more strategically, the location of the Hub in the old Lang Tannery (once the largest in the Commonwealth), in the heart of downtown Kitchener, is part of a broader set of moves by the City of Kitchener to shift its urban economy away from the declining manufacturing sector towards some of the high-technology activities that Waterloo has traditionally been associated with. Long the manufacturing centre and the larger city, Kitchener has suffered in recent years through the closure of some of its major employers, including Electrohome, Uniroyal, Budd Automotive, and even B.F. Goodrich, whose president, Ira Needles, was the author of the famous Waterloo Plan, which laid out the strategy for the founding of the university and laid the basis for the region's high technology future. In a series of far-sighted moves to shift the economy towards more knowledge-intensive activities, the City of Kitchener has used its own financial reserves and resources leveraged from other levels of government to attract the Faculty of Social Work at Wilfrid Laurier University (which is primarily based in Waterloo), a new satellite of the McMaster medical school, and the renovation of the old tannery building. In addition to the Communitech Hub, the renovated Lang Tannery building also houses the corporate headquarters of Desire2Learn (one of the University of Waterloo's successful spin-offs) and the Canadian headquarters of Google. The most recent piece of the strategy is the purchase of a nearby site to accommodate a new transportation hub, which will connect the region more effectively to metropolitan Toronto through the province's Go Transit system. The combined effect of these moves is to tie the Kitchener and Waterloo parts of the regional economy together more effectively, and to help overcome the old/new technology divide that has characterized the region since the 1970s (English 2011). Taken together, these initiatives are part of a series of strategic actions to help the region adapt to the ongoing restructuring of its traditional industrial base, and move into some of the expanding sectors of the knowledge economy.

CONCLUSION

The Waterloo case is an example of a region that has embarked on a series of successful initiatives in collaborative governance to provide the institutional supports to maintain its regional resilience. Over time, the scope and number of initiatives has increased, and participation has expanded to include a wider variety of actors. The region is characterized by a high degree of civic engagement and well-developed organizational linkages, which have coalesced behind a relatively

broad-based local development coalition. Those collaborative networks are being deployed effectively to reposition the local knowledge infrastructure in support of future economic growth, through
initiatives such as the CACDM and the Communitech Hub that draw
upon available federal and provincial funding to expand the region's
knowledge infrastructure and innovative capabilities. Rather than
become absorbed in grand strategic planning exercises as have some
other Canadian and American cities, the business and civic leadership in the region has focused its efforts on a more targeted set of
initiatives to support and reposition its knowledge infrastructure.
Similarly, the political fragmentation of the region into a number of
smaller municipalities has been offset, to some extent, by the high
level of civic capital outside of the public sector that links the different municipalities into one broader regional economy. Most of the
key leaders, groups, and initiatives that have been influential in
promoting the regional agenda have emerged from the private and
higher education sectors.

The degree of resilience found in the region has not gone unno-
ticed by the Canadian public and media, as senior government representatives regularly point to the Waterloo example as a model for
other small and medium-sized cities in the country to follow.
However, the region is not without its continuing challenges, as the
recent announcements of major layoffs and corporate reorganization by Research in Motion indicate. Nonetheless, it is clear from the
preceding discussion that the strategy currently being followed is to
diversify the region's economic base of emerging technology sectors
and to foster a start-up culture to avoid staking its future on the success of one or two leading firms.

This raises a key question concerning the extent to which the success enjoyed by the region has been the product of a set of unique
circumstances that are not easily replicated elsewhere, or whether
there are key elements in the Waterloo story that can serve as guidelines for other communities working to recover from an external
economic shock or challenge. In this respect, the Waterloo example
may point us towards policy mechanisms that are part of a formula
for ensuring long-term economic resilience and durability. In his
comparison of the economic growth trajectories in the two "rustbelt" cities of Youngstown, Ohio, and Allentown, Pennsylvania,
Sean Safford (2009) attributes the relative failure of the first, and the

success of the second, to the quality of social networks in each place, and argues that the respective differences in the density and nature of organizational relationships shaped the strategic choices made in response to the economic crises they faced, and ultimately were the source of their economic divergence. While the economic challenges faced in the Waterloo region were not as severe as those in the two regions mentioned above, this case study demonstrates that the foundations of the region's resilience have been developed over a long period of time, and have rested on a collaborative and inclusive governance model as well as a close engagement and ongoing dialogue between public research institutions and the private sector. The current challenges being faced by one of its flagship firms will provide a true indication of whether the region is resilient enough to adapt to the latest round of competitive and market changes.

NOTES

1 Refer also to the discussion of "institutional thickness" in chapters 11 and 12, this volume.
2 A fourth city located in a neighbouring county, Guelph, was also an early participant in the partnership, but withdrew in 1999.

REFERENCES

Bramwell, A., J. Nelles, and D.A. Wolfe. 2008. "Knowledge, Innovation and Institutions: Global and Local Dimensions of the ICT Cluster in Waterloo, Canada." *Regional Studies* 42 (1): 1–16.

Bramwell, A., and D.A. Wolfe. 2008. "Universities and Regional Economic Development: The Entrepreneurial University of Waterloo." *Research Policy* 37 (September): 1175–87.

Bunnell, T.G., and N.M. Coe. 2001. "Spaces and Scales of Innovation." *Progress in Human Geography* 24 (4): 569–89.

Christopherson, S., J. Michie, and P. Tyler. 2010. "Regional Resilience: Theoretical and Empirical Perspectives." *Cambridge Journal of Regions, Economy and Society* 3 (1): 3–10.

Communitech. 2006. *State of the Industry Report 2006: Technology in Waterloo Region*. Waterloo, ON: Communitech, Waterloo Region Technology Association.

Communitech and Waterloo Region Record. 2010. *Waterloo Region Technology Directory 2010*. Waterloo, ON: Author.

English, J. 2011. "Kitchener Meets Its Waterloo." *Maclean's*, 8 August.

Feldman, M.P., J. Francis, and J. Bercovitz. 2005. "Creating a Cluster While Building a Firm: Entrepreneurs and the Formation of Industrial Clusters." *Regional Studies* 39 (1): 129–41.

Gertler, M.S. 2010. "Rules of the Game: The Place of Institutions in Regional Economic Change." *Regional Studies* 44 (1): 1–15.

Henton, D., J. Melville, and J. Parr. 2006. *Regional Stewardship and Collaborative Governance*. Monograph Series. Denver: Alliance for Regional Stewardship.

Henton, D., J. Melville, and K. Walesh. 1997. *Grassroots Leaders for a New Economy: How Civic Entrepreneurs Are Building Prosperous Communities*. San Francisco, CA: Jossey-Bass Publishers.

Hill, E.W., H. Wial, and H. Wolman. 2008. *Exploring Regional Resilience*. Working Paper 2008–04. Building Resilient Regionalism, Institute of Government Studies. Berkeley, CA: University of California Berkeley.

Jacobs, J. 1969. *The Economy of Cities*. New York: Random House.

Kenney, M., and D. Patton. 2011. "Does Inventor Ownership Encourage University Research-Driven Entrepreneurship? A Six University Comparison." *Research Policy* 40 (8): 1100–12.

Knowles, P. 2011. "Building a Better Sandbox." *Exchange* 28 (5 May): 15–18.

Krashinsky, S. 2011. "Lighting up the Screen for a New Generation." Toronto: *The Globe and Mail*, 19 July.

Leibovitz, J. 2003. "Institutional Barriers to Associative City-Region Governance: The Politics of Institution-Building and Economic Governance in Canada's Technology Triangle." *Urban Studies* 40 (13): 2613–42.

Lorenzen, M. 2007. "Social Capital and Localised Learning: Proximity and Place in Technological and Institutional Dynamics." *Urban Studies* 44 (4): 799–817.

Martin, R., and J. Simmie. 2008. "Path Dependence and Local Innovation Systems in City-Regions." *Innovation: Management, Policy & Practice* 10 (2–3): 183–96.

Maskell, P. 2000. "Social Capital, Innovation and Competitiveness." In *Social Capital*, edited by S. Baron, J. Field, and T. Schuller. Oxford, UK: Oxford University Press.

Nelles, J., A. Bramwell, and D.A. Wolfe. 2005. "History, Culture and Path Dependency: Origins of the Waterloo ICT Cluster." In *Global Networks and Local Linkages: The Paradox of Cluster Development in an Open*

Economy, edited by D.A. Wolfe and M. Lucas. Montreal and Kingston: McGill-Queen's University Press for the School of Policy Studies, Queen's University.

Nelles, J. 2009. "Civic Capital and the Dynamics of Intermunicipal Cooperation for Regional Economic Development." Unpublished PhD thesis. Toronto: Dept. of Political Science, University of Toronto.

Pike, A., S. Dawley, and J. Tomaney. 2010. "Resilience, Adaptation and Adaptability." *Cambridge Journal of Regions, Economy and Society* 3 (1 March): 59–70.

Porter, M.E., Monitor Group, ontheFRONTIER, and Council on Competitiveness. 2001. *Clusters of Innovation: Regional Foundations of US Competitiveness*. Washington, DC: Council on Competitiveness.

Roy, J. 1998. "Canada's Technology Triangle." In *Local and Regional Systems of Innovation*, edited by J. de la Mothe and G. Paquet. Amsterdam: Kluwer Academic Publishers.

Safford, S. 2004. *Searching for Silicon Valley in the Rustbelt: The Evolution of Knowledge Networks in Akron and Rochester*. Working Paper. Cambridge, MA: MIT Industrial Performance Centre.

– 2009. *Why the Garden Club Couldn't Save Youngstown: The Transformation of the Rust Belt*. Cambridge, MA, and London: Harvard University Press.

Simmie, J., and R. Martin. 2010. "The Economic Resilience of Regions: Towards and Evolutionary Approach." *Cambridge Journal of Regions, Economy and Society* 3 (1): 27–43.

Swanstrom, T. 2008. *Regional Resilience: A Critical Examination of the Ecological Framework*. Working Paper 2008–07. Berkeley Institute of Urban and Regional Development. Berkeley, CA: University of California Berkeley.

Walker, B., C.S. Holling, S.R. Carpenter, and A. Kinzig. 2004. "Resilience, Adaptability and Transformability in Social-Ecological Systems." *Ecology and Society* 9 (2).

Wolfe, D.A. 2009. *21st Century Cities in Canada: The Geography of Innovation*. Ottawa: The Conference Board of Canada.

– 2010. "The Strategic Management of Core Cities: Path Dependence and Economic Adjustment in Resilient Regions." *Cambridge Journal of Regions, Economy and Society* 3 (1): 139–52.

Wolfe, D., and A. Bramwell. 2008. "Innovation, Creativity and Governance: Social Dynamics of Economic Performance in City-Regions." *Innovation: Management, Policy & Practice* 10 (2–3): 170–82.

Wolfe, D., and M.S. Gertler. 2006. "Local Antecedents and Trigger Events: Policy Implications of Path Dependence for Cluster Formation." In *Cluster Genesis: Technology-Based Industrial Development*, edited by P. Braunerheim and M. Feldman, 243–63. Oxford, UK: Oxford University Press.

Wolfe, D., and J. Nelles. 2008. "The Role of Civic Capital and Civic Associations in Cluster Policies." In *Handbook of Research on Innovation and Cluster Policies*, edited by C. Karlsson, 374–92. Cheltenham, UK: Edward Elgar Publishers.

10

The Environmental Governance
of Canadian City-Regions:
Problems, Actions, and Challenges

LOUIS GUAY AND PIERRE HAMEL

Over the last decades, the experience of urban life has been profoundly transformed. As underlined by Scott et al. (2001), the development of a new city-regionalism has become "central to modern life" (11). It is not only that city-regions are offering new models of urban organization, but also that national economies are ever more organized around the capacity of city-regions to face global threats or to adapt to the new opportunities coming from globalization.

Social and economic actors thus increasingly encounter social, economic, urban, and environmental problems at the scale of city-regions. Even though city-regions rarely exist as administrative entities, their existence through social and cooperative networks is nevertheless central for defining the challenges of contemporary urban life as well as the potential solutions.

In this chapter, we specifically focus on those pressing challenges related to sustainability and the environment, and in doing so, we contend that environmental governance must necessarily be defined at a city-regional scale. For this purpose, we have divided this chapter into four parts. First, we explore the ways in which environmental problems have so far been approached. Second, we introduce the important influence of a federalist context that necessarily affects Canadian cities' and city-regions' capacity to cope with environmental problems. Third, we make reference to the recent example of metropolitan planning in Montreal as a case study of city-regional environmental governance, and its current limitations as a means of managing environmental challenges. Finally, going back to the issue of environmental governance, we consider the main environmental challenges cities are facing, assessing the promises of sustainable urban policies. One of these challenges is climate change, which will be dealt with in some detail. If cities were at first reluctant to confront climate change, they are now getting involved in planning for what is being labelled the "post-carbon economy." The goal may still be very far ahead, but steps in the right direction are being taken through public policy and investment.

CITIES AND THE ENVIRONMENT

Cities are thoroughly human-made and artificial environments. They are best thought of as socio-technical systems. One of the greatest and most complex inventions of humanity, they are nonetheless inextricably natural environments as well, themselves situated in wider natural environments and ecosystems. The natural environments that cities contain are composed of plants and animals, parks, and waterways, whether they are natural or built. Animals and plants are adapted to an urban environment, even to a polluted one. We increasingly recognize that cities are not separated by clean lines drawn between society and nature, or between town and country, but rather, situate human activity within an urban ecology.

There are two perspectives on cities as ecological systems (Pickett et al. 2001). One is to see a whole city as itself an ecosystem; the other is to view cities as comprising many different and evolving ecosystems. The two views are examined by new research under the general heading of urban ecology (Gaston 2010). Considering a city as a whole ecosystem leads to understanding and measuring energy and material exchange inside a city, and between a city and its surroundings, including with other types of ecosystems. An approach that focuses on intra-urban ecosystems will study different natural environments within a city, such as a park, a water area, or a river, and will look at the ecological dynamics of such ecosystems: how they are structured, how they change, and what forces affect them. This research may be conducive to conservation measures, but sociologists and other social scientists have not had much to say about it. Nevertheless, in a truly human ecology perspective, social scientists are interested in the interactions between human life and urban environments (Moran 2010). Some years ago, Stephen Boyden (1981;

1992) explored the field of *urban human ecology*, where human beings interact with nature in cities. Recent developments are provided by the new *urban political ecology*, led by geographers and highly influenced by Marxism, which looks at capitalism's material metabolism (importing, transforming, using, and wasting energy and material on a large scale) (Harvey 1996; Sassen and Dotan 2011; Heynen, Kaika, and Swyngedouw 2006). This last "critical" political ecological perspective adopts a system approach and is less concerned with the role of social actors, individually or collectively, in bringing about change to urban environmental problems.

A further perspective arising out of research in environmental sociology takes the view that ecological problems are socially constructed. This does not mean that they only exist in the minds of people, but that to be socially relevant, problems have to be socially appropriated as social problems (Guay 2002; Hanningan 2006; Irwin 2001). There has been some debate inside environmental sociology between "realists" and "constructivists" (Mol 2006). The former group asserts that ecological problems are real and are determinants (whatever that means) of social conscience and action, and even perhaps of institutions. A good case in point is global environmental change, and climate change in particular. If, as we are more and more certain, climate change is anthropogenic – that is, caused in great part by human activities – then there is no way to avoid taking steps to reduce humanity's contribution and to start adapting to a warmer climate once the ecological reality is known (IPCC 2007). This great capacity of human beings to produce such large-scale change has implications for social development and institutional building. According to human ecologists, there is an urgent need not only to act and adapt, but also to change our mindset, our ways of life, and the industrial and technological civilization we have been building and promoting across the world.

Changing our basic philosophy towards nature entails adopting, in the terms of realist sociologists, a *New Ecological Paradigm* (NEP) questioning and reversing the old "Human Exemptionalism" (or "Exceptionalism") Paradigm.[1] Constructivist sociologists see the reality differently. Ecological problems are always socially appropriated, and since people are different and live in different conditions, their responses are bound to differ, leading to debates or controversies over the nature of the problem and the changes that can be made.

REFLEXIVE MODERNITY

Modernity, and the unceasing transformation of nature and the environment for human purposes, is now widely recognized as a risky venture. Industrial development has taken its toll on environmental integrity and quality. During the nineteenth century, the great industrial cities of the world became so polluted that actions had to be taken. The air was foul and water quality was often poor. But other problems that didn't emerge at that time were smouldering, evolving slowly, and only became major problems years and decades later. Climate change is not the product of recent developments, but a long and slow process of industrialization and economic growth. Already in the 1820s, mathematician and physicist Joseph Fourier had put forward the hypothesis that, owing to industrial production that emitted the air gases rich in carbon, the Earth's atmosphere was likely to warm, which later research confirmed (Weart 2003).

This discovery of a long-term and, for a long time, hidden environmental effect of industrial society is the starting point of Ulrich Beck's theory of risk in what he calls "second modernity" (Beck 2009), or "reflexive modernity" (Giddens 1990; Beck 1992; Beck, Giddens, and Lash 1994). Beck is much concerned with risk, ecological as well as technological. Many technological risks show an ecological dimension. For instance, it is through the environment that technological risk – and disaster, such as the catastrophic nuclear accident at Chernobyl – manifests itself. Technological failures can directly affect people's health and security, but many technical disasters reveal risks and potential future hazards related to wider, indirect impacts on the environment. In response, modernity takes on a second order of modernization, "re-modernizing" itself to respond to these risks (Beck 2009).

Beck's works are highly relevant to understanding the post-industrial city. The reflexive modernity thesis suggests the need to understand the challenges of the city in relation to the unhappy and unintended consequences of modernity implicit within the rise of the city. Yet few urban analysts have drawn from his work. Risk is generally not an important topic in urban research; risk analysis belongs to other areas of sociology and the social sciences. But it would be a mistake not to be aware as urban researchers of the major contribution of the sociology of risk, and especially the writings of Beck, who has provided one of the most elaborate theoretical conceptions of the risk society, to urban environmental problems. Though there are still local environmental problems in cities, and large cities in particular, many of the new problems are less local, more regional, and, in some instances, truly global. The urbanization process and the urban way of life aggravate large environmental problems such as climate change, ozone depletion, resource scarcity, forest decline, and biodiversity loss. These are not always considered typical urban problems, but the global urban way of life and the process of urbanization have, directly and indirectly, contributed to ecosystem stress and degradation (MEA 2005).

THE INSTITUTIONAL CONTEXT OF CANADIAN FEDERALISM AND CONSTRAINTS ON URBAN ENVIRONMENTAL GOVERNANCE

It is necessary to locate the environmental problems that Canadian city-regions are facing in their social, historical, and geographic context. And for that matter, the evolution of Canadian federalism is necessarily at stake. Contrary to the representations that are often transmitted by external observers regarding its territory or the wilderness character of its landscape, Canada is a very highly urbanized country. Less than twenty percent of the Canadian population currently lives in rural areas. One can thus expect some tensions between cities and the countryside, but this is not generally the case, even though it can happen from time to time.

Over the last twenty years, the study of public policies, defined as the intervention of an authority granted public power and governmental legitimacy regarding a specific domain of society or territory (see Thoenig, quoted in Lascoumes and Le Galès 2007, 11), has increasingly been replaced by the study of public action. If it is true that considering public action rather than public policies results in moving the focus onto social actors and their interests, it does not mean that institution-building and the production of norms are put aside. However, the fact remains that these are looked upon with a bottom-up approach instead of a top-down one. This is to remind us that it is equally important to consider the sustainable interactions that prevail among different social subsystems as well as examining the contribution of social actors (including municipal and other governmental bodies, the public, institutions, and transnational coordinating bodies such as the United Nations or the OECD) to policy-making (Muller 2005).

Environmental Problems in Canada: Their Urban Specificity

Canada remains a strong decentralized federation where regions and subregions have access to specific resources. Environmental governance is thus considered and enacted across multiple levels, and unsurprisingly, can often be inconsistent, incomplete, or characterized by conflict. Of particular interest here is that within the decentralized context of Canadian federalism, cities and city-regions have largely been left on the governmental sidelines when it comes to dealing with today's emergent environmental challenges, and specifically those risks such as climate change that flow across local, regional, and global boundaries. This is important because, alongside being strongly decentralized, Canada is a highly urban country, suggesting at least some degree of urban specificity in the way we produce, experience, and manage environmental risks.

Over 80 percent of Canadians live in cities, and increasingly, they tend to concentrate in large urban agglomerations or city-regions. In 2011, 69 percent of the Canadian population lived in metropolitan areas, defined as Census Metropolitan Areas (CMAs),[2] and 81 percent in settlements over 10,000 inhabitants (calculated from Statistics Canada, Census 2011). This concentration of urban density in Canada is even more astonishing if we consider that the majority of the population is concentrated in the corridor between Windsor and Quebec City, two cities anchoring an axis across the south of Ontario and Quebec: "More than half of the population of Canada resides in this corridor, and seven out of ten manufacturing jobs in the country are located there" (Hiller 2010, 28).

In addition to this concentrated density of urban population, it is important to underline that, in the past, urbanization has taken a variety of forms in different regions according to demographic pressures, but also due to the history and geography of these regions. More recently, the emergence of the post-industrial era has had a huge impact on the shaping of urbanization. Fostered by immigration and the growth of the service sector, Canadian cities have had to face new challenges, including environmental issues (Lorinc 2006).

In other words, in a strongly urbanized country such as Canada, it is very difficult to deal with environmental issues without taking into account cities and their models of urban planning and/or urban development. It is therefore not surprising to note that issues of urban development and those of sustainable development are converging.

This does not mean that we do not find environmental problems outside cities or metropolitan regions. We can discuss the problems raised by the exploitation of the oilsands in Alberta or those raised by the exploitation of other natural resources, which activity continues to characterize Canadian society and its economy. Even if the country has long been associated with the so-called industrial societies and the service and knowledge industries, it has continued to rely on its natural resources to increase its exports and boost economic development.

In addition, we must consider the context of Canadian federalism within which cities and city-regions are evolving. In other words, to better understand the capabilities of municipalities to take action and resolve environmental issues, it is necessary to better understand their constitutional legitimacy and the reason for the weak support the federal government seems willing to give them.

Cities and the Evolution of Canadian Federalism

According to the division of powers and responsibilities among the main tiers of the state within Canadian federalism, municipalities, and more extensively, local governments are under the authority of provinces. When the British North America Act (BNAA) was signed in 1867 by the representatives of the North American British colonies to create a federal dominion, municipalities were not part of the transaction. They were not recognized as legitimate, autonomous entities. Local issues fell entirely under provincial jurisdiction; in other words, following the division of powers between the federal government and the provinces, it is the provinces that have to guarantee that land management and planning meet the demands and needs of Canadians. Since then, nothing has changed, even though local governments are now playing a more central role in social and economic development.

Despite the establishment of a clear separation of powers between the provinces and the federal government (what is not taken care of by the provinces is automatically the responsibility of the federal government), some gray areas and, therefore, disputes were quick to arise between the two tiers of the state. Without recalling the conflicts between the federal government and the provinces that marked the transformation of Canadian federalism, one must mention that the spending power of the federal government as defined by the

Constitution has allowed the federal government to intervene in a more or less important way towards municipalities, influencing their development.

In spite of this, the fact remains that the federal government has been very weak in supporting the involvement of city-regions with regards to environmental problems. Except for some limited support to public transport, assistance with environmental performance in the field of building construction, and the creation of the Canadian Environmental Assessment Agency dedicated to reviewing major projects in connection with sustainable development, in general, the federal government has been of little help in improving the environmental record of metropolitan areas. How is it possible to explain this?

To restate, the weak presence of the federal government regarding environmental – as well as urban – issues is directly linked to the history of Canadian federalism. However, since the mid-2000s, and more specifically, with the arrival to power of the Conservative Party in 2006, it is also a consequence of political choices.

At the start of the new millennium, governments were being pressed by an active coalition to bring cities and urban affairs back onto the policy agenda (Andrew, Graham, and Phillips 2002). In response, former Liberal prime minister Jean Chrétien established a working group on urban issues, and created a secretariat for cities. His successor, Paul Martin, was even more enterprising in these matters. He suggested a "new deal for cities," and in "declaring that there is 'no question that the path to Canada's future runs through municipal governments large and small, urban and rural,' Prime Minister Martin called his New Deal 'a national project for our time' equal in significance to earlier 'generational' federal railway and welfare state commitments" (Bradford 2007, 9). The wide-reaching aims of the project were remarkable when viewed against the recent history of the 1980s and 1990s, during which a preoccupation with managing deficits meant that the federal interventions concerning urban matters had become more discreet.

Out of former prime minister Martin's statement came three primary strategies. First, municipalities should be provided with long-term stable revenue. Second, the establishment of cooperative agreements involving the three levels of government in the case of large urban centres would support specific urban projects. Third, investment in the production of knowledge should be supported for improving the impact assessment of federal intervention in cities.

However, the initiatives taken by the Martin government produced very few consequences. Following its electoral victory in
January 2006, the Conservative Party was quick to put aside Martin's
"New Deal." Although some measures have been renewed, such as
the sharing of gas tax revenue with municipalities to support investment in public transport, many of them have been abolished. The
Conservative federal government has been less directly involved in
urban planning and policy, and the far-reaching visions of the "New
Deal" have been largely abandoned.

The recall of the "New Deal" strategies helps to emphasize that we
are dealing here with opposing and contradictory visions of federalism. On one hand, in the case of the Liberals, we encounter a "deep
federalism" recognizing the importance of a federal presence in matters traditionally occupied entirely by provinces and municipalities.
On the Conservative side, the vision is consistent with a federal with-
drawal. This is what Prime Minister Harper has termed a "federalism
of openness" (open federalism), based on a long-established division
of powers between the federal government and provinces. According
to some researchers, this vision is compatible with the recognition of
the dual character of Canada, and with the collective choices that
provincial governments should promote (Montpetit 2007). However,
this solution is clearly oriented towards decentralization with the aim
of reducing the direct intervention of the federal government.

One has to understand that the clash between deep and open federalism reiterates an old confrontation between two visions of federalism that are difficult to reconcile: one that relies on a multicultural
vision of the country while supporting universal liberal values, and
another that focuses on biculturalism, sticking to the initial recognition of the "two founding nations" thesis – that the Act of Union of
1840 and the BNAA of 1867 confirmed – with greater devolution of
powers to the provinces.

But the crisis of Canadian federalism is not just about constitutional issues. The capacities of the federal government and local governments alike to solve current urban and environmental problems
are at stake. In this situation, it is unlikely that the federal government will choose to revise its current position concerning the urban
and the environment. At the same time, despite their limited resources
and the weak support they can expect from the federal government,
local governments are still able to take action on environmental
problems.

URBAN AND METROPOLITAN INITIATIVES

The capacity of local and metropolitan actors is largely related to the intergovernmental support they can count on. We agree with Hank V. Savitch and Paul Kantor (2002) that cities are "neither prisoners nor masters" with regards to economic and urban development; contextual factors related to market conditions and intergovernmental support can shed light on the path chosen by a particular city.

In Canada, generally, cities are more vulnerable to market pressures than is the case in the European context. This is due to their weak constitutional autonomy and to the inadequate support received from upper tiers of the state to produce and manage urban infrastructures. In Canada, municipal revenues come mainly from property taxes. The conditional or unconditional transfers received from provincial governments are argued by some to be negligible (Tindal and Tindal 2004) and vary from province to province.

Nonetheless, this situation has not prevented municipalities from being increasingly concerned with matters of the environment and sustainability. Accordingly, cities and city-regions can increasingly be found to be developing municipal policies and actions in response to such concerns. This has been observed recently in the Montreal city-region, where the Communauté Métropolitaine de Montréal (CMM) has chosen to give the environment major attention in recent metropolitan planning documents concerning Montreal metropolitan land use and development.

THE COMMUNAUTÉ MÉTROPOLITAINE
DE MONTRÉAL

The CMM was created in 2001 by the Quebec government. This was part of a general reform of the municipal system at the turn of the millennium. The provincial government has since decided to modernize anew its municipal system through, first, the amalgamation of municipal entities, and second, a realignment of functions between various types of municipalities in both metropolitan and non-metropolitan areas (Hamel 2005). In the case of Montreal, the creation of a regional body for planning, coordination, and management of city-regional facilities and functions had been requested since the 1980s by planners and local reformers, but constantly delayed by elected provincial officials.

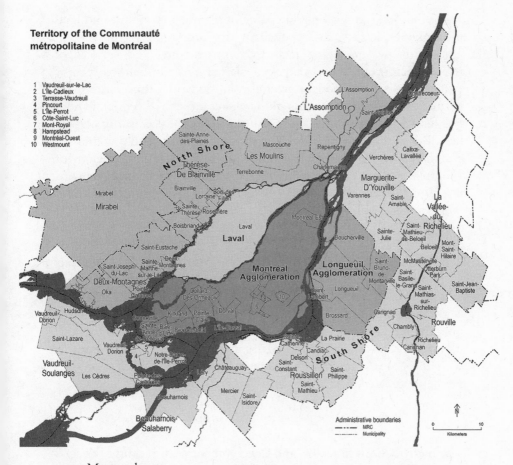

Territory of the Communauté
métropolitaine de Montréal

1 Vaudreuil-sur-le-Lac
2 L'île-Cadieux
3 Terrasse-Vaudreuil
4 Pincourt
5 L'île-Perrot
6 Côte-Saint-Luc
7 Mont-Royal
8 Hampstead
9 Montréal-Ouest
10 Westmount

10.1 Montreal

The CMM covers the territory of the Montreal Census Metropolitan Area. Twenty-eight elected officials (fourteen from Montreal, three from Longueuil, three from Laval, four from the North Shore, and four from the South Shore) representing the eighty-two municipalities form the CMM's council, which is the organ of policy and decision-making (Figure 10.1). The mandate of the CMM, as defined in Bylaw 134 – specifying also its status and functions – was to elaborate a "metropolitan plan for land use and economic development" for the entire city-region. The objective was to establish "a strategic vision of economic, social, and environmental development aiming to facilitate the coherent exercise of the Community's powers" (Gouvernement du Québec, quoted in Hamel 2006, 106).

But the CMM is not only in charge of planning economic and land use activities. It also has responsibility for promoting the city-region internationally; managing facilities, infrastructure, and services of regional importance; and playing a planning role in matters such as public transit, metropolitan arterial road networks, and waste management. The rescaling trends of managing urban and economic policies, as suggested by the Montreal example, are necessarily at play here. But in this case, the rescaling process remains caught within the contradictions of supporting and promoting the city-region of Montreal as a key Canadian city-region while the Quebec state remains in a confrontational position vis-à-vis the federal government.

The general objectives defined by the provincial state for the CMM are broad: 1) to develop a shared vision with a "consistent" economic plan and a metropolitan land use and development plan that will "make the region internationally competitive"; 2) to favour harmonious and equitable development for the entire city-region that will provide "a quality living environment for the region's citizens"; 3) to create a metropolitan financing system able to support metropolitan and municipal activities in "specific sectors"; and 4) to "harmonize government and regional organization policies and programs with the CMM's activities" (Gouvernement du Québec, quoted in Hamel 2006, 106; CMM 2011).

Environmental Issues and Metropolitan Planning

The metropolitan land use and development plan recently released by the CMM (2011) was required by the same law that instituted the CMM as a key tool for exercising its own responsibilities in regards to land use planning and territorial development. A general consensus exists among the municipalities included in the metropolitan region supporting the planning statement.

The CMM has defined three main orientations in the general philosophy that frames the planning processes. The first one focuses on sustainable living spaces. The second pertains to networks and transport systems in order to enhance their performance and structural capacity. The third targets environmental protection and development. For each of these orientations, a series of objectives and criteria for their implementation are defined. In total, fourteen objectives are specified. The criteria – being descriptive, prescriptive, or evaluative – are necessarily more numerous.

The targeted horizon for the planning document is twenty years. The concern for environmental protection is central. The framework of sustainable development in this document is thus also central. In the Foreword, this is clearly stated by the general manager of the CMM. In 2010, the total population of the Montreal metropolitan region was 3,735,066 inhabitants. According to CMM planners, the population increase during the next twenty years should follow, to a certain extent, the current trend. The demographic increase from now to 2031 should be 530,000 new inhabitants. Beginning in 2016, however, a slowing down of population growth will be followed by a more rapid aging of the population, which is worrying.

In the planning document, preserving the environment in line with a sustainable development perspective has entailed a series of choices regarding the main territorial components. Concerning the access to transit networks – which is at the heart of the strategy underlying the planning document – a choice has been made in favour of a Transit-Oriented Development (TOD). This will be compulsory for municipalities' future development.

In relation to TOD, the plan includes promoting urban density in some areas. At the same time, an emphasis is also put on agricultural land. An increase of six percent of arable land is targeted. In addition, the protection of wetlands, metropolitan forests, and flood areas, to name some of the main metropolitan milieux at risk, is clearly taken care of. Finally, CMM planners are concerned with global warming. They mention that with this metropolitan plan it is possible to contribute in a significant way to the reduction of greenhouse gas emissions produced by the Quebec population as a whole.

Two concerns must be raised in regards to the implementation of this metropolitan planning approach. The first pertains to the degree of cooperation between the several categories of actors involved in the achievement of the metropolitan planning process. To be successful, this metropolitan plan requires the support not only of the municipalities that are part of the CMM, but of other intermediary organizations also involved in local and metropolitan development. For that matter, beyond localities, Regional County Municipalities (RCM) beyond the borders of the CMM are influencing choices made by municipalities, particularly on the North and South Shores of Montreal. The same should be said about the diverse administrative regions, represented by the *Conférences regionales des élus* (CRÉ), that reside within the CMM. Finally, the Quebec government – and, to a lesser extent, the federal government – should also be taken into account. All of these various actors are involved in making decisions related to metropolitan development. They are also engaged in joint projects with one another. The result is that the metropolitan planning program elaborated by the CMM has become an object of controversy.

The capacity of the CMM to convince these actors to support its planning program has yet to be demonstrated. More importantly, we do not know the effective support – beyond their formal agreement – that municipalities are going to give to this planning process. Even though we can find progressive ways of engaging with growth and sustainability in the planning document produced by the CMM, the barriers to such ideas are numerous. To begin with, the authority and legitimacy of the CMM are at stake. So far, the CMM has not acquired the legitimacy to convince the majority of social, economic, and political actors that its leadership can make a difference. The status of planning documents must also be carefully examined. While these documents can be useful if produced through consultation and large popular participation – contributing to informing and animating public discussion around metropolitan issues – their impact remains linked to the quality of the consultation process. In other words, planning documents are less important than the planning processes. Finally, as David Imbroscio (2011) recalls in reference to urban policies in general in the United States, it is the dominant mobility paradigm as linked to liberal values that makes the integration of public concerns into planning processes difficult. So far, this paradigm has favoured an individualized form of urban development, putting aside public and collective preoccupations. We do not think the CMM planning document addresses this serious limit.

This brings us to our second concern. Nowhere in the document are the resources required to implement the main projects of the plan specified. Who is going to pay for these projects? To take only one example, the implementation of TODs is expansive. As neither the municipalities nor the provincial government have the resources, the future of these TODs is quite obscure, to say the least.

URBANISM AND PLANNING AS AN ECOLOGICAL URBAN WAY OF LIFE[3]

Since cities are complex socio-technical systems, they can be subject to failure, breakdown, and aging. The idea of a socio-technical system is borrowed from technology studies that study large technical systems, such as electricity production and distribution or transport systems, and their evolution in a changing social and institutional environment (Geels 2004; Hughes 1987). It has been applied, *mutatis mutandis*, to city-building, taken to mean the built urban environment in all its aspects, from houses, industrial plants and shops, parks, and public spaces, to large urban infrastructure projects such as water supply. Urban technical networks are an important part of the urban landscape. A period of more than a century (from 1780 to roughly 1960) rules the first modernity of city construction. Let us call it the first urban modernity, to echo Beck's first modernity – that is, before the ecological crisis and ecological awareness of the 1970s (Beck 1992; 2009). The second urban modernity, to again follow Beck's expression, is concerned with the ecological consequences of the first urban modernity.

What are these consequences? What are the new problems of cities, and large cities in particular? There are, of course, many problems, but these are of a different nature from the ones that plagued the industrial city. Some problems are directly caused by urban evolution, and others by the near-universal quality of urban lifestyles. Many of the problems of the second urban modernity are caused by the expansion of cities over wider and wider areas. Urban sprawl has become, in the planning profession, a curse in search of a cure. Sprawl consumes valuable space that could otherwise be used for conservation and other purposes. It not only encroaches on land that is allocated to agriculture, but it destroys forests, woodlands, and wetlands. Nature performs ecological services for free, such as water purification and climate regulation. In an urbanizing world, cities are bound to increase their ecological footprint, that is, the quantity of space and resources needed to sustain an urban way of life (York, Rosa, and Dietz 2003). Moreover, since urban populations are generally richer, they consume more resources and land, not to mention produce more waste, which must then be disposed of.

A second set of problems relate to large-scale ecological crises. The global urban world has a great impact on global problems, such as climate change, biodiversity loss, and deforestation. To tackle these problems, cities can do their part, even though, in cases such as biodiversity loss, other actors and institutions (such as national governments and international institutions) are at the forefront.

Cities and Climate Change

Climate change is truly a global problem with local consequences. Cities have only recently begun to get involved in climate change policy, either because their national governments were, as in Canada and the United States, reluctant to act and legislate decisively, or because they were incited by a higher tier of government, such as the European Union, to do something to reduce their greenhouse gas (GHG) emissions and to prepare themselves for the consequences of a warmer climate (Bulkeley and Betsill 2003; Bulkeley and Kern 2006; Broto and Bulkeley 2013).

The measures for climate change policy have been defined by the United Nations Framework Convention on Climate Change as comprising two types of action in order to achieve the goal of stabilizing the climate system: measures "to *mitigate climate change* by addressing anthropogenic emissions by sources and removals by sinks of all greenhouse gases not controlled by the Montreal Protocol," and measures "to facilitate adequate *adaptation to climate change*" (UN 1992, article 4.1.B; emphasis added). Mitigation measures are, to put it simply, actions taken now, or in the near future, to reduce current emission levels. Adaptation measures are anticipating what the future will bring, and support actions that prepare communities and people to exist in a warmer climate and to plan for a wide range of anticipated impacts.

Both types of measures in tandem are needed to face climate change. What actions have cities preferred and chosen? Some authors have suggested classifying urban policies with regard to climate change according to whether they are self-governed, governed through enabling, governed by provision, or governed by authority (Alber and Kern 2009, 6; Bulkeley and Kern 2006). Self-governed actions do not need to be explained; they are self-evident. Municipalities and local governments can decide, in the areas they control and are responsible for, what the best measures are for them. Governing by means of enabling means that urban citizens are prompted to change their behaviours through education and advice. For instance, campaigns for energy efficiency, waste reduction, and recycling waste products lead to behavioural change. Governing by provision refers to the public sector buying goods and services that are "climate-friendly." Governing by authority is more in tune with what governments are expected to do: legislate and impose regulations on activities and people's choices.

For instance, the enacting of transport policy to limit urban car use is an authority-governed type of governance. However, it may also belong to the provision type, as governments may impose certain regulations on manufacturers for energy efficiency. Some overlap between governance types exists, and one can expect that effectiveness in climate policy should rely on combining two, three, or all types.

All large Canadian cities have recently produced *Climate Action Plans*. They can be divided into two styles: (1) a "corporate" strategy dealing with how the municipality is going to reduce its own emissions, and (2) a larger plan aimed at engaging other stakeholders (such as businesses, households, and other public institutions) to constitute a broader community, or whole area, plan. Greenhouse gas reductions vary accordingly. Self-governed measures may come rather easily, but they concern only municipal organizations, buildings, and activities for which the municipality is responsible. However, whether the measures are self-governed or not, urban authorities have to act in the four main sectors of activities, as identified by researchers: that is, energy, transport, waste, and urban planning and land use (Alber and Kern 2009, 6).

Let us give a few examples of urban objectives on climate change. Toronto wants to reduce its GHG emissions by 6 percent in 2012, 30 percent in 2020, and 80 percent in 2050. The base year is 1990. In other words, the Toronto community and Toronto municipality are determined to more or less respect past Canadian engagements in the Kyoto Protocol, and, in accordance with the best scientific estimates, plan to reduce by a large amount (80 percent) total greenhouse gas emissions. Among the large Canadian cities, Toronto seems in the vanguard.

The City of Montreal's plan is less ambitious. It aims to reduce GHG emissions by 20 percent based on the year 2005, but this policy applies only to the city's activities and buildings. Vancouver distinguishes between its own corporate objectives and those of the community as a whole. The former are more ambitious, whereas the latter are more modest. If corporate Vancouver intends to reduce its GHG emissions by 20 percent (base year 1990) in the years to come, it is even less forward-looking for the community as whole, planning a 6 percent reduction by 2012.

Most of the urban plans and measures for these cities are concerned with mitigation. Adaptation measures (as of 2009) are far from being as developed as mitigation measures. Toronto is again at the forefront

(Toronto Environmental Office 2008). Vancouver has also examined how the whole urban region can prepare itself for a warmer climate and has set up a working group on climate adaptation. Other large cities and urban regions are concerned with planning for adaptation, but they have only recently discovered that the problem concerns them as well. Adaptation is, at times, subsumed under a sustainable development plan, as in Montreal, Ottawa, and Calgary.

It is more and more obvious that climate change policy is a stepping-stone in sustainable development. When the climate change issue reached the international polity, the problem was couched in terms of a challenge for all humanity. The more the global debate and controversy over climate change has penetrated all institutions, nations, the larger public, and different populations of the world, the more the debate has switched to a focus on the differentiated impacts of a warmer world (Stern 2009). As a consequence, the debate has turned to equity and justice concerns. If large Canadian cities are moving along the adaptation path in their urban governance, they will have to be more concerned with equity and environmental justice issues as well (Adger et al. 2006).

CONCLUSION

We tend to think of ecological problems as problems of ecosystems outside of cities, but they are, on the contrary, profoundly linked to the global urban way of life. If the world climate is changing and warming, cities may be important causes and culprits. If forests are, as is the case almost everywhere, declining, it is due not only to demographic growth, but also to a higher demand for food – particularly energy-rich food – for a growing and richer urban population. Not all urban populations are rich, but the choice of city living rests on better economic prospects and better living conditions.

Environmental governance is complex, and increasingly multilevel. Complexity in governance is due to the complexity of natural systems, but also to social complexity. Social complexity is the historical evolution of a highly differentiated society, as many sociologists (e.g. Luhmann 1982) have insisted. Some complexity is the result of contingent historical institution-building and political arrangements. Canada is a federal state, where two tiers of government share power, and where each rules over its own constitutional responsibilities. The environment is a relatively new area of political and administrative action that various tiers of government have had to learn how to deal with.

The city has not been a great concern to the federal state, because the municipalities were the creation of the provinces. However, administrative and ad-hoc cooperation are frequently arrived at. The climate change issue has pitted the federal government and certain provinces against other provinces and cities wanting to do their part on the climate front. Large Canadian cities have taken steps to achieve the stabilization of the Earth's climate and, though still timidly, to adapt themselves to a warmer climate. Many sustainable development initiatives have a direct and indirect effect on climate change.

Environmental urban governance has broadened with new global problems. Climate change, biodiversity, and sustainability are problems best tackled at the metropolitan and regional scale of urban areas, and not solely at the scale of one municipality, such as the main central city. But to face these problems, cooperation and institutional experience are needed. Metropolitan governance is challenged by these new and global ecological problems, but it must learn to adapt them to its own reality and practices.

Finally, planning ideas have been rich in innovation. New urbanism and smart growth are leading the innovation march. However, the two models may come up short in creating the expected sustainable city, and it is not clear, in a globalizing and urbanizing world, if their main intellectual inventions are the most daring and the best solutions there are. There are many local actions taken to "green" cities (more parks, green spaces, green roofs and green walls, etc.), but an overall vision is still needed, one that can encompass developed and developing countries as well. The sustainable development idea and ideal of the UN World Commission on the Environment and Development was very helpful in providing new inputs to city planning and urban growth. Sociologists (Mol, Sonnenfeld, and Spaargaren 2009) have observed that industry seems to have taken the ecological modernization path. It is worth asking if or when large cities will invent and embark on their own urban ecological modernization process.

Confronting climate change, planning for greater biodiversity protection and restoration in cities (and large cities in particular), acting on the urban form, and investing in technological developments, notably in infrastructure and transport systems, are all measures and policies that can help bring about urban ecological modernization.

But the challenge may be even greater. It is not clear whether people believe that an urban sustainable society is an easily achievable goal, or even desirable, as sustainable development means different things to different people. For instance, is it true that compact cities, promoted by some planning schools of thought and by urban analysts such as Glaeser (2011), will be enthusiastically adopted by urban dwellers, who still often aspire to residential choices according to the low-density model they know and value, at least in North America? The trade-off between expansive cities and greater environmental protection may face cultural challenges and social resistance. The idea of urban sustainable development is taken up when the development dimension is in the forefront. It may be relatively easy for the advanced technology industry to embark on ecological modernization and considerably reduce its impact on the environment, but there are limits. Some, in the perspective of human ecology and Malthusianism, claim that a deliberate and conscious shift from one way of life to another is doomed, and that only necessity will make people and society change. However, if "reflexive modernity" has any meaning and reality, one can hope that, with the help of science, environmental social movements, and a greater public awareness of ecological impacts and footprints, people and societies will change, though this will likely occur gradually and not without conflict, as the international debate on climate change vividly shows. The dual process of world urbanization and world development raises the challenge. The ecological modernization thesis has been criticized for only and restrictively applying to some parts of the industrial (or post-industrial) world, namely northwestern Europe, which is not the best representative of the world at large (Buttel 2000). Since cities are, in large part, unique and anchored in local cultures, power relations, and economies, there may be no ready-made and universal solution to creating an ecological urbanity.

NOTES

1 According to this paradigm, human beings are largely exempt from ecological constraints that are regularly lifted. It also asserts that human beings and the societies they live in are a different and superior species (Catton 1980; Catton and Dunlap 1978). Critics of this neo-human ecology perspective complain that such a view is reductive and even false, for people

are reflexive and thinking beings. No ecological change has a direct impact on social actions and institutions, at least in non-extreme cases.

However, we can hypothesize that with rising environmental conscious-ness socially, it is also necessary to incorporate an understanding of the complex interrelationships between urban and (for lack of a better term) wider rural environments in finding integrated ways of managing a sus-tainable environment with more attention.

2 A CMA is an urban agglomeration with a population of at least 500,000 including an urban centre with no fewer than 50,000 inhabitants.

3 This section relies on a chapter on "Cities and the Environment" in Guay and Hamel 2014.

REFERENCES

Adger, W.N., S. Hug, M.J. Mace, and J. Paavola, eds. 2006. *Fairness in Adaptation to Climate Change*. Cambridge, MA: MIT Press.

Alber, G., and K. Kern. 2009. "Governing Climate Change in Cities: Modes of Urban Governance in Multi-Level Systems." Paper presented at the *Competitive Cities and Climate Change* conference, October. Milan, Italy: 171–96.

Andrew, C., Graham, K.A., and S.D. Phillips. 2002. *Urban Affairs Back on the Policy Agenda*. Montreal & Kingston: McGill-Queens's University Press.

Beck, U. 1992. *The Risk Society. Towards a New Modernity*. London: Sage.

– 2009. *World at Risk*. Cambridge: Polity Press.

Beck, U., A. Giddens, and S. Lash. 1994. *Reflexive Modernization: Politics, Tradition and Aesthetics in the Modern Social Order*. Stanford, CA: Stanford University Press.

Boyden, S. 1992. *Biohistory: The Interplay between Human Society and the Biosphere*. Paris: UNESCO.

Boyden, S., et al. 1981. *The Ecology of a City and Its People: The Case of Hong Kong*. Canberra: Australian National University Press.

Bradford, N. 2007. *Whither the Federal Urban Agenda? A New Deal in Transition?* Working Paper. Ottawa: Canadian Policy Research Network Inc.

Broto, C.V., and H. Bulkeley. 2013. "A Survey of Urban Climate Change Experiments in 100 Cities." *Global Environment Change* 23: 92–102.

Bulkeley, H., and M.M. Betsill. 2003. *Cities and Climate Change*. London: Routledge.

Bulkeley, H., and K. Kern. 2006. "Local Governance and the Governing of Climate Change in Germany and the UK." *Urban Studies* 43 (12): 2237–59.

Buttel, F.H. 2000. "Ecological Modernization as a Social Theory." *Geoforum* 31 (1): 57–65.

Catton, W.R. 1980. *Overshoot. The Ecological Basis of Revolutionary Change*. Urbana, IL: Illinois University Press.

Catton, W.R., and R.E. Dunlap. 1978. "Environmental Sociology: A New Paradigm." *American Sociologist* 13 (1): 41–9.

Communauté Métropolitaine de Montréal. 2011. *Un Grand Montréal attractif, compétitif et durable. Projet de Plan métropolitain d'aménagement et de développement*. Montreal: Author.

Gaston, K.J., ed. 2010. *Urban Ecology*. Cambridge: Cambridge University Press.

Geels, F. 2004. "From Sectoral Systems of Innovation to Socio-Technical Systems: Insights About Dynamics and Change From Sociology and Institutional Theory." *Research Policy* 33 (6–7): 897–920.

Giddens, A. 1990. *The Consequences of Modernity*. Stanford, CA: Stanford University Press.

Glaeser, E. 2011. *The Triumph of the City*. London: Macmillan.

Guay, L. 2002. "The Science and Policy of Global Biodiversity Protection." In *Governing Global Biodiversity*, edited by P. Le Prestre, 207–33. Aldershot, UK: Ashgate.

Guay, L., and P. Hamel. 2014. *Cities and Urban Sociology*. Don Mills, ON: Oxford University Press.

Hamel, P. 2005. "Municipal Reform in Quebec: The Trade-off between Centralization and Decentralization." In *Municipal Reform in Canada. Reconfiguration, Re-Empowerment, and Rebalancing*, edited by J. Garcea and E.C. LeSage Jr, 149–73. Don Mills, ON: Oxford University Press.

– 2006. "Institutional Changes and Metropolitan Governance: Can De-amalgamation Be Amalgamation? The Case of Montréal." In *Metropolitan Governing: Canadian Cases, Comparative Lessons*, edited by E. Razin and P.J. Smith, 95–120. Jerusalem: The Hebrew University Magnes Press.

Hannigan, J.A. 2006. *Environmental Sociology*. London: Routledge.

Harvey, D. 1996. *Justice, Nature and the Geography of Difference*. Oxford, UK: Blackwell.

Heynen, N., M. Kaika, and E. Swyngedouw, eds. 2006. *In the Nature of Cities. Urban Political Ecology and the Politics of Urban Metabolism.* London: Routledge.

Hiller, H.H. 2010. "The Dynamics of Canadian Urbanization." In *Urban Canada*, 2nd ed., edited by H.H. Hiller, 19–39. Don Mills, ON: Oxford University Press.

Hughes, T.P. 1987. "The Evolution of Large Technological Systems." In *The Social Construction of Technological Systems*, edited by W.E. Bijker, T. Pinch, and T.P. Hughes, 51–82. Cambridge, MA: MIT Press.

Imbroscio, D. 2011. "Beyond Mobility: The Limits of Liberal Urban Policy." *Journal of Urban Affairs* 34 (1): 1–19.

IPCC (Intergovernmental Panel on Climate Change). 2007. *Climate Change 2007. The Physical Science Basis.* Cambridge: Cambridge University Press.

Irwin, A. 2001. *Sociology and the Environment.* Cambridge: Polity Press.

Lascoumes, P., and P. Le Galès. 2007. *Sociologie de l'action publique.* Paris: Armand Colin.

Lorinc, J. 2006. *The New City. How the Crisis in Canada's Urban Centres Is Reshaping the Nation.* Toronto: Penguin Canada.

Luhmann, N. 1982. *The Differentiation of Society.* New York: Columbia University Press.

Millennium Ecosystem Assessement (MEA). 2005. *Ecosystems and Human Well-Being: Synthesis.* Washington, DC: Island Press.

Mol, A.J.P. 2006. "From Environmental Sociologies to Environmental Sociology: A Comparison of U.S. and European Sociology." *Organization & Environment* 19 (1): 5–27.

Mol, A.J.P., A. Sonnenfeld, and G. Spaargaren, eds. 2009. *The Ecological Modernization Reader: Environmental Reform in Theory and Practice.* London and New York: Routledge.

Montpetit, É. 2007. *Le fédéralisme d'ouverture. La recherche d'une légitimité canadienne au Québec.* Quebec: Septentrion.

Moran, E.F. 2010. *Environmental Social Science. Human-Environmental Interactions and Sustainability.* Chichester, UK: Wiley-Blackwell.

Muller, P. 2005. "Esquisse d'une théorie du changement dans l'action publique." *Revue française de science politique* 55 (1): 155–87.

Pickett, S.T.A., M.L. Cadenasso, J.M. Grove, C.H. Nilon, R.V. Pouyat, W.C. Zipperer, and R. Costanza. 2001. "Urban Ecological Systems: Linking Terrestrial Ecological, Physical, and Socioeconomic

Components of Metropolitan Areas." *Annual Review of Ecology and Systematics* 32: 127–57.

Sassen, S., and N. Dotan. 2011. "Delegating, Not Returning, to the Biosphere: How to Use the Multi-Scalar and Ecological Properties of Cities." *Global Environmental Change* 21 (3): 823–34.

Savitch, H.V., and P. Kantor. 2002. *Cities in the International Market Place*. Princeton, NJ: Princeton University Press.

Scott, A.J., Agnew, J., Soja, E.W., and M. Storper. 2001. "Global City-Regions." In *Global City-Regions: Trends, Theory, Policy*, edited by A.J. Scott, 11–32. Oxford, UK: Oxford University Press.

Statistics Canada. 2011. *Census 2011. Population and Dwelling Counts*. http://www12.stat.gc.ca/census-recensement/2011. Accessed 29 May 2013.

Stern, N. 2009. *The Global Deal*. New York: Public Affairs.

Tindal, C.R., and S. Nobes Tindal. 2004. *Local Government in Canada*. Scarborough, ON: Thomson/Nelson.

Toronto Environmental Office. 2008. *Ahead of the Storm: Preparing Toronto for Climate Change*. Toronto: Author.

United Nations. 1992. *United Nations Framework Convention on Climate Change*. New York: Author.

Weart, S.R. 2003. *The Discovery of Global Warming*. Cambridge, MA: Harvard University Press.

York, R., E.A. Rosa, and T. Dietz. 2003. "Footprints on the Earth: The Environmental Consequences of Modernity." *American Sociological Review* 68 (2): 279–300.

The Tensions and Benefits of Regionalizing Palliative Care Services: Considerations for City-Regionalism

KYLE Y. WHITFIELD AND ALLISON M. WILLIAMS

INTRODUCTION

At what geographical scale should health care provision be organized? Echoing long-running debates regarding the logic and legitimacy of state control, Canada is characterized by experiments in both regional and city-regional governance of health care. The oscillation between regional and city-regional geographies of service provision and the practical issue of finding a spatial fix that "works" throw into sharp relief questions relating to how regions and city-regions are defined, understood, and occupied, and the manner in which they codify a relationship between service providers and end users. In this chapter, we consider the recent history of spatial reorganization in Canadian health care provision, using three provinces as case studies: Alberta, Saskatchewan, and Manitoba. We unpack how shifting geographies of health care have affected the evolution of an essential health service: palliative and end-of-life care. City-regionalization is examined as a potential turning point in the evolution of a health care service, with specific attention paid to the value of networks as an essential element of successful regional planning and city-regional–level decision-making. Guiding this chapter are questions about the function of the city-region considered through an analysis of the impact of regional planning on the development of health services in three provinces in western Canada.

THE REGIONALIZATION OF HEALTH CARE
IN CANADA

We begin by describing the story of health service planning in Canada, and then in the prairie provinces of Alberta, Saskatchewan, and Manitoba, specifically. This narrative is informed by a research investigation of the evolution of end-of-life palliative care services in Canada involving a series of key-informant interviews and case study comparisons.[1] Here, specifically, we employ the outcomes of this research to explore the evolution of regionalization of health service planning in Canada and to consider the implications for the city-region.

At its heart, regionalism is about politically dividing space and creating unique regional scales at which to govern. The regionalization of the health care system in Canada has involved a process of experimentation over four decades, with the goal of finding the most appropriate scale at which to manage health services. In doing so, regionalism has significantly altered how health care systems are now being understood and delivered (Schroeder 2009). Beginning in the 1960s, regional experiments began taking place, as governments sought to modernize and formalize a largely fragmented and dispersed health care system. As Church and Barker (1998) note, a plethora of attempts at reform have been made within Canada since then. Commonly reforms have envisioned the region as an intermediary level between communities and the province. From the 1960s onwards, regional bodies have been created across the country by provinces to deliver health care services that integrate service delivery, motivated by the desire to create greater efficiencies in the system while also reducing costs. About regionalizing health care services in Canada, Decter (1997) explains: "Regionalization involves both consolidation of multiple health sector boards, as well as the devolution of authority from provincial departments of health to regional authorities [and it] is expected to result in more efficient and effective allocation of resources, because decision making can take into account local circumstances and population health needs" (0872).

Prior to regionalization, acute care services were provided in hospitals governed by independent local boards. Similarly, public health and continuing care were governed by independent local boards. Provincial governments identified the separateness of these local boards as barriers to providing a coordinated approach to health care delivery (Decter 1997). Integration in a regionalized model was intended to streamline services into one coordinated health care system for patients, eliminating duplication of inefficient services and creating a more coordinated approach to care. Choosing a regionally focused model of health care delivery aims to achieve cost savings by rationalizing health services and centralizing authority into regional organizations from local boards, all the while shifting authority to manage health care from provincial governments to these regional authorities. Regionalizing health care has been seen as a means of devolving authority and de-centring management away from provincial departments, which worked across numerous local boards. The process is one of decentralizing the management of health services from provincial governments to centralized regional health authorities (Decter 1997).

Moreover, the restructuring of health services in Canada has reflected another of the dominant logics shaping processes of regionalization. The creation of regional health boards has also been imagined to further benefit citizens by aligning service delivery closer to local needs, fostering engagement, and making health systems more accountable to regional communities. It is this pairing of regional efficiencies and cost savings with local accountability that places regionalism as an accommodation between centralized and more diffuse systems, and that has strongly influenced health service delivery in Canada.

The influence of city-regional planning has been much less direct in shaping health service delivery. However, as regions become more closely linked to growing urban centres, it is becoming more relevant. In this sense, it is important to note that city-regionalism shares many of the attributes of regionalism, and is guided by many of the same logics. As Harrison (2008) notes, it is not that city-regionalism replaces regionalism; rather, it joins the city to the region. As a number of chapters in this volume suggest, its meanings are multiple and contested, and city-regions take many forms in practice (Jones et al., Harrison, and Glass, this volume; see also Hamedinger 2011). Nelles (2012, 2) too says that city-regions are many things, but at their most basic they are a combination of spaces, scales, nodes of action, and structures. Out of this context, city-regions are imagined as spaces for policy development, knowledge creation, collective learning, and projects for economic, social, and political interaction. They also embody attempts to rationalize governance and motivate efficiencies in local service delivery. As is the case for regionalization, their success or benefit in these regards is uncertain.

In terms of the Canadian health care system, the city-region may become an important focal point for further rescaling of service provision. Canada is a disproportionately urban country, with almost eighty percent of the population living in cities.[2] This number has increased steadily since Confederation, and the country's primary cities are increasingly the destination for immigrants to Canada and migrants within the country. It is therefore unsurprising that health services, particularly those of a specialized nature, are highly centralized within Canada's cities, and within the large city-regions in particular (Sanmartin and Ross 2006). A constant challenge for health care planners has been to provide equitable access to service for Canadians in both rural and urban locales, while also controlling costs. The consequence is that most rural communities must rely upon urban areas for at least part of their health care needs (Romanow 2000, 159–269). Canada's large cities and city-regions are, in other words, both where most of the demand for health services resides and the source of services to wider, regional communities. Moreover, as the city-region has become more prominent in Canadian planning, so too has the focus on service delivery at the urban, and even neighbourhood, scale. Regional rationales for integration, efficiency, and local accountability remain the same, but are becoming increasingly expressed at the urban scale.

HEALTH SERVICE PLANNING IN CANADA'S PRAIRIE PROVINCES

Few studies place health services in a regional planning context to assess the outcomes of efforts at rescaling service delivery (c.f. Gambardella et al. 2009). In response to this deficit, the following discussion provides an account of regionalism and city-regionalism, and their impact on palliative care services, in each of Canada's three prairie provinces: Alberta, Saskatchewan, and Manitoba.

Health Canada describes palliative and end-of-life care services as those that support people living with life-threatening illnesses.[3] Care is focused on achieving comfort and ensuring respect for the person nearing death, and maximizing quality of life for them, their family, and other loved ones. Services can be those that help manage pain and other symptoms; that provide social, psychological, cultural, emotional, spiritual, and practical support; that help caregivers; and that support bereavement. This care can be offered in institutional and community (non-institutional) settings.

Beginning with Alberta, the use of a regional and city-regional planning model for the development of palliative care services has had significant impacts, both positive and negative. Regionalization of this particular service sparked a major turning point in the evolution of palliative care delivery, because it allowed each region to set its own health care priorities, thus setting a precedent for end-of-life care in the province. Regionalization forced new insights about the differences in rural versus urban palliative care needs, and gave each region in Alberta its own decision-making power. The use of regionalization as a planning model, however, also compromised provincial palliative care services in a number of ways. Services were said to be unequal and unfair between regions, contributing to regional competition and making collaboration between key decision-makers, service providers, and other palliative care–related stakeholders extremely difficult. In the process of moving to a regionalized model in 1994, several local-level palliative care services were cut. With the shifting number of regions in Alberta – from seventeen to nine regions, then to one health super board, with the Health Quality Council of Alberta in the process of being disbanded at the time of this writing – service planning and implementation were described as being very slow to develop.

In Saskatchewan, a regional model of health care planning brought palliative care to the forefront. It created a new and positive link between urban and rural communities, resulting in better care provision in less-populated areas of the province. In Saskatchewan, the role of individual champions of palliative care services was essential to its success. Regional-level decision-making became independent and autonomous from the province, and has been described as being of terrific value to palliative care services. It may be that this occurred because service delivery was being supported by the creation of mutually supportive networks at the regional level which had not necessarily been present, or as influential, at the local level. "Red tape" and high levels of bureaucracy, however, hindered palliative care services in Saskatchewan. This has implications for family members in rural areas who, while caring for their loved ones, have to start an intravenous drip, for example, having had no prior training.

Manitoba implemented a model that used a palliative care coordinator at the provincial level. This aided in the planning, implementation, and prioritization of palliative care services, and coordinators became essential in the creation of a provincial palliative care network in 2000, which linked together regions and key stakeholders. Because localities and regions were strategically brought together, inter-institutional relations and synergies were permitted to grow (MacLeod 1997). Similar to Alberta and Saskatchewan, decision-making power at the regional level in Manitoba allowed services to be regionally customized, enabling regions to provide different services according to need. Along with decision-making power being closer to the community, support for service planning and service provision by local communities had a critical impact on success, as did having key individuals who championed palliative and end-of-life care services in the province. As in Saskatchewan and Alberta, however, these individuals' need to travel enormous distances between the thirteen regions to provide direct support to Manitobans at the end of their lives, and to their families, significantly hindered the ability to meet people's urgent needs.

Considerations for the City-Region

Decentralized decision-making and integration are two major characteristics of a regional planning framework. Since one aim of regionalization has been to decentralize resources and their allocation from the provincial ministries to regional authorities so as to locally coordinate planning (Marchildon 2006), it is intended to allow for more place-based care, as local factors and local-level citizen engagement are high priorities. Ultimately, as Schroeder (2009) states, decentralized decision-making is about ensuring that health services are responsive to local needs.

All three provinces commonly fostered integration, collaboration, partnerships, and resulting networks. Such characteristics suggest a degree of "institutional thickness." Usually found in literature on the role of regions in fostering economic and community development, the idea of a "thickness" of institutional relations seeks to capture the value of having regional policy supported by a strong institutional presence and positive interactions between varied stakeholders, as well as having clearly defined structures for decision-making (MacLeod 1997; see also Keeble et al. 1999, and Amin and Thrift

1995). Such robustness is seen to support cooperation and the development of shared purpose across a region, foster innovation, and embed the benefits of integration within local development contexts.

In regards to service delivery, Glover et al. (2007) similarly suggest that "good" regionalism happens when there is positive collaboration. Schroeder (2009) echoes this sentiment: "the need to integrate services has led to the widespread use of partnership arrangements between public, private and voluntary sector organizations" (19). When developing a specialized geriatric service in the province of Ontario (central Canada), Glover et al. (2007) found that their success was dependent on establishing a regional network. In this instance, a regional network helped because there was integration between services; their main focus was on building local capacity and collaboration so that equality between all regional partners existed.

City-regionalism may create a spatial and scalar context in which successful partnerships can emerge, so long as openness to partnership and citizen engagement is maintained (Counsell and Haughton 2003), and so long as publics and communities are engaged as part of the planning process. Community engagement strategies should therefore be consistent between regions (Schroeder 2009). At the heart of good regional planning and health service delivery, we discovered how important it is to overcome inequities between regions, and even between provinces. Facilitating such equity is a key role of city-regional thinking. The core question driving the city-region, therefore, is how to build regional capacity that fosters partnerships, ongoing citizen engagement, and overall equity. It is further necessary to recognize that partnership cannot stop at the boundaries of a city-region; good policy must also emphasize the value of building relationships across and between city-regions as allies in pursuing enhanced capacity.

Even though there has been a long history of regional planning in Canada, it is still not clear whether regionalization has been beneficial or not (Counsell and Haughton 2003), or if it has benefited Canada's health services (Schroeder 2009). As a planning model, regionalization continues to be debated. For many, it remains inadequate in providing sufficient evidence that the system is meeting the population's needs. Alberta, Saskatchewan, and Manitoba experienced some of the same and some different effects amongst themselves, but overall, there was little variation. This does not necessarily mean that regionalization is a faulty model; factors such as timing, existence of local champions, and autonomy in decision-making certainly influence the success and provision of a health service (Hinings et al. 2003). As Marchildon (2005) points out, a regional model in and of itself does not necessarily improve or cause harm. Moreover, it may not be that regionalization is misguided; rather, its potential benefits may not yet have been realized (Schroeder 2009). This has implications for city-regionalism.

HEALTH SERVICE PLANNING TRENDS IN CANADA

With continued development and ongoing progress of the concept of the city-region in Canada, what are the key health service planning trends and their implications for the city-region? The most fundamental change occurring in health care in Canada that impacts health planning is the transfer of care and planning from the province to the local, regional, municipal, and even neighbourhood levels. In the past, there was greater reliance on hospitals to provide care; now, care is often planned and provided through community clinics, community health centres, and through informal systems of support: that is, friends, family, and neighbourhoods. The growth of Canada's aging population – and with that, the rise in chronic disease – reminds us that the health needs of Canadians are always in flux, and that the health system and planning processes have to continually adapt and respond accordingly (Health Canada 2011). It is necessary to ensure the following: 1) that there is greater coordination of fragmented, difficult-to-access health services; 2) that there is citizen engagement and input into health service–related decision-making; and 3) that the health needs and realities of those living in rural and remote locations are seen as highly relevant and are responded to. If Health Canada's strategic outcomes for 2010–11 are to create a sustainable health system that is responsive to the health needs of Canadians (Health Canada 2010, 9), the role of planning is a central requirement.

Considerations for the City-Region

These health service planning issues both influence and are influenced by city-regionalism through concepts and priorities such as quality of place, by creating greater opportunities for civic engagement, and by building decision-making systems that are open to opportunities. The quality of the place in which health services are provided is an important characteristic for the city-region. Health services that are place-based must ensure that the specific attributes of the people of that place are taken into account, such as age, disease prevalence, and other similar attributes. It acknowledges the particular aspects of the overall health system, such as services available, and considers the influence of environmental factors on people such as air and water pollution.

Well-developed, or successful, city-regions are said to be areas where an important role exists for civic engagement – where community members are not only valuable sources of local information, but are integrated as leaders of such engagement (Krueger and Savage, 2007).

Gambardella et al. (2009) examined the effect of openness as a broad decision-making concept in a regional context. Openness, they argue, is characteristic of regional excellence, as it is associated with knowledge, services and skills, assets, or linkages. Openness in decision-making, they state, contributes to opportunities for advanced performance in the specified region as well as those regions surrounding it. In particular, if there is openness in a region, it is open to external opportunities. Moreover, if it is open, it is embedded in broad networks. An open region is defined as "a region ... [that] is hooked into wider networks ... these networks provide exposure to knowledge, resources, learning processes, or to more advanced benchmarks or best practices that enable the regions to produce better or more advanced goods and services, or to make more productive investments" (936). Openness happens very slowly; however, it can, when measured, have beneficial impacts on a region in terms of boosting scientific and technological activities that affect regional economic performance.

THE VALUE OF CITY-REGION CONSTRUCTS
FOR NEW HEALTH SERVICE PLANNING
DIRECTIONS IN CANADA

Having looked at how a regional model has affected one health service in three prairie provinces, we now examine several factors that contributed to the momentum towards a regional focus. We then highlight several key tensions that show inconsistencies between the logics of regional and city-regional models. Finally, we end this chapter by asking about the usefulness of city-region constructs for developing new directions in health service delivery in Canada.

In the 1990s, palliative and end-of-life care services shifted in these three Canadian provinces because the region became a new means of conceptualizing and approaching many significant health service problems. It was a solution. It provided greater decision-making autonomy at the regional level, helping to create services more reflective of the expressed needs of communities. It helped reduce service costs and eliminate service duplication, thus better integrating services. It reversed the trend towards centralization and built "new institutional spaces through which to secure the promise of increased accountability and participatory democracy under devolution" (Harrison 2010, 17). It is no wonder then that city-regional thinking became essential to the planning and implementation of this significant and growing service need. In evaluating the evolution of city-regionalism in the United Kingdom, Harrison describes the process as one creating "spaces of flow," where there is "spatiality of flow, porosity and connectivity" (18).

In our case, this movement towards a regional model also created problems: the cutting of palliative care services, severe competition between regions – especially between rural and urban areas – and service planning being slow in its delivery of actual services. Service inequity between regions increased, as did levels of service bureaucracy. There are obvious inconsistencies between the purpose, intent, and logic of city-regional thinking and its actual outcomes on the ground. The conceptual vagueness of the city-region and the fact that it rarely (if ever) corresponds to its intended outcomes are, however, triggering a new line of thinking about how to best conceptualize regions and regional change (Harrison 2011). As a result, questions are now being asked about the politics of transformation in an actual region, the combinations that may be more suited to stabilizing society in our current "regional world," how best to represent space, and most recently, Harrison's (2011) exploration of the role and strategies of individual and collective agents, organizations, and institutions to create multiple dimensions of socio-spatial relations.

Finally, we must ask about the usefulness of certain city-region constructs for new directions in health service delivery in Canada, considering what we have learned about the application of a region-centred model to health care services. The work of Krueger and Savage (2007) offers an extremely valuable perspective on the city-region that is necessary for future directions of health service planning in Canada. According to these authors, the success of a region is founded on what they refer to as "social reproduction," which, amongst other things, is about improving access to services such as health care. It is about responding to issues relevant to quality of life and concepts of social justice. A successful city-region, these authors assert, must consider the people engaged in struggles and their efforts to sustain families and communities (216). "Social reproduction," they say, is characteristic of the sustainable development of a city-region – a concept or term they, along with Agyeman et al. (2003), argue has been too centred on the environment. Sustainable development has an important social context, as social equity is an essential component of sustainability (Krueger and Savage 2007, 217).

CONCLUSION

In this chapter, we considered the recent history of spatial reorganization in Canadian health care provision, using the case of one health service, palliative care, and its evolution in three western Canadian provinces to view the effects of the continued changing geographies of health care. Themes examined have been city-regionalization as a turning point in the evolution of a health care service, the value of networks and "institutional thickness" as being conducive to good regional planning, and the benefits and challenges of regional- and city-regional–level decision-making. Overall, we asked about the function of the city-region after looking at the impact of regional planning on the development of palliative care in Alberta, Saskatchewan, and Manitoba.

From the outset, we noted that regionalization, and more recently the expression of its core rationales in terms of the city-region, have promised much to many. Yet, as our case study of palliative care in Canada's prairie provinces demonstrates, such benefits are difficult to achieve. Rather, the consequences of re-territorializing palliative care services has been contradictory (as has the experience of the regionalization of health services more generally; see Church and Barker 1998). Redrawing service boundaries has inevitably granted services to some communities while creating access challenges for others. An unintended outcome of regional thinking has thus been an increase in conflicts between regions for service access, and between rural regions and urban communities. Moreover, intended efficiencies have led to greater bureaucratic burdens, potentially ostracizing communities instead of making health services account-able to them. Regional and city-regional planning are not a panacea for the persistent and, in many ways, intractable challenges facing Canadian health care planners. Geographic distance, budget ratio-nalizations, urban growth, and the ongoing challenge of making services accountable to citizens persist within regional scenarios, as they do elsewhere. The persistence of these challenges draws our attention back to engaging regionalization as a politics of change, and guides planning to engage directly with justice and sustainabil-ity challenges at their heart. Rationalized regional planning exercises may help focus our attention on these challenges, but caution should be taken in assuming that they impose positive change on complex and uncertain health service contexts.

NOTES

1 For a full discussion of this research, its methods, and conclusions, please refer to Williams et al. 2010.
2 http://www.statcan.gc.ca/tables-tableaux/sum-som/l01/cst01/demo62a-eng. htm.
3 http://www.hc-sc.gc.ca/hcs-sss/palliat/index-eng.php.

REFERENCES

Agyeman, J., R.D. Bullard, and B. Evans, eds. 2003. *Just Sustainabilities: Development in an Unequal World.* Cambridge, MA: MIT Press.

Amin, A., and N. Thrift. 1995. "Globalisation, Institutional 'Thickness' and the Local Economy." In *Managing Cities: The New Urban Context*, edited by P. Healey, S. Cameron, S. Davoudi, S. Graham, and A. Madani-Pour. Chichester, UK: John Wiley.

Church, J., and P. Barker. 1998. "Regionalization of Health Services in Canada: A Critical Perspective." *International Journal of Health Services* 28 (3): 467–86.

Counsell, D., and G. Houghton. 2003. "Regional Planning Tensions: Planning for Economic Growth and Sustainable Development in Two Contrasting English Regions." *Environment and Planning C: Government and Policy* 21 (2): 225–39.

Decter, M.B. 2007. "Canadian Hospitals in Transformation." *Medical Care* 35 (10): OS70–OS75.

Friedman, T.L. 2000. *The Lexus and the Olive Tree*. Toronto: Anchor Books.

Gambardella, A., M. Mariani, and S. Torrisi. 2009. "How Provincial is Your Region? Openness and Regional Performance in Europe." KITes Working Paper 006. Milan, Italy: KITes, Centre for Knowledge, Internationalization and Technology Studies, Università Bocconi.

Glover, C., L. Hillier, and I. Gutmanis. 2007. "Stakeholder Engagement and Public Policy Evaluation: Factors Contributing to the Development and Implementation of a Regional Network for Geriatric Care." *Healthcare Management Forum* 20 (4): 6–12.

Hamedinger, A. 2002. *Longitudes and Attitudes: Exploring the World after September 11*. New York: Farrar, Strauss and Giroux.

– 2011. "Understanding City-Regional Governance – The Integration of 'Space' into Governance Theory." Regional Studies Association Winter Conference 2011, London. http://www.regional-studies-assoc.ac.uk/events/2011/winterconf/presentations/Hamedinger.pdf. Accessed 20 March 2012.

Harding, A. 2007. "Taking City-Regions Seriously? Response to Debate on 'City-Regions': New Geographies of Governance, Democracy and Social Reproduction." *International Journal of Urban and Regional Research* 31 (2): 443–58.

Harrison, J. 2008. "Stating the Production of Scales: Centrally Orchestrated Regionalism, Regionally Orchestrated Centralism." *International Journal of Urban and Regional Research* 32 (4): 922–41.

– 2010. "Networks of Connectivity, Territorial Fragmentation, Uneven Development: The New Politics of City-Regionalism." *Political Geography* 29 (1): 17–27.

– 2013. "Configuring the New 'Regional World': On Being Caught between Territory and Networks." *Regional Studies* 47 (1): 55–74.

Health Canada. 2010. "Health Canada 2010–2011 Estimates Part III – Report on Plans and Priorities." http://www.tbs-sct.gc.ca/rpp/2010-2011/inst/shc/shc-eng.pdf. Accessed 19 March 2012.

– 2011. *Canada's Health Care System*. http://www.hc-sc.gc.ca/hcs-sss/ppubs/system-regime/2011-hcs-sss/index-eng.php. Accessed 19 March 2012.

Hinings, C.R., A. Casebeer, T. Reay, K. Golden-Biddle, A. Pablo, and R. Greenwood. 2003. "Regionalizing Healthcare in Alberta: Legislated

Change, Uncertainty and Loose Coupling." *British Journal of Management* 14 (S1): S15–S30.

Jonas, A., and K. Ward. 2007. "There's More than One Way to Be 'Serious' about City-Regions." *International Journal and Urban and Regional Research* 31 (3): 647–56.

Keeble, D., C. Lawson, B. Moore, and F. Wilkinson. 1998. "Collective Learning Processes, Networking and 'Institutional Thickness' in the Cambridge Region." *Regional Studies* 33 (4): 319–32.

Krueger, R., and L. Savage. 2007. "City-Regions and Social Reproduction: A 'Place' for Sustainable Development?" *International Journal and Urban and Regional Research* 31 (1): 215–23.

MacLeod, G. 1997. "'Institutional Thickness' and Industrial Governance in Lowland Scotland." *Area* 29 (4): 299–311.

Marchildon, G. 2006. "Regionalization and Health Services Restructuring in Saskatchewan." In *Health Services Restructuring in Canada: New Evidence and New Directions*, edited by C.M. Beach, R.P. Chaykowski, S. Shortt, F. St-Hilaire, and A. Sweetman, 33–58. Montreal: McGill-Queen's University Press.

Nelles, J. 2012. "Cooperation and Capacity? Exploring the Sources and Limits of City-Region Governance Partnerships." *International Journal of Urban and Regional Research* 37 (4): 1349–67.

Romanow, R. 2002. *Building on Values: The Future of Health Care in Canada. Final Report*. Commission on the Future of Health Care in Canada. http://www.cbc.ca/healthcare/final_report.pdf. Accessed 18 March 2012.

Sanmartin, C., and N. Ross. 2006. "Experiencing Difficulties Accessing First-Contact Health Services in Canada." *Healthcare Policy* 1 (2): 103–19.

Schroeder, H. 2009. "The Art and Science of Transforming Canada's Health System." *Healthcare Management Forum* 22 (4): 17–22.

Williams, A., V.A. Crooks, K. Whitfield, M. Kelley, J. Richards, L. DeMiglio, and S. Dykeman. 2010. "Tracking the Evolution of Hospice Palliative Care in Canada: A Comparative Case Study of Seven Provinces." *BMC Health Services Research* 10: 147. http://www.biomedcentral.com/1472-6963/10/147. Accessed 25 April 2013.

Conclusion: Prospects?

KEVIN EDSON JONES, ALEX LORD,
AND ROB SHIELDS

The promises of the city-region have been prophesied loudly, but its reality is less clear and its benefits less direct, ambiguous, and sometimes contradictory. The overwhelming impression is that the city-region concept has evolved to mean different things in different contexts; it is not a readily accessible solution to the multifaceted social and economic challenges posed by an urbanizing world.

A principal aim of this volume has been to address how the city-region has evolved in theory and practice through a series of detailed case studies. It has sought to create a reflexive account rooted in place and community from which meaningful lessons may be derived (Innes 1995).

RE-PLACING THE CITY-REGION

The city-region denotes a series of spatial interrelationships. On either side of a hyphen, the term connects growing urban centres within inter-reliant regional territories. The city-region may simply appear as a means of territorial rationalizing – redrawing boundaries in the attempt to overlay urban geographies with appropriate and functional systems of governance. This restructuring of geographic space is a persistent theme in the work of planners and municipal policy officials. It is also often the source of a great deal of politics and conflict at the local level in the form of difficult urban-rural partnerships, amalgamation strategies, annexation, identity politics, or struggles over autonomy and electoral representation. However, while the politics of municipal restructuring can appear dominant within the political landscape of the city-region, the contributors to this book also point to the importance of acknowledging a normative politics of the city-region. Less visible, such politics impose a series of contexts, or discourses (Smart and Tanasescu, this volume), which impose a series of logics, or even assumptions, about what cities ought to be doing.

The city-region is not simply an articulation of policy, but is situated within (and co-producing) a series of more elusive and seldom acknowledged political trajectories. In particular, alongside the geographic shifting of local boundaries, the concept of the city-region has further evolved to encompass a series of spatial relations with abstract global networks. As we noted in the opening of this book, the city-region is imagined as a bridge between the local and the global. As a conceptual framework, it is a vision that responds to the demands and sense of rescaling brought about by competitive, globalized relationships. The "city-region" is something that metropolitan governments have reached out for as they have sought additional status and powers to respond to calls for cities to take centre stage in a number of policy contexts. Dominantly, these areas are most often narrowly defined in terms of economic competitiveness in relation to the logics of growth, market liberalization, and the development of knowledge economies.

In this sense, the "city-region" has also been a compelling touchstone of success in this globalized drama: through their architecture and new infrastructure such as airports, cities have sought to demonstrate their centrality to regional networks. In some cases, the new or redeveloped cores of cities confirm their economic success; in other cases, they mimic success by offering environments that are deemed conducive to global business, to innovation and activities associated with buzzwords such as "creativity." Every city needs to ask itself which of these categories it falls into.

Where city-regionalism can often fail is when abstract ideals, supported by narrowly defined prescriptive policy measures (i.e. scalar restructuring), obscure locally rooted policy options. Local context matters, and as Geddes (1915) argued a century ago, successful participation in global networks is built upon a foundation of knowledge of local needs, cultures, and strengths. Even a perceived weakness such as isolation can be a strength in allowing retreat and contemplation, or becoming a reward for the effort made to get to such a distant destination, for example. It is best, in other words, to develop global relationships from these local virtues outward, rather than to impose desirable qualities on communities from the outside. "In this way a community can take meaningful action at the local level: action aimed at providing long-term, shared social and economic benefits in ways that account for issues of equity, liveability and sustainability" (Jones 2010).

Re-emphasizing the local should not be interpreted as a retreat from relational planning or regionalism. The impetus remains on approaching planning and city-regional development as complex and dynamic processes that understand city-regions as produced through "social actions within and between places" (Graham and Healey 1999; see also Shields, this volume; 1990). As Harrison (2007, parentheses added) has identified elsewhere, city regions have been "defined in economic terms (travel to work areas, functional economic ties, labour market geographies) [but] all too often what is missing is how city-regions are constructed politically, and ... the processes by which they are rendered visible spaces." In her analysis of the absence of narrative in planning Canada's capital, Andrew similarly argues that too often matters of scale, boundaries, and bureaucracy come readily to the fore in planning exercises. Dynamic contexts, social relations, and the politics of city-regional planning are potentially left lurking unattended in the background (also see Glass, this volume). The cases of city-regions surveyed in this and other volumes often turn out to be logics that serve highly rationalized, systematic practices, such as regional administration, or narrow sectoral interests such as transportation, without reference to the history and commitment of populations and cultures that drive and perpetuate places and regions with strong identities.

This problematic situation is compounded when highly relational and contestable notions such as globalization are not reflexively engaged with, but instead are either ignored or treated too literally as *faits accomplis*. The outcome of this relational blind spot is that cities leave themselves open to the imposition of definitions of place and logics of development from above or from outside. For instance, as Smart and Tanasescu (this volume) demonstrate, increasingly popular global ranking systems that rate cities against criteria for development and against each other impose narrow discourses onto places, and shape planning action in ways that ignore local context. Etherington similarly raises concerns about city-regionalism acting as a means by which neoliberal tenets of entrepreneurship and competitiveness are imposed on communities and local labour markets. In each case, external logics take precedence in creating priorities for development, and therefore risk ignoring local needs, persistent inequities, community cultures, and identities (see also Amin and Thrift 1995). Forcing cities to fit into externally imposed niches requires eliminating local initiatives that diverge from this direction and also cutting the locality off from those forces, flows, and opportunities that nurture these efforts. The result is considerable dislocation. Rankings may also recognize the opposite case, of new external linkages that offer new niches and opportunities. These also often result in conflicts over land use, local identity, and recognition of status as groups compete for recognition and control of the polity. But in the longer historical run, local needs tend to reassert themselves or create a situation of stasis (see Glass; Smart and Tansescu, this volume).

In this regard, the practice of city-regionalism to date has often embodied a notable contradiction. It has charted the importance of cities as spatial actors in a global world, while at times failing to account for locales, people, and their communities within these very places. To address this paradox it is essential (i) to re-engage community and place (see also Bradford 2005); and (ii) to foster a spatial and global reflexivity – asking "what does this mean for us, here and now?" – as two central constituents of planning scholarship and practice.

For scholars in the field, acknowledging the political as an important animator of specific city-regional geographies identifies the potential for future research even though it gives the lie to blanket pronouncements. Scholars still need to investigate more systematically the local politics and spatializations that inform how policy-makers select which of the competing articulations of a city-region is *the* version that they choose to stress, and *how* – visually, textually – they present that particular account. This would make a valuable contribution to opening up the contested articulations of globalization, competition, and development bound up in the term "city-region." Furthermore, doing so would create a basis for less naïve and more engaged dialogues between researchers, planners, and elected leaders.

One consequence of this approach is that active and dynamic processes of collaboration and engagement come to the fore, and are deserving of serious attention by scholars and practitioners alike. As Morgan (2010) has noted, city-regionalism has often carried with it a narrow range of assumptions about local government and planning (see also Jonas and Ward 2007). First, it is often naïvely presumed that regionalization inevitably carries with it economic advantages, expressed simply in terms of competitive advantage. Alternately, Morgan calls for the development of a more polycentric approach that situates economic aims within wider collaborations about sustainability, transportation, and waste (see also Guay and Hamel, this volume; Sandercock 1999). A second conviction of regional approaches is that re-territorializing government to the city brings democracy closer to people and embeds it in everyday life. However, Morgan warns that, while such logics appear obvious at the time, "the formal realm of local politics can be remote and inaccessible in spite of its proximity" (1249).

Engagement and collaboration should not be assumed, but require active attention. Efforts are needed that shift city-regional planning away from questions of governance and the restructuring of Euclidean space to include a greater emphasis on interdisciplinary approaches to planning and the complexities of access and history that warp relations between places in ways not apparent on a map. This includes paying greater heed to place-making as a socially constructed and contested activity, rooted in processes of conflict and culture. For instance, in his examination of the resiliency of Waterloo, Ontario, David Wolfe (this volume) roots adaptation in the ability of communities to work across sectors and communities, and to open economic development to a wide range of participants. Likewise, Glass's history of regionalism in Pittsburgh points to the capacity of communities and municipalities to be flexible in their approach to city-regionalism. This requires knowledge of the relationships, contexts, and conflicts shaping collaboration, as well as the knowledge of how to reflexively adapt practice (see also CRSC 2010). Choosing whether city-regionalism, and what form of city-regionalism, fits within a local context are essential skills for successful governance, and an area where engaged scholarship can play a vital role in assisting communities (Harrison, this volume). City-regional planning requires close partnerships between scholars, practitioners, and a wide range of publics and communities. These and other contributors such as Andrew, Wolfe, and Shields advocate for bottom-up approaches to city-regionalism rooted in communities. In this sense, the "institutional thickness" (also see Whitfield, this volume) of cities is important. Coalition-building is a key skill.

There are good logics for rethinking the scale at which we organize and govern our urban municipalities and regions. Urban areas are rarely static, but are rather in constant states of geographic and demographic flux. Trends towards rapid urbanization suggest that the mutability of cities around the world is increasing (see Introduction, this volume). Moreover, processes of reterritorialization mean that governance is taking place at multiple scales within the urban landscape. Boundaries are necessarily flexible, or even contradictory, and systems of appropriate governance should be considered (see also Sancton 2008). The challenge is for cities and regions to adapt municipal governance to the changing nature of our communities and the challenges they face. This is very different from a great deal of current practice, which has sought to impose communities within restructured global city-regions. Across various sectors, concepts including smart growth, integrated land-use planning (Olson 2013), ecological management (Guay and Hamel, this volume), social planning, and economic clustering (Wolfe, this volume) might all inform, as well as benefit from, the development of effective and meaningful city-regional scales of governance.

As a term, the "city-region" is thus most useful when it is nuanced and adapted to encapsulate the changing nature of a particular place in a global world whose uncertainty is mirrored in the ambiguity of the term "city-region," an entity that is never one single set of things, such as a local labour market, but is the coming together of disparate local elements into a hyphenated whole. Understanding this local specificity is achieved through reflexivity in thought and practice. This is institutional in the sense of thoughtful mission statements and business plans, but also community-based in the sense of pulling together tacit and idiosyncratic elements that create the character and ethos of a place or region.

The city-region can help make sense of a transition from one economic model, or model of prosperity, to another as part of a set of processes, and in doing so, can provide some guidance for economic actors, communities, and governments to react in a coordinated way to a changing context. It can open patterns of urban growth, development, and sustainability up to scrutiny, and provide a means of supporting communities to consider their own positions, needs, and planning practices from these viewpoints. Where the term is least helpful is when it restricts thinking and acting about cities and is foreign to the scales of community life.

Together, the contributors to this book have charted an alternate framing of the city-region, and have approached the re-spacing of cities in ways that emphasize flexibility, adaptability to local contexts, social robustness, and community engagement. The future prospects of the city-region lie in reasserting an emphasis on emergence over imposition; focusing on community dynamics over boundaries; facilitating networks and relationships over bureaucracy; and facing up to the necessary political renegotiation and settlements rather than masking stresses with rhetoric.

REFERENCES

Amin, A., and Nigel Thrift. 1995. "Institutional Issues for the European Regions: From Markets and Plans to Socioeconomics and Powers of Association." *Economy and Society* 24 (1): 41–66.

Bradford, N. 2005. *Place-Based Public Policy: Towards a New Urban and Community Agenda for Canada*. Ottawa: CPRN.

CRSC. 2010. *Partnerships: Responding to the Changing Dynamics of Urban-Rural Interdependency*. Edmonton: CRSC, University of Alberta.

Geddes, P. 1915. *Cities in Evolution*. London: Williams and Margate.

Innes, J.E. 1995. "Planning Theory's Emerging Paradigm: Communicative Action and Interactive Practice." *Journal of Planning Education and Research* 14: 183–9.

Jonas, A.E.G., and K. Ward. 2007. "Introduction to a Debate on City-Regions: New Geographies of Governance, Democracy and Social Reproduction." *International Journal of Urban and Regional Research* 31 (1): 169–78.

Jones, K.E. 2010. "Putting the 'Local' into Economic Development Planning." *CURB* 1 (2): 12–15.

Graham, S., and P. Healey. 1999. "Relational Concepts of Space and Place: Issues for Planning Theory and Practice." *European Planning Studies* 7 (5): 623–46.

Morgan, K. 2010. "The Polycentric State: New Spaces of Empowerment and Engagement." *Regional Studies* 41 (9): 1237–51.

Olson, D. 2013. "Landscape, Nature and Urbanism, a Nested Approach." Keynote address. Edmonton: Regional Planning Speakers Series, 26 March. http://crsc.ualberta.ca/en/EventsArchive/2013-04-26-Sustainabil ityandRegionalPlanning.aspx.

Sandercock, L. 1998. "Expanding the 'Language' of Planning: A Meditation on Planning Education for the Twenty-First Century." *European Planning Studies* 7 (5): 533–44.

Shields, R. 1990. *Places on the Margin*. London: Routledge.

Contributors

CAROLINE ANDREW is the director of the Centre on Governance, School of Political Studies, University of Ottawa. Her research interests include urban development, municipal immigration and immigrant integration policies, gender and local governance, and place-based policy and relations between community groups and municipal governments. Caroline serves on the board for Women in Cities International and the steering committee of the City for All Women Initiative in Ottawa.

DAVID ETHERINGTON serves as principal researcher for the Centre for Enterprise and Economic Development Research at Middlesex University Business School, London. His research interests include welfare to work, employment relations, and social exclusion. Previous to his experience as an academic, David worked in local government as a senior policy officer, including ten years (1984–94) at Sheffield City Council within the planning and economic development directorate.

MICHAEL R. GLASS is a lecturer with the Urban Studies Program at the University of Pittsburgh. His research interests include political boundary reform, urban governance, and the use of performativity theory in political geography. His current research project is a comparative analysis of the consulting networks which attempt to transfer global best practices in metropolitan governance to specific urban settings through regional visioning programs in mid-sized American cities.

LOUIS GUAY is a professor in the Department of Sociology and a research member of the *Institut en environnement, développement et société* at Laval University. He specializes in global environmental problems, such as climate change and biodiversity protection, and issues in urban planning and sustainability. He focuses on science and policy interaction in the decision-making process. He also is interested in the social impacts of scientific and technological change.

PIERRE HAMEL is professor of sociology at the University of Montreal. His research addresses the evolution of metropolitan governance in Canada, and investigates the development of new state spaces and civic-public relationships. It is specifically motivated by an interest in public debate and the participation of civil society in emerging systems of urban and regional government. More recently, Professor Hamel's research is investigating the link between sustainability, environment, and local governance.

JOHN HARRISON is senior lecturer of human geography at Loughborough University, UK. He is also associate director of the Globalization and World Cities Research Network. In his research projects, he seeks to connect the new politics of economic development with transitions in the regulation and governance of capitalism and its territorial form. He publishes on city-regions as key sites for economic development, models of city-region governance, the political construction of city-regions, and challenges for sustaining competitive city-regions.

KEVIN EDSON JONES is director and senior research scientist at the University of Alberta's City-Region Studies Centre. His research investigates interrelationships between locality, community, and regional innovation and development strategies. His training is in the social study of science and society, and he also publishes on the topics of risk, engagement, and environmental governance.

ALEXANDER LORD is lecturer of planning at the University of Liverpool. His research interests revolve around the use of financial instruments in the design of spatially targeted policy. This is reflected in publications on aspects of the reform of the English planning system as well as on wider changes in the institutional geography of the United Kingdom and Europe.

JAMES REES is a research fellow at the Third Sector Research Centre at the University of Birmingham, UK. His recent research concentrates on transformations in UK public services, including the role of the third sector, but his longer-term interests have been in the governance of urban and regional governance, with a particular focus on the politics of city-regionalism; critical perspectives on urban housing market restructuring and housing policy; and more broadly on issues in urban regeneration, neighbourhoods, and community.

ROB SHIELDS is Henry Marshall Tory Chair at the University of Alberta. His research has focused on urban cultural studies, particularly the social use and meanings of the built environment and urban spaces and regions, including tourist destinations, local identities, and the impact of changing spatializations on cultural identities.

ALAN SMART is professor of anthropology at the University of Calgary. His research and teaching interests include political economy, urban anthropology, anthropology of law, Hong Kong, China, and North America.

ALINA TANASESCU has worked in a variety of capacities in the academic and non-profit sectors on immigrant, poverty, and homelessness issues. She holds a PhD in anthropology at the University of Calgary, where her research has focused on immigration, housing careers, and housing stress across Calgary migrant communities. Alina is the VP of strategy at the Calgary Homeless Foundation, the organization leading the implementation of Calgary's 10-Year Plan to End Homelessness.

KYLE Y. WHITFIELD is a scholar in the field of community planning. At the core of her research, teaching, and service are such areas of scholarship as: community development; social citizenship and health justice; health service planning; citizen engagement; and concepts and practices relevant to inclusion and exclusion. Dr Whitfield is an associate professor at the University of Alberta in the Faculty of Extension.

ALLISON M. WILLIAMS is trained as a social geographer, specializing in health research addressing health care services, quality of

Contributors

life, informal caregiving, critical policy/program evaluation, and therapeutic landscapes. She currently is a professor at McMaster University.

DAVID A. WOLFE is professor of political science at the University of Toronto Mississauga and co-director of the Innovation Policy Lab at the Munk School of Global Affairs, University of Toronto. He holds a BA and an MA in political science from Carleton University and a PhD from the University of Toronto. He has served as national coordinator of the Innovation Systems Research Network since 1998 and was principal investigator on its two SSHRC-funded major collaborative research initiatives. His most recent book is *Innovating in Urban Economies*, published in 2014.

Index